VISUAL QUICKSTART GUIDE

iPHOTO '09

FOR MAC OS X

Adam C. Engst

Peachpit Press

Visual QuickStart Guide
iPhoto '09 for Mac OS X
Adam C. Engst

Peachpit Press

1249 Eighth Street · Berkeley, CA 94710
510/524-2178 · 510/524-2221 (fax)
Find us on the Web at www.peachpit.com.
To report errors, please send a note to errata@peachpit.com.
Peachpit Press is a division of Pearson Education.

Editor: Cliff Colby
Production Coordinator: Lisa Brazieal
Copyeditor: Tonya Engst
Compositor: Adam C. Engst
Indexer: James Minkin
Cover Design: Peachpit Press

Notice of liability
The information in this book is distributed on an "As Is" basis, without warranty. While every precaution has been taken in the preparation of the book, neither the author nor Peachpit Press shall have any liability to any person or entity with respect to any loss or damage caused or alleged to be caused directly or indirectly by the instructions contained in this book or by the computer software and hardware products described in it.

Trademarks
Visual QuickStart Guide is a registered trademark of Peachpit Press, a division of Pearson Education. iPhoto, iTunes, iDVD, and iMovie are registered trademarks and/or registered service marks of Apple Inc. Many of the designations used by manufacturers and sellers to distinguish their products are claimed as trademarks. Where those designations appear in this book, and Peachpit was aware of a trademark claim, the designations appear as requested by the owner of the trademark. All other product names and services identified throughout this book are used in editorial fashion only and for the benefit of such companies with no intention of infringement of the trademark. No such use, or the use of any trade name, is intended to convey endorsement or other affiliation with this book.

ISBN 13: 978-0-321-60131-5
ISBN 10:   0-321-60131-9

9 8 7 6 5 4 3 2 1

Printed and bound in the United States of America

Dedication

To my son, Tristan Mackay Engst, the subject of so many of my photographs.

About the Author

Adam C. Engst is the publisher of *TidBITS,* one of the oldest and largest Internet-based newsletters, and the Take Control electronic book series (with print collections published by Peachpit Press), both of which have helped tens of thousands of readers (find them at `www.tidbits.com`). He has written numerous computer books, including the best-selling *Internet Starter Kit* series, and many articles for magazines, including *Macworld,* where he is currently a contributing editor. His photos have appeared in juried photography shows.

His indefatigable support of the Macintosh community has resulted in numerous awards and recognition at the highest levels. In the annual MDJ Power 25 survey of industry insiders, he consistently ranks as one of the top five most influential people in the Macintosh industry, and he was named one of MacDirectory's top ten visionaries. And how many industry figures can boast of being turned into an action figure?

Please send comments about this book to Adam at `iphoto-vqs@tidbits.com`.

Other Books by Adam C. Engst

Take Control of Your Wi-Fi Security

Take Control of Buying a Mac

The Wireless Networking Starter Kit

Internet Starter Kit for Macintosh

Special Thanks

No book is the work of a single person, and many people helped with this one, including:

- Tonya Engst (not only my wonderful wife, but also a great copyeditor)

- Cliff Colby (my first new Peachpit editor in years!)

- Lisa Brazieal (spotter of wayward pixels!)

- Nancy Ruenzel (for giving me the nod on this book way back when with iPhoto 1.0)

- Scott Cowlin (for marketing wizardry)

- Chris Engst (for watching Tristan!)

- Glenn Fleishman, Marshall Clow, Fred Johnson, and David Blatner (without whose help I could never have explained color management and resolution)

- Keith Kubarek, Sandro Menzel, Cory Byard, and Laurie Clow (for their photography knowledge and tips)

- Jeff Carlson, Glenn Fleishman, Joe Kissell, Doug McLean, Tonya Engst, Matt Neuburg, and Mark Anbinder (for helping keep *TidBITS* running)

- The High Noon Athletic Club, whose noontime runs kept me more or less sane.

Technical Colophon

I wrote this book using the following hardware and software:

- An 8-core 2.8 GHz Mac Pro with a pair of 24-inch Dell monitors, and Canon PowerShot S100, S400, and SD870IS digital cameras

- Mac OS X 10.5 Leopard, iPhoto '09, Adobe InDesign CS3, Snapz Pro X for screen shots, and the Peachpit VQS template

Featured Photographers

I took most of the photos in this book, but I also included some pictures from my sister, Jennifer Upson, and my father, Chris Engst. And of course, any photos that I'm in were probably taken by Tonya Engst or Tristan Engst (who is now 10 years old and loves to take pictures with his own Canon PowerShot SD850IS).

CONTENTS AT A GLANCE

TABLE OF CONTENTS

TABLE OF CONTENTS

1

GETTING STARTED

Digital cameras have become commonplace, and few people even consider purchasing a traditional analog camera anymore. But with digital photos, the camera is only part of the equation. Once you've taken photos, you need software to help you import, organize, edit, and share your photos. Since 2001, the most popular application for that task on the Mac has been Apple's iPhoto.

But iPhoto's popularity doesn't stem just from the fact that Apple bundles it—it's a genuinely useful program, providing a broad set of features while remaining easy to use. With iPhoto, you can organize your photos, perform common editing tasks, and create professional-looking printed works (prints, greeting cards, hardcover books, and even calendars).

If iPhoto is so easy, why write this book? Even though iPhoto '09 is the best version of the program that Apple has released so far, it still doesn't entirely demystify the process of importing a digital photograph, editing it, and presenting it on paper or on the computer screen. And iPhoto comes with no documentation beyond minimal and often incomplete online help. Read on, then, not just for the manual iPhoto lacks, but also for the help you need to take digital photos and make the most of them.

iPhoto '09, not iPhoto 8

Annoyingly, Apple refers to iPhoto '09 interchangeably as "iPhoto '09" and "iPhoto 8," the latter of which is the actual version number. Although I prefer the actual version number to the year, I fear it would be too confusing to call it iPhoto 8, given that the previous version, iPhoto 7, was also called iPhoto '08. As a result, I'll use the iPhoto '09 name throughout this book, except when I'm referring to a very specific version of iPhoto '09, such as the current-as-of-this-writing iPhoto 8.0.2.

Hardware and Software Requirements

iPhoto '09 has fairly steep system requirements thanks to the resources needed to work with large numbers of digital images.

To run iPhoto, you need:

◆ A Macintosh with a PowerPC G4 (867 MHz or faster), PowerPC G5, or Intel processor with 512 MB of RAM (though 1 GB of RAM is better). Realistically, the more CPU power and RAM you can throw at iPhoto, the better its performance. You'll also find a large monitor extremely helpful.

◆ Mac OS X. Specifically, Mac OS X 10.5.6 or later and QuickTime 7.5.5 or later.

◆ An optical drive that can read DVD discs, since iLife '09 comes on DVD. Burning DVDs directly from iDVD requires a drive that can write to DVD as well, such as an Apple SuperDrive or a third-party DVD burner.

◆ A source of digital images, which could be an iPhoto-compatible digital camera, scanned images, Kodak Photo CDs, or a service that provides digital images along with traditional film developing.

✔ Tips

■ Some features—such as Places; purchasing print products; or uploading to MobileMe, Flickr, and Facebook—require an Internet connection. And you're really going to want a high-speed Internet connection; dialup will be painful.

■ On PowerPC G4- and some PowerPC G5-based Macs, some slideshow themes won't be available. See http://support.apple.com/kb/TS2576 for details.

✔ More Tips

■ iPhoto can import photos in *RAW* format, which is an uncompressed image file format used by some high-end cameras. However, there are multiple flavors of RAW, and iPhoto does not support all of them.

■ Some of the other components of the iLife '09 suite, such as iMovie and GarageBand, have steeper system requirements. See www.apple.com/ilife/systemrequirements.html for details.

Acquiring iPhoto

Apple offers several methods of acquiring iPhoto, although it's worth noting that Apple does not offer free upgrades between major versions of the program. In other words, even if you got iPhoto 6 bundled with your last iMac, you must still buy iLife '09 to get iPhoto '09.

Ways to get iPhoto '09:

◆ Look in your Applications folder. If you purchased your Mac since January 2009, iPhoto '09 may already be installed.

◆ Buy a $79 copy of Apple's iLife '09, which is a DVD package containing all five of Apple's digital hub applications: iPhoto '09, iMovie '09, iDVD 7, GarageBand '09, and iWeb '09. Although these applications come free with new Macs, the iLife package is the only way for current owners of iPhoto, iMovie, iDVD, GarageBand, and iWeb to get updates for those products. For details, visit www.apple.com/ilife/.

◆ Buy a new Mac, which will come with iPhoto preinstalled. Steve Jobs and his private jet thank you!

✔ Tip

■ Rather than buy multiple copies of iLife '09 to use on all the Macs in your house, you can buy a $99 family pack that's licensed for up to five users.

Installing iPhoto

Installing iPhoto from the iLife '09 package requires almost no effort at all. Be sure to read "Updating to iPhoto '09" on page 6 too!

To install iPhoto:

1. Insert the iLife DVD into your Mac's optical drive.

2. In the Install window that appears after the DVD mounts, double-click the iLife '09 icon (**Figure 1.1**).

3. Click through the Introduction (**Figure 1.2**), Read Me, License, Destination Select (select your hard disk here), Installation Type, Installation, and Summary steps.

   When you're done, you end up with iPhoto (and the rest of the iLife applications) in your Applications folder.

✔ Tips

■ The iLife installer won't allow you to install if any of the iLife applications are currently running; you must quit them before installing.

■ If you don't want to install some of the iLife applications (iDVD and GarageBand in particular take up a lot of disk space), click Customize in the Installation Type screen and select only the applications you want (**Figure 1.3**).

■ The installer calculates whether or not you have enough disk space; if you're on the edge, install only iPhoto.

Figure 1.1 Double-click the iLife '09 icon to start the installation process.

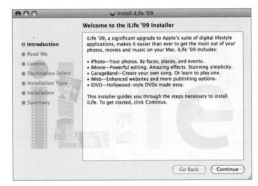

Figure 1.2 The Introduction screen describes the iLife applications briefly.

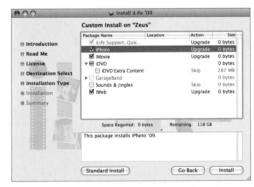

Figure 1.3 If you don't want to install all the iLife applications, click Customize in the Installation Type screen and select only those you do want.

INSTALLING iPHOTO

Figure 1.4 Click Check Now to make Software Update look for iPhoto updates.

Figure 1.5 To install an update, select the checkbox next to its name, and then click the Install button.

Updating iPhoto via Software Update

Although you can't get iPhoto '09 for free via Software Update, Apple will release minor revisions via Software Update.

To update iPhoto via Software Update:

1. From the Apple menu, choose System Preferences.

2. To display the Software Update pane, choose Software Update from the View menu.

3. To check for updates, make sure you're connected to the Internet, and then click the Check Now button (**Figure 1.4**).

   If Software Update finds any updates, it launches another application that displays updates that make sense for your Mac, including iPhoto, if any exist.

4. Select the checkboxes next to the updates you want to install (**Figure 1.5**).

5. Click the Install button, and when the installer prompts you for it, enter your administrator password.

   Software Update proceeds to download and install the selected updates.

✔ Tips

- Choose Check for Updates from the iPhoto application menu at any time to see if you have the latest version.

- To set Software Update to kick in on its own, select the Check for Updates checkbox, and from the pop-up menu choose how often you wish it to check.

- When Software Update fails to find updated software appropriate for your computer, it tells you none is available.

Watching for Updates

I recommend setting Software Update to check for updates automatically, and iPhoto can do so itself too (select Check for iPhoto Updates Automatically in the General pane of iPhoto's Preferences window). You can also visit Apple's iPhoto Web page at www.apple.com/ilife/iphoto/ every so often for news about iPhoto or updates that might not have been released via Software Update.

Updating to iPhoto '09

In theory, updating from an earlier version of iPhoto should be merely a matter of installing iPhoto '09 and letting it upgrade your iPhoto Library. However, a few simple actions can prevent future problems.

Tips when updating to iPhoto '09:

◆ Make sure to back up your iPhoto Library (located in your user account's Pictures folder) before installing iPhoto '09. Then, if something bad happens, or if you need to revert to your earlier version for some reason I can't imagine, you won't lose all your photos. I'm sure you have a backup, but another one can't hurt.

◆ Before updating your iPhoto Library, run Software Update to make sure you have the latest version of iPhoto '09.

◆ If you have installed third-party export plug-ins (see "Other Web Export Tools," on page 145), it's best to remove them before updating (and to install new versions that are confirmed to work with iPhoto '09). To find them, [Control]-click iPhoto's icon in the Finder, choose Show Package Contents, and navigate to the PlugIns folder. Drag any third-party plug-ins to the Desktop.

◆ For a clean installation (and don't bother doing this unless you suspect trouble), move the com.apple.iPhoto.plist file (in your user account's Preferences folder) and the iPhoto application to the Trash, but leave your iPhoto Library alone. Then install iPhoto '09.

◆ If you have trouble immediately after updating, delete the preference file mentioned in the previous tip and the iPhoto application, and then reinstall iPhoto '09.

New Features in iPhoto '09

iPhoto '09 offers a number of welcome enhancements that are covered throughout this book. Here are my favorites:

◆ iPhoto now boasts face recognition, so you can organize your photos by people whose faces you've trained iPhoto to recognize.

◆ iPhoto can now read *geotags,* which indicate the latitude and longitude at which a photo was taken with a camera (like an iPhone) containing a GPS receiver. You can also assign locations to photos that don't yet have geotags. Geotagged photos can be viewed on a map within iPhoto and included on maps in printed books.

◆ A new Definition slider in the Adjust window improves clarity and detail.

◆ A new checkbox in the Adjust window prevents the tools from oversaturating skin tones as you make other changes.

◆ An Auto button in the Red-Eye display uses face recognition to remove red-eye automatically.

◆ The Retouch tool now handles edges and non-skin tones better, and the Enhance tool does a better job and avoids oversaturating skin tones.

◆ Slideshows gain themes, use face detection to keep faces onscreen, and can be synced with an iPhone, iPod touch, or Apple TV.

◆ You can now upload photos to the photo-sharing site Flickr and the social networking site Facebook.

◆ Hardcover books ordered from Apple can now have a photo on the front cover, as well as on the dust jacket.

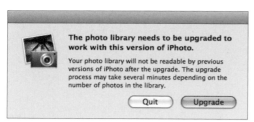

Figure 1.6 On the first launch with an old iPhoto Library, iPhoto prompts you to upgrade the library. Click Upgrade unless you want to quit first and make a backup before proceeding.

Recovering Photos on Upgrade

When iPhoto 6 upgraded your iPhoto Library, if it found photos that weren't properly tracked in iPhoto's database, it offered to recover them, putting them in an album called Recovered Photos.

I can't be sure that iPhoto '09 will do the same, having not seen this myself, but if you are presented with such a message, I strongly encourage you to heed it and let iPhoto recover the photos.

In some cases, the recovered photos may actually be duplicates, at which point you can easily delete them. To figure out which are duplicates, search in iPhoto on the filename of the photo (it's usually the sequential number assigned by your camera). If only the recovered photo appears in the search results, you know it's unique and should be kept; if two or more photos that are obvious duplicates show up, you can probably delete any extras.

Launching iPhoto

Once you have installed iPhoto, the next step is to launch it. The first time you launch iPhoto differs from subsequent launches.

Ways to launch iPhoto:

◆ Double-click the iPhoto icon in your Applications folder.

◆ If iPhoto's icon already appears in your Dock, click the Dock's iPhoto icon.

◆ Drag the iPhoto icon to your Dock to add it to the Dock permanently, and then click the Dock's iPhoto icon.

◆ Use a third-party launcher utility like LaunchBar. I really like LaunchBar, and you can find more about it at www.obdev.at/products/launchbar/.

iPhoto's initial launch

The first time iPhoto '09 launches and sees an iPhoto Library created with a previous version of iPhoto, it prompts you to upgrade it (**Figure 1.6**). Click Upgrade to proceed (this can take quite some time, depending on how many photos you have in your iPhoto Library), or click Quit if you want to make a backup first.

✔ Tips

■ You can put off the decision to make a backup or use a different iPhoto Library, but upgrading isn't optional if you wish to use photos in your existing iPhoto Library with iPhoto '09.

■ Don't interrupt the relatively slow upgrade process or work in other iLife applications while it's upgrading.

LAUNCHING iPHOTO

iPhoto's Modes

When you use iPhoto, you'll find yourself in one of five modes at all times. The rest of the book looks at these modes, focusing on the tasks you perform in each mode. Here's a quick summary of the modes.

Import mode

To add photos to your photo library, you import them, either from files or from a digital camera. All you can do in import mode is select which photos to import, but note that you can keep working in other parts of the program while iPhoto imports photos.

Organize mode

Once you have images in iPhoto, you'll want to organize them into events and albums, assign them keywords, and delete the lousy ones. All that and more happens in organize mode, where you'll spend most of your time.

iPhoto's organize mode also provides tools for running slideshows, creating Web pages, setting your screen saver and Desktop picture, sending photos via email, exporting photos, and more.

Faces mode

New in iPhoto '09 is Faces mode. When you teach iPhoto to recognize a person's face, the controls change to focus on that task, with screens and controls for identifying faces in photos, confirming that the face iPhoto has identified in other photos is correct, and browsing through identified photos.

Places mode

Also new in iPhoto '09 is Places mode, which provides controls for showing the locations of geotagged photos on a map or displaying the photos taken in a particular location.

Edit mode

Even the best photographers edit their images. iPhoto provides the basic image-editing tools you need to crop pictures, enhance colors, remove red-eye, retouch unsightly blemishes, and apply a variety of effects.

iPhoto also provides more advanced editing tools that let you adjust exposure, play with the colors in your photo, and straighten photos, among other things. If you need even more advanced tools or tools that let you work on only selected portions of a photo, iPhoto can work with another image editor, such as Adobe Photoshop Elements.

Slideshow mode

With iPhoto's powerful slideshow tools, you can create highly customized slideshows containing music, elegant transitions, per-slide timings, and the Ken Burns Effect for panning and zooming photos. Once you create the slideshows, you can replay them as many times as you like; export them to QuickTime movies that you can share with your friends and relatives; or even sync them with an iPhone, iPod touch, or Apple TV.

Book/calendar/card/print mode

One of iPhoto's great strengths is the way it helps you design and order professional-looking books, calendars, and cards. All those tasks take place in very similar modes with controls dedicated to the task of designing pages.

You're not limited to buying things from Apple; iPhoto also provides theme-based printing that uses a similar interface to help you create and print photo designs on your own printer.

Interface Overview

Before we dive into the specifics of using iPhoto in the upcoming chapters, let's take a bird's-eye view of the main window so you can orient yourself and get a feel for the program's primary functions (**Figure 1.7**).

I assume here that you already know about standard Mac OS X window widgets like the close, minimize, and zoom buttons, the scroll bars and scroll arrows, and the resize handle in the lower right. If not, let me recommend that you visit your local bookstore and look for a beginner title that will help you with the basics of Mac OS X.

Source pane. Create and work with albums, folders, Web galleries, books, calendars, cards, and slideshows here. Cameras and card readers also appear here when importing.

Drag to resize the Information pane.

Drag to resize the source pane.

Display pane. Your events and images show up here in a variety of sizes, as do thumbnails of book, card, calendar, and print pages you create.

Information pane. Info about events, images, and albums shows up here.

Event names (shown here) or photo titles, ratings, and keywords appear below the images.

Click to enter full-screen editing mode.

Click to add an album or other project.

Click to hide or show the Information pane.

Size slider. Adjust this slider to resize the contents of the display pane. In organize mode, the slider displays more or fewer thumbnails; in edit and book mode, it zooms in or out.

Figure 1.7

Search by title, keyword, date, or rating (choose from the pop-up menu).

Click to play a basic slideshow with the selected photos.

Number of events and photos selected.

The controls available here change with your current mode (organize mode shown).

Importing and Managing Photos

2

One of the most common things you'll find yourself doing in iPhoto is importing photos. iPhoto provides a number of ways you can import photos, including the most obvious: from a digital camera or iPhone.

You can also import files that you downloaded from your camera previously, acquired on a CD, scanned in from prints, downloaded from the Internet, or received from a photo-processing company that provides digital images along with traditional prints. It's also possible to use a *card reader*—a USB or FireWire device into which you put the memory card from your camera and which presents the contents of your memory card as files on a disk—with the twist that iPhoto recognizes many card readers and can import from them just as though they were cameras. And lastly, you can copy photos that other iPhoto users make available to you on disc or over a network.

In this chapter, we'll look at all the ways you can import pictures into iPhoto and manage them afterward, including such tasks as trashing and recovering photos, making and switching between different iPhoto libraries, backing up your images to CD or DVD, and learning exactly how iPhoto stores images on your hard disk.

Multitasking While Importing

You may not realize it, but you can work in other parts of iPhoto while it is importing images. Although this is worth keeping in mind, it's not always as much of a help as you might think, since you usually want to work with the images that are being imported.

Entering Import Mode

It's easy to bring your photos into iPhoto no matter where they may originate because iPhoto offers four different importing approaches, all of which switch you into import mode automatically. The only time you need to switch into import mode manually is if you switch modes after connecting a camera but before clicking either Import Selected or Import All.

Ways to enter import mode:

◆ Connect your digital camera to your Mac's USB port and turn the camera on. iPhoto need not be running; it launches automatically if necessary (**Figure 2.1**).

◆ Insert your camera's memory card into the card reader. iPhoto need not be running; it launches if necessary.

◆ From iPhoto's File menu, choose Import to Library (Cmd Shift I). iPhoto displays an Import Photos dialog from which you can select a file, a folder, or multiple items before clicking Import.

◆ From the Finder, drag and drop one or more files or an entire folder of images into the iPhoto window or onto the iPhoto icon in the Dock.

✔ Tips

■ The Last Import album in the Recent list remembers the last set of images you imported. Click it to see just those images (**Figure 2.2**).

■ By default, iPhoto shows you all the photos on your card, but if you have already imported some of them, select Hide Photos Already Imported to avoid seeing the already imported photos.

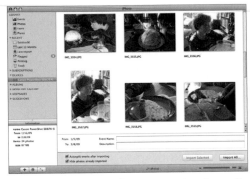

Figure 2.1 After you attach a camera or insert a media card, it shows up in the source pane, and thumbnails of its pictures appear in the display pane.

Figure 2.2 To see the last set of images you imported, click the Last Import album in Recent.

Launching Automatically

iPhoto launches automatically only if you allow it to do so. The first time iPhoto runs, it asks if you want it to launch automatically from then on. If you agree, iPhoto takes over as the application that launches when you connect a camera. You can change this setting in iPhoto's General preference pane, if you wish.

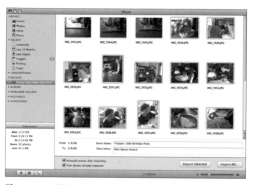

Figure 2.3 Click either Import Selected or Import All to import photos from your camera.

Figure 2.4 While iPhoto imports photos, it displays the image being downloaded along with a progress bar. To stop the process before it completes, click the Stop Import button.

Figure 2.5 When iPhoto finishes importing, it gives you the choice of keeping or deleting the original photos on the camera. I recommend keeping them and deleting them later from the camera itself.

Importing from a Camera

Most people will probably import most of their photos directly from a digital camera.

To import from a digital camera:

1. Connect your camera to your Mac using the USB cable included with the camera, turn it on, and make sure the camera is set to view pictures.

   iPhoto switches into import mode (**Figure 2.1**, previous page).

2. Either select one or more photos to import and click Import Selected, or click Import All (**Figure 2.3**).

   iPhoto imports the photos, showing thumbnails as it works (**Figure 2.4**). If you've made a mistake, click Stop Import.

   iPhoto asks if you'd like it to delete the original photos from the camera after importing (**Figure 2.5**).

3. Click the Keep Photos button.

✔ Tips

- To be safe, **always** click Keep Photos. Then erase the card in your camera after verifying that the import succeeded.

- You can name and describe the event that will be created by the import. The name and description are applied only to the first event if more than one are created.

- Select Autosplit Events After Importing unless you're importing photos from one event that spans multiple days.

- If you attempt to import an already-imported photo, iPhoto asks if you want duplicates or only new images.

- Some cameras mount on your Desktop like a hard disk. Eject such a camera using the eject button next to its name in the source pane before disconnecting it!

Importing from a Card Reader

Importing images via a memory card reader works almost exactly like importing from a digital camera.

To import from a card reader:

1. Connect your card reader to your Mac using USB or FireWire, as appropriate.

2. Insert your memory card.

   iPhoto switches into import mode.

3. Either select one or more photos to import and click Import Selected, or click Import All.

   iPhoto starts importing the photos. If you've made a mistake, click the Stop Import button. iPhoto then asks if you'd like it to delete the original photos from the card after importing.

4. To remove the memory card from the card reader, first click the eject button next to the card's name in the source pane, and then eject the card from the card reader (**Figure 2.6**).

✔ Tips

- When using a card reader, you may be able to preview your pictures in the Finder's column view, or using Mac OS X's Quick Look feature by selecting the photo and pressing (Spacebar) (**Figure 2.7**).

- You can drag files from the card into iPhoto to import them manually.

- Never eject the card while importing!

Eject button.

Figure 2.6 Be sure to click the eject button next to the card's name in the source pane before removing the card.

Figure 2.7 For a quick glance at a photo on a memory card, make sure you're in column view, navigate to where the images are stored, and select one to see a preview. Or just select it and press the Space bar to use Quick Look.

Kodak Photo/Picture CD

iPhoto can import digital images from Kodak Photo CDs and Picture CDs, which you can get when having analog film developed. Insert the CD and iPhoto sees it as though it were a memory card.

Laptop Memory Card Adapters

If you use a MacBook Pro or PowerBook with an ExpressCard or PC Card slot, you can buy an adapter for your memory cards. Then, instead of mucking about with a bulky USB card reader, you can insert your memory card into the credit card-sized adapter, and then insert the adapter into the laptop to import the photos on the memory card.

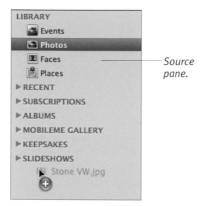

Source pane.

Figure 2.8 The easiest way to import files into iPhoto is to drag the desired files or folders into the display pane or the source pane, as I've done here.

Figure 2.9 To import existing image files into iPhoto, choose Import to Library from the File menu, navigate to your images, select the desired files, and click Import.

Supported File Formats

iPhoto can import images in any file format supported by Apple's QuickTime technology, including BMP, GIF, FlashPix, JPEG, MacPaint, movies (read-only), PICT, PNG, Photoshop, RAW (those flavors supported by Mac OS X in general), SGI, Targa, and TIFF.

Importing from Files

If you have photos already on your disk, or if someone gives you a CD or DVD of photos, iPhoto can import these files in several ways.

Ways to import files into iPhoto:

◆ From the Finder (or some photo cataloging applications), drag the desired files or folders into iPhoto's display pane or source pane (**Figure 2.8**).

◆ From the File menu, choose Import to Library (Cmd Shift I). In the Import Photos dialog, navigate to your images, select the desired file(s) or folder(s), and click Import (**Figure 2.9**).

With either approach, iPhoto starts importing the images. If you want to halt the import, click Stop Import. When the import finishes, the photos appear in the display pane.

✔ Tips

■ Hold down Shift or Cmd to select multiple files in the Import Photos dialog.

■ By default, iPhoto copies the files you import, so make sure you have enough hard disk space before starting.

■ If you drag a file or folder onto the Albums list in the source pane, iPhoto imports the photos *and* creates an album.

■ You can drag photos into a specific album, Web album, book, calendar, card, or slideshow to import and add the photos to that collection.

■ iPhoto retains the EXIF camera information stored with images along with filenames you've given the images.

■ iPhoto creates a new event for each import. Events created from folder imports pick up the name of the folder.

Importing from Mail, Safari, and Other Apps

Many people share photos via the Internet, either sending them via email or posting them on Web pages. The details vary by application, but one of these techniques will always work.

To import from Mail:

◆ Click the Quick Look button in the message header to view the photo(s) (**Figure 2.10**) and then click the Add to iPhoto button (**Figure 2.11**).

◆ Drag the photo to iPhoto's source pane or display pane.

To import from Safari:

◆ [Control]-click the image in Safari and choose Add Image to iPhoto Library from the pop-up menu (**Figure 2.12**).

To import by dragging:

◆ From applications such as Eudora that identify dragged data appropriately, drag the photo to iPhoto's source pane or display pane.

To import by saving, then dragging:

◆ From applications like Firefox that don't allow direct dragging into iPhoto, [Control]-click the image, use one of the commands in the contextual menu to save it, and then drag it from the Finder into iPhoto.

✔ Tip

■ There's no way to know in advance if an application will allow direct dragging into iPhoto, like Eudora, or not, like Firefox. Trial and error is the only way.

Figure 2.10 To view and import photos in a Mail message, click the Quick Look button in the header.

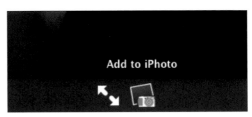

Figure 2.11 Click the Add to iPhoto button to add the photo to your iPhoto library.

Figure 2.12 In Safari, Control-click a photo and choose Add Image to iPhoto Library to, well, add it to your iPhoto library.

Figure 2.13 iPhoto discs appear in your source pane with any albums on the disc showing up under the disc name.

Figure 2.14 The easiest way to import pictures from an iPhoto disc into iPhoto is to drag the desired photos into the source pane, as I've done here.

No Keywords from iPhoto 5

Unfortunately, iPhoto 5 did not save keywords when burning to an iPhoto disc, which makes importing from an old backup disc less desirable if you've put much effort into keywords. Luckily, later versions of iPhoto fix the problem, including keywords on iPhoto discs and importing them along with photos.

Importing from an iPhoto Disc

iPhoto helps you protect your photo collection by making backup copies to CD or DVD (see "Backing up Your Photos," on page 26). Should something go wrong with your main iPhoto Library, you can restore your photos from these backup discs.

Also, friends or relatives who use iPhoto might send you discs of photos; although you can view photos from the disc, if you want to edit a photo or create a book, you must first import the desired images.

To import from an iPhoto disc:

1. Insert the iPhoto disc into your Mac's optical drive and switch to iPhoto.

   iPhoto displays the disc in the source pane under Shares (**Figure 2.13**).

2. Select one or more photos or albums, and then drag them to the source pane to import them into the iPhoto library and create an untitled album (**Figure 2.14**). Alternatively, drag them into an album to import them and add them to that album.

   iPhoto starts importing the photos, showing the images and a progress bar. Click Stop Import to halt if necessary.

✔ Tips

- Importing from an iPhoto disc works almost exactly the same as copying photos from a shared photo album.

- iPhoto performs duplicate checking, just as with the other import methods.

- Dragging a disc's album to the source pane copies the album to your iPhoto Library.

Importing via Image Capture

Before Apple released iPhoto, the way you transferred images from a digital camera to a Mac running Mac OS X was with an included utility called Image Capture (found in your Applications folder). Image Capture is still useful for downloading images from your camera if you *don't* want them to go into iPhoto for some reason.

To import using Image Capture:

1. Launch Image Capture.

2. Connect your camera or insert a memory card into your card reader, as appropriate.

3. Either click Download All (**Figure 2.15**), or click Download Some, select several photos to import, and click Download (**Figure 2.16**).

    Image Capture imports the photos to your Pictures folder as normal files.

✔ Tips

- You can download photos to any folder using Image Capture. Choose Other from the Download To pop-up menu, and then select the desired folder in the dialog.

- To adjust Image Capture's options, click the Options button in Image Capture's main window. In particular, make sure it doesn't delete after downloading for safety's sake. It's always best to erase photos in your camera after you're sure they have imported properly (**Figure 2.17**).

Figure 2.15 To download photos via Image Capture, connect your camera or insert your memory card, open Image Capture, and click Download All.

Figure 2.16 Alternatively, to import only particular photos, click Download Some, Shift- or Command-click to select a set of desired images in Image Capture's thumbnail listing, and then click the Download button.

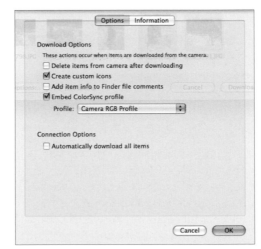

Figure 2.17 Make sure to set Image Capture's options so photos aren't deleted from the camera or card, both for safety's sake and in case you also want to import into iPhoto.

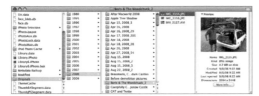

Figure 2.18 iPhoto uses an event-based directory structure that starts in your Pictures folder.

iPhoto Directory Structure

iPhoto creates its entire directory structure in the Pictures folder inside your user folder, starting with a *package* (a special folder you can't open normally) called iPhoto Library. Inside it, iPhoto creates three special folders: Originals, Modified, and Data. Inside each are folders for years; inside those are folders corresponding to events, and inside those event folders you finally get to the actual image files (**Figure 2.18**).

The top-level Originals folder contains your original photos. The Modified folder contains, in its event folders, modified versions of your photos. Until you make a change to an original image, there won't be a corresponding file in the Modified folder. The Data folder holds thumbnail images of your photos; they look the same in the Finder's preview, but are much smaller in size.

✔ Tips

- To open the iPhoto Library package, (Control)-click it and choose Show Package Contents.

- Other than the items mentioned in "Old Stuff That Can Go," do **not** move, rename, or delete anything inside the iPhoto Library in the Finder because you'll risk confusing iPhoto and corrupting your library! (And always work with a backup!)

- If you ever have to recover your photos from a corrupted iPhoto Library package, look in the Originals and Modified folders. Originals contains the photos as you imported them and Modified contains the versions that you edited.

- To locate a file corresponding to a photo in iPhoto, (Control)-click it in iPhoto and choose Show File. If you have edited the file, you can choose Show Original File to display the original file in the Finder.

Old Stuff That Can Go

Although you shouldn't mess with files and folders in the iPhoto Library package generally, there are a few items you can delete without harm—if they're present—because they're relics from previous versions and are no longer used. You likely won't save much disk space by deleting these unused items, but sometimes it's nice to have things be a bit more tidy.

Starting with iPhoto 6, the structure of the iPhoto Library changed significantly. Previous versions of iPhoto used a year/month/day hierarchy of folders, storing originals and modified images separately within the final day folder. If there were errors in upgrading your library when you first launched iPhoto 6, those year folders may still exist at the top level. As long as you allowed iPhoto to recover the photos nested inside, you can delete all the year folders with impunity (it's worth checking inside each one first, of course!).

Other items you can delete include the Desktop, iDVD, and Screen Effects folders. These folders merely contain aliases used by previous versions of iPhoto for your Desktop picture, iDVD, and the Mac OS X screen saver.

Leaving Photos in Place

Since iPhoto 6, iPhoto has had the capability to import photos from the Finder *without* copying the original files into the iPhoto Library package. The lack of this feature in early versions of iPhoto drove some users nuts, since they weren't sure they trusted iPhoto to manage all their laboriously arranged photos.

iPhoto now provides a simple checkbox in the Advanced pane of its Preferences window: Copy Items to the iPhoto Library. Uncheck this checkbox (**Figure 2.19**), and iPhoto will create aliases to your original photos in the Originals folder, leaving the original files wherever they're located on your hard disk.

Honestly, I generally don't recommend using this feature because it separates your original photos from the modified versions that iPhoto creates, which could cause confusion, particularly with backups. It might have been useful in iPhoto 1.0, but at this point, the feature is simply unnecessary for most people.

✔ Tips

- Turning off Copy Items to the iPhoto Library has no effect on photos imported from cameras or card readers.

- When you edit a photo, iPhoto stores the edited version in the Modified folder, just as you'd expect. But the changes you make are not reflected in the version stored outside of your iPhoto Library.

- To locate a file corresponding to a photo in iPhoto, (Control)-click it in iPhoto and choose Show File. If you have edited the file, you can instead choose Show Original File to display the original file in the Finder.

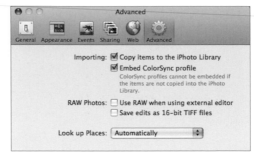

Figure 2.19 Uncheck Copy Items to the iPhoto Library to leave photos imported from your hard disk in their original locations.

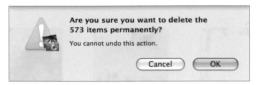

Figure 2.20 iPhoto checks to make sure you really want to delete photos from your hard disk before doing so.

Deleting Photos

Many of the pictures any photographer takes are lousy, and you need to cull the ones of your spouse wearing a stupid expression. Believe me, you really do. But that's the best part of digital photography; there's no cost to taking a photo and trashing it immediately.

You can trash photos only if you're viewing photos in Events, Photos, Last Import, or Last 12 Months, and *not* in a normal album.

Ways to trash photos:

◆ Select one or more photos (see "Selecting Photos," on page 45), and press (Delete), drag them to the Trash album, or (Control)-click the selection and choose Move to Trash from the contextual menu that appears.

◆ While viewing a photo from Events, Photos, Last Import, or Last 12 Months in a basic slideshow or in edit mode, press (Delete).

To delete photos for good:

1. From iPhoto's application menu, choose Empty iPhoto Trash ((Cmd)(Shift)(Delete)). iPhoto asks if you really want to remove the pictures (**Figure 2.20**).

2. Click OK to delete the photos.

✔ Tips

■ Deleting a photo from a normal album (or book, calendar, card, or slideshow) does not delete the original image but removes it from that album.

■ The only way to remove a photo from a smart album is to change the photo's criteria so the smart album doesn't see it.

■ Dragging a photo to the Trash icon on the Dock does nothing.

■ Remember, backups are your friends!

Culling Photos Quickly

Now that you know how to delete photos, you need to learn how to delete them as quickly and effectively as possible. There are four ways to cull photos, but the best approach isn't necessarily the most obvious. In order of worst to best...

Ways to cull imported photos:

◆ In organize mode, use the size slider to zoom your thumbnails, then click each one you want to delete and press Delete. Because this method requires so much clicking, it's clumsy.

◆ Select up to eight photos and choose Full Screen from the View menu (Cmd Option F) to enter full-screen mode with the photos showing at the largest possible size (**Figure 2.21**). Click a photo in full-screen mode to select it, and press Delete to trash it. Cycle through photos by pressing the arrow keys. This method works well for comparing similar photos but doesn't display the photos as large as when you view them one at a time.

◆ In organize mode, magnify a photo by double-clicking it (or Option-double-clicking it, depending on the setting in iPhoto's preferences), then cycle through the photos with the arrow keys, pressing Delete to trash those you don't like.

◆ In editing mode, either full-screen or in iPhoto's display pane, cycle through the photos with the arrow keys, pressing Delete to trash those you don't like (see full instructions in the sidebar).

✔ Tip

■ You can no longer delete photos while viewing them in a slideshow. Don't fret—it wasn't a good method before anyway, due to the lack of Undo support.

Figure 2.21 In full-screen mode, you can compare up to eight photos; click any one to select it, and send it to the Trash by pressing Delete.

The Best Way to Cull Photos

So you've just imported a bunch of photos and you want to get rid of the worthless ones. Here's my favorite method, which can be done entirely from the keyboard and shows each photo at full size.

1. Switch into full-screen mode by selecting the first photo in the event you want to clean up and clicking the full screen button or choosing Full Screen from the View menu (Cmd Option F).

2. If necessary, rotate the image to the correct orientation with Cmd R or Cmd Option R. You can also do other minor edits at this point, but don't get bogged down.

3. If you like it, press → (the right arrow key) to move on to the next photo.

4. If you don't like it, press Delete to move it to the Trash and move on to the next photo automatically. If you delete a photo accidentally, press Cmd Z to bring it back.

5. Repeat steps 2–4 as necessary.

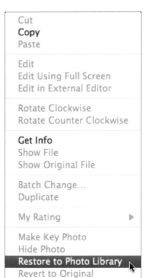

Cut
Copy
Paste

Edit
Edit Using Full Screen
Edit in External Editor

Rotate Clockwise
Rotate Counter Clockwise

Get Info
Show File
Show Original File

Batch Change...
Duplicate

My Rating ▸

Make Key Photo
Hide Photo
Restore to Photo Library
Revert to Original

Figure 2.22 To remove photos from the Trash, select them and choose Restore to Photo Library from the Photos menu.

Recovering Photos

iPhoto sports a special Trash album that holds all your deleted photos, just like the Finder's Trash. And like the Finder's Trash, you can pull mistakenly deleted photos out.

Ways to recover photos:

◆ Select one or more photos in the Trash album and choose Restore to Photo Library (Cmd Delete) from the Photos menu (**Figure 2.22**).

◆ Select one or more photos in the Trash album, Control-click the selection, and choose Restore to Photo Library from the contextual menu that appears.

◆ Drag one or more photos from the Trash album onto Events or Photos or, if you want to create an album from the recovered photos, to the Albums list in the source pane.

✔ Tips

■ You can't magnify or edit photos stored in the Trash, nor can you create a book, calendar, or card using the Trash album. Well, duh!

■ You can't drag a photo from the Trash album into another album without first restoring it.

■ iPhoto doesn't move the actual image files when you put them in the Trash; it merely tracks which ones are in the Trash album. Only when you empty the Trash are the actual files deleted.

Use Your Trash!

I strongly recommend that you make full use of iPhoto's Trash and empty it only occasionally. The whole point of having a Trash is to save you from mistakes, and you never know if you'll realize a mistake right away. Instead, let photos sit in the Trash for a while before deleting them for good. Or wait until you feel like you need the disk space they take up before deleting them.

Creating Multiple iPhoto Libraries

Although there's little outward indication of this, iPhoto lets you create and maintain multiple iPhoto libraries.

Reasons to create multiple iPhoto libraries:

◆ You might want to keep two different types of photos completely separate, such as personal snapshots and location shots for your real estate business.

◆ You might want different iPhoto libraries for different purposes. For instance, I have a special iPhoto Library that holds a small set of specific images that I use when giving presentations.

◆ You might want an iPhoto Library for miscellaneous photos sent to you by other people that you don't want cluttering your main collection.

To create an iPhoto Library:

1. Quit iPhoto.

2. Hold down ⌐Option⌐ and click iPhoto's icon in the Dock to launch it.

   In the dialog that appears, click Create New (**Figure 2.23**), and in the save dialog, enter a name and select a location for your new iPhoto Library (**Figure 2.24**).

✔ Tip

■ If you want a second iPhoto Library to contain *all* your photos to start with, select the original iPhoto Library package in the Pictures folder in the Finder and choose Duplicate (⌐Cmd⌐⌐D⌐) from the Finder's File menu.

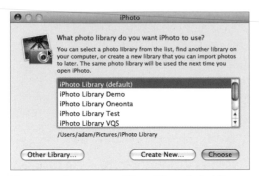

Figure 2.23 Create a new iPhoto Library by holding down Option while launching iPhoto and then clicking Create New in the dialog that appears.

Figure 2.24 Name and save your new iPhoto Library however and wherever you like.

Figure 2.25 If you double-click an iPhoto Library package in the Finder while iPhoto is running, click Relaunch to switch from the current library to quit iPhoto, and switch to the selected library.

Figure 2.26 iPhoto Library Manager enables you to switch among multiple iPhoto libraries easily.

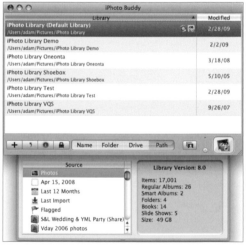

Figure 2.27 You can also use iPhoto Buddy to switch among multiple iPhoto libraries.

Switching between iPhoto Libraries

So you now have two (or more) iPhoto libraries. How do you switch between them?

Ways to switch between iPhoto libraries:

◆ Double-click an iPhoto Library package in the Finder. If iPhoto is not running, it launches and opens the iPhoto Library you clicked. If it is running, it asks you if you want to switch (**Figure 2.25**).

◆ Hold down Option and click iPhoto's icon in the Dock to launch it. In the dialog that appears, click Choose (**Figure 2.23**, previous page), and locate the desired iPhoto Library.

◆ With iPhoto not running, manually rename or move your main iPhoto Library package, then rename or move the desired iPhoto Library package so it's called just "iPhoto Library" and is located in your Pictures folder. If you launch without renaming, or if the name doesn't match exactly, iPhoto prompts you to choose a photo library (**Figure 2.23**, previous page).

◆ Use Fat Cat Software's $19.95 iPhoto Library Manager, with which you can manage the iPhoto libraries you want to switch among (**Figure 2.26**). Find it at www.fatcatsoftware.com/iplm/. iPhoto Library Manager can also copy photos between libraries, split large libraries, merge libraries, and much more.

◆ Use Rick Neil's free iPhoto Buddy (www.iphotobuddy.com), which also provides a simple interface for switching quickly among multiple iPhoto libraries (**Figure 2.27**).

Backing up Your Photos

The most important thing you can do when managing your photos is to make a backup.

To back up photos:

1. Select the items you want to back up, which is best done by selecting events in the display pane (**Figure 2.28**), or folders, albums, books, calendars, cards, or slideshows in the source pane.

2. From the Share menu, choose Burn, insert a blank disc, and click OK.

   Below the display pane, iPhoto shows the name of the disc and information about how much data will be burned to the disc (**Figure 2.29**). The disc's icon will be red if it can't hold the selected photos.

3. Select fewer or more photos to use the space on your destination disc as desired.

4. Change the name of the disc if you want.

5. When everything looks right, click the Burn button to start the burn, and when iPhoto asks you to confirm one last time and lets you set additional burning options, click Burn (**Figure 2.30**).

   iPhoto creates a disk image, copies the selected photos to it, and burns the disc.

✔ Tips

■ Don't believe statistics reported about the size of the selection in the Information pane; the only numbers that matter are those that iPhoto reports in step 2 above.

■ On the disc, your photos are stored in an iPhoto Library *folder*, not a *package*, so it's easier to get into (but otherwise has the same structure). If you want to give the disc to someone who doesn't use iPhoto, see "Sharing Photos on Disc with Windows Users," on page 155.

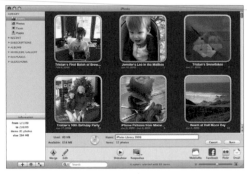

Figure 2.28 To get started, select the items you want to burn, choose Burn from the Share menu, and then insert a blank disc.

Figure 2.29 Once you've inserted the disc, iPhoto lets you name your disc and gives you information about how much data will be burned to it.

Figure 2.30 iPhoto verifies that you really want to burn a disc with one last dialog that also provides additional burn options if you click the triangle button in the upper-right corner (for more information, see the sidebar "Burn Options," next page).

A Proper Backup Strategy

I'll be honest. I think backing up just your photos by burning them to CD or DVD is only a small step above useless. If you value the contents of your Mac, and if you value having a working Mac as a communications device for email and iChat, you need a real backup strategy. To learn more, I recommend Joe Kissell's *Take Control of Mac OS X Backups* ebook (www.takecontrolbooks.com/backup-macosx). It's only $15 and will help you figure out exactly what hardware and software you need and how to set it up.

Burn Options

I recommend that you select Verify Burned Data for safety; if you have trouble burning, try reducing the burn speed.

The options for erasing media and leaving a disc appendable apply only to rewritable media like CD-RW, but iPhoto won't erase no matter what; use Disk Utility.

The choice of ejecting the disc after burning or mounting it on the Desktop is minor, though I recommend a quick visual inspection of the contents of the disc in iPhoto after burning.

True Archiving

If you want to *archive* photos, that is, burn them to disc and then remove them from your hard disk, I recommend the following:

◆ Make at least two copies and store one off-site, like at a friend's house.

◆ Work methodically by making albums from events to retain organization and by selecting *everything* in order.

Other Backup Options

What if you don't have a writable optical drive or don't want to end up with your photos existing only in an iPhoto Library? You have a few options.

Other backup options:

◆ Copy your iPhoto Library (remember that it's in your Pictures folder) to an external hard disk.

◆ Use a dedicated backup program, such as Mac OS X's own Time Machine or Carbon Copy Cloner (www.bombich.com) to back up your entire Mac. I also like CrashPlan (www.crashplan.com) for backing up just your Home folder to a friend's house as an off-site backup.

◆ Export photos to folders in the Finder, then manually burn them to CD or DVD to back them up with your desired organizational approach. It's more work, but you get exactly what you want at the end.

✔ Tips

■ No matter which backup method you choose, I recommend having more than one backup copy and storing one of them off-site. That way, should your house or office burn down or be burglarized, your backup would remain safe.

■ To avoid wasting media (though CD-R discs are awfully cheap), buy the more expensive CD-RW discs and erase them in Disk Utility between uses.

■ Don't use CD-RW discs for true archiving, since anything that can be erased is a lousy permanent medium.

■ Don't assume that *any* backup media will last forever. Every year or so, check to make sure your backups are readable, and recopy them to new media, just to be safe.

Merging iPhoto Libraries

If you have two Macs, you may want to merge the contents of two iPhoto libraries, one from each computer.

To merge iPhoto libraries (I):

1. Network your Macs via AirPort, Ethernet, or even FireWire (using IP over FireWire, which you can enable in the Network system preference pane).

2. On both Macs, turn on photo sharing in iPhoto's Preferences window (**Figure 2.31**). For more information, see "Sharing Photos via iPhoto Sharing" on page 150.

3. On the destination Mac, in the source pane, drag the desired photos or albums from the source Mac's shared album to Events or Photos.

To merge iPhoto libraries (II):

◆ If one of your Macs has a writable optical drive that supports CD-R, CD-RW, or DVD-R, burn a disc containing all the photos you want to transfer from the source iPhoto Library. Then import them into the destination iPhoto Library as explained in "Importing from an iPhoto Disc," on page 17.

To merge iPhoto libraries (III):

1. From the source iPhoto Library, export the desired images by album or event into folders (see "Exporting Files," on page 152).

2. Copy those folders to the Mac with the destination iPhoto Library via a network or FireWire Target Disk Mode.

3. Drag the folders into iPhoto to import their photos (see "Importing from Files," on page 15).

Figure 2.31 To turn on photo sharing, select Look for Shared Photos and Share My Photos in the Sharing pane of iPhoto's Preferences window.

To merge iPhoto libraries (IV):

◆ Use Fat Cat Software's $19.95 iPhoto Library Manager, which can merge iPhoto libraries automatically, retaining all titles, keywords, ratings, and albums, along with face and place information. Download it from: `www.fatcatsoftware.com/iplm/`. This option is the most costly, but by far the easiest if you're merging a lot of photos, or need to merge libraries frequently.

✔ Tips

■ If you're burning to disc, use CD-RW media if you want to reuse that disc; use CD-R media if you want a backup.

■ When exporting via the third method, I recommend using the photo title as the filename or else you'll lose any work you put in titling your photos.

3

ORGANIZING PHOTOS

Switching to Organize Mode

iPhoto keeps you in organize mode, except when you're importing photos; editing photos; creating a slideshow; or working on a book, card, or calendar. Thus, there are two basic ways to return to organize mode from another mode:

◆ In the source pane, click any item in Library, Recent, Subscriptions, or Albums to switch to organize mode and display the contents of the selected album.

◆ When you have switched into edit mode from organize mode but are not using the Crop, Red-Eye, or Retouch tools, double-click the picture to switch back to organize mode.

Faces and Places, Oh My!

New in iPhoto '09 are Faces and Places. Put briefly, iPhoto '09 can automatically organize your photos by recognizing the people in them. And it can use location information stored in (or added to) photos as a way of placing photos on a map. These features are wildly useful for organizing photos, so much so that I've given them their own chapters, coming next.

One of the best things, in my opinion, about digital photographs is that they come with their own organizational tags built in. We may not have cameras that can recognize specific people, but every modern digital camera records a great deal of information about when each picture was taken and its associated settings. For many people, including me, that information alone provides enough organizational power.

However, many people want to do more, and iPhoto provides a wide variety of tools for assigning keywords to your photos, collecting them in albums, and more. We'll look at each of those capabilities in this chapter.

Of course, the only reason to organize photos at all is so you can find them quickly and easily later, and iPhoto also shines in that department, making it easy to scroll through your entire photo collection chronologically or home in on a specific set of photos with sophisticated yet simple searching tools. Want to find all the photos taken in June, July, and August of the last 5 years? Want to find all the photos whose titles or descriptions mention your mother? No problem. You can even make smart albums that constantly search your entire library for matching photos and present them in an album.

Let's take a look.

What's New in Organize Mode

If you've used the previous version of iPhoto, you'll want to pay attention to the new interface elements iPhoto '09 brings to organize mode (**Figure 3.1**).

New features in organize mode:

◆ A new Faces mode uses face detection and recognition technology to help you organize photos by the people who appear in them. Faces is a sufficiently significant addition to iPhoto that Apple gave it a prominent entry in the source pane, under the Library list. For more information about Faces, see Chapter 4, "Working with Faces," starting on page 63.

◆ Joining Faces in the Library list of the source pane is Places, which reads location information stored in photo files to show photos on a map and let you search for them by location. For more information on Places, see Chapter 5, "Working with Places," which begins on page 71.

◆ Apple has renamed the Projects list in the source pane to Keepsakes—it still contains all your books, cards, and calendars. Also, Web Gallery is now called MobileMe Gallery.

◆ iPhoto '09 gains new lists for your Facebook and Flickr albums.

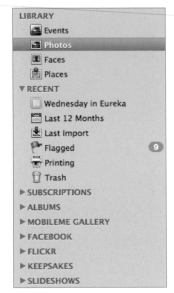

Figure 3.1 iPhoto '09 adds Faces and Places to the Library list, creates new lists for Facebook and Flickr, and swaps the Projects name for Keepsakes and the Web Gallery name for MobileMe Gallery.

Source Pane?

I follow Apple's lead in calling the items in the left-hand area in iPhoto "sources" and the area itself the "source pane," even though iPhoto no longer explicitly labels it as some previous versions did. In most cases, things you can do to one type of source (like delete it, move it around, or add photos to it), you can do to all the types of sources. When that's the case, I'll use the term "sources;" when there is an exception, I'll use the specific term or call out the exception.

Organize Tools Overview

Here's a quick reference to the controls available in organize mode (**Figure 3.2**). Note that this screenshot shows the Photos view; the Events view displays a single photo for each event, making for faster navigation.

✔ Tip

■ The Keepsakes pop-up menu replaces the Book, Calendar, and Card buttons when the window is too narrow for them all to fit comfortably.

Source pane. Create and work with collections of photos here.

Drag the divider to change the size of the source pane.

Event, showing its thumbnail, name, date, and number of photos. Drag a photo to the thumbnail to set it as the key photo; double-click the title to change it. Click an event's triangle to open and close it.

A folder containing other items. Click its triangle to open and close.

Information pane. Info about the selected item(s) shows up here. Modify titles, dates, and descriptions.

Click to add a new item to the source pane.

Photo metadata: title, rating, and keywords. Click any one to change it.

Size slider. Adjust this slider to display more or fewer thumbnails. Drag the slider or click the desired location. Click the end icons for smallest and largest sizes.

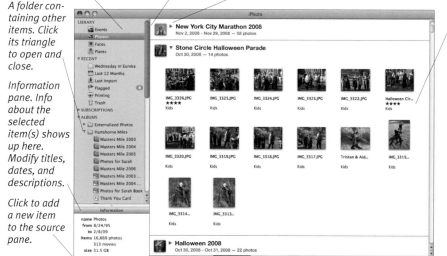

Click to hide and show the Information pane.

Figure 3.2

Click to enter full-screen mode.

Click to assign names to faces.

Search field. Enter text here to find matching photos.

Click to hide or flag the selected photos.

Click to play a basic slideshow.

The buttons in the organize mode's toolbar help you switch between modes and offer different methods of sharing photos.

ORGANIZE TOOLS OVERVIEW

Changing the Display Pane's Layout

There are various things you can do to change the way the display pane looks.

To change the display pane layout:

◆ Switch among Events, Photos, Faces, and Places by clicking them in the source pane.

◆ Move the size slider (or click in the desired location) to adjust the size of the thumbnails from moderately large (**Figure 3.3**) all the way down to as many photos as fit in the window (**Figure 3.4**).

◆ Double-click a photo to magnify it such that it occupies the entire window.

◆ To show or hide titles, ratings, and key-words (**Figure 3.5**), choose the desired item from the View menu.

◆ To add or remove sharing tools from the toolbar, choose the desired one from the Show in Toolbar submenu in the View menu (**Figure 3.6**).

✔ Tips

■ The keyboard shortcuts for zooming work only on photos, not events.

■ You can shrink the source pane by dragging the line that divides it from the display pane to the left. Expand it by dragging back to the right.

■ Viewing titles in the display pane isn't useful when you use smaller thumbnail sizes, but remember that the current photo's title is in the Information pane.

■ Event titles help show where you are when in Photos view, so I recommend leaving them showing and giving them names. Option-click an event expansion triangle to hide or show all events.

Figure 3.3 To view thumbnails at a moderately large size, move the size slider all the way to the right, or press the 1 key.

Figure 3.4 To view as many thumbnails as possible, move the size slider all the way to the left or press the 0 (zero) key.

Figure 3.5 For an uncluttered look in the Photos view, turn off display of titles, ratings, and keywords in the View menu.

Figure 3.6 Choose which sharing tools you want in the tool-bar using the Show in Toolbar submenu.

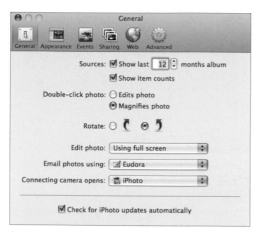

Figure 3.7 Use the Sources settings in iPhoto's General preference pane to control the Last Months album and the display of the item count in sources.

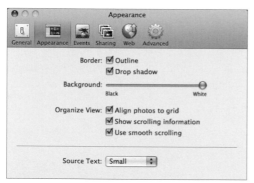

Figure 3.8 The Appearance pane of iPhoto's Preferences window provides settings that control how iPhoto draws and scrolls through photos, and the size of source name text.

Figure 3.9 In the Events preference pane, you can choose what double-clicking an event does and set whether you'll see event reflections and the translucent scrolling feedback display.

Other Display Preferences

You can set options in iPhoto's Preferences window that affect the display pane.

From the iPhoto application menu, choose Preferences (Cmd ,) to open the Preferences window; you can find display preferences in the General, Appearance, and Events panes (**Figure 3.7** through **Figure 3.9**).

Display preferences you can change:

◆ In the General preference pane, use the Sources controls to choose if the Last Months album appears and how many months it contains.

◆ Select Show Item Counts to append the number of photos in each source item to its name in the source pane.

◆ In the Appearance pane, select Outline and/or Drop Shadow border styles, and use the Background slider to change the darkness of the background.

◆ To align all your photos to a regular grid in which the width of the widest picture sets the width for all photos, check the Align Photos to Grid checkbox.

◆ Use the Show Scrolling Information checkbox to toggle whether the translucent Information dialog appears when scrolling. In the Appearance preferences, this setting affects the Photos view; in Events preferences, the Event view.

◆ The Use Smooth Scrolling option makes scrolling via the Page Up and Page Down keys smoother.

◆ For a more spartan look, turn off event reflections in the Events preference pane.

◆ Set what happens when you double-click an image in the General preference pane and what happens when you double-click an event in the Events pane.

Contextual Menu Shortcuts

Although iPhoto does a good job of making most of what you can do visible in the interface, you can also [Control]-click (or, if you have a two-button mouse or appropriately configured trackpad, right-click) a photo to bring up a contextual menu that lets you perform a number of actions directly on the photo you clicked (**Figure 3.10**).

Contextual menu shortcuts:

◆ You can cut, copy, or paste photos, for use both inside iPhoto and in other applications. Cutting a photo removes it from the current album and pasting a photo adds it to the current album (neither is true of smart albums).

◆ The Edit commands are particularly useful for opening photos in alternative ways without switching iPhoto's preferences.

◆ Show File and Show Original File switch you to the Finder. Show File selects the original file if no changes have been made; if changes have been made, it selects the edited version. And if changes have been made, Show Original File selects the original. Yeah, it's confusing.

◆ The rest of the commands—Rotate, Get Info, Batch Change, Duplicate, My Rating, Make Key Photo, Hide Photo, Move to Trash, and Revert to Original—are like those in iPhoto's Photos and Events menus, but using the contextual menu to apply them may feel more intuitive.

✔ Tip

■ You can often drag photos from iPhoto to other applications instead of using copy and paste.

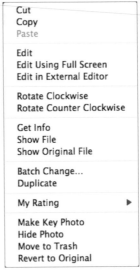

Figure 3.10 Control-click one or more selected photos to display iPhoto's contextual menu shortcuts.

✔ More Tips

■ Some of the menu items become unavailable when they don't make sense (for example, you can't paste into the Events and Photos views, and Revert to Original doesn't apply to original photos).

■ Move to Trash changes to Delete From Album when you're not in the Events or Photos views.

CONTEXTUAL MENU SHORTCUTS

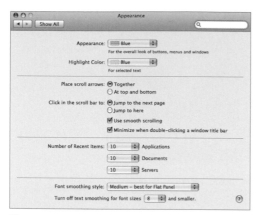

Figure 3.11 You can change Mac OS X's scrolling behavior in the Appearance preference pane.

Moving around in iPhoto

Obviously, you can move around in iPhoto by scrolling, but knowing a few tricks and techniques can make navigating through your photos easier.

Ways to move around:

◆ Click or drag in the scroll bar, just as you would in any other Mac application.

◆ Option-click the scroll bar to jump to the particular spot you clicked.

◆ Click a photo to make sure the display pane is active; then use the arrow keys to move around.

◆ With the display pane active, use Page Up and Page Down to scroll through your photos one screen at a time.

◆ With the display pane active, use Home and End to move to the top and bottom of the currently displayed photos.

✔ Tips

■ The Option-clicking (Jump to Here) behavior applies to Mac OS X in general, and you can make it the default clicking behavior by selecting the Jump to Here radio button in Mac OS X's Appearance preference pane (**Figure 3.11**). I find the Jump to Here setting disconcerting, since it's counter to the way I've used scroll bars on the Mac forever.

■ If you're having trouble scrolling to a desired location, it might help to reduce the thumbnail size so you can see many more thumbnails on the screen at once.

■ Hold down Option when scrolling to scroll smoothly. This feature may not help many people, but it made arranging the iPhoto window (to take nicely aligned screen shots) a lot easier for me while I was writing this book.

Working with Events

Events are key to iPhoto, and Apple has provided lots of ways to work with them.

To rename an event:

◆ Wherever you see an event title, click it to edit, and then type the new name (**Figure 3.12**).

To view photos in an event:

◆ In Events view, move the mouse pointer horizontally over the key photo to view all the photos in the event. This is called *scrubbing*, and it's wildly cool.

◆ In Events view, double-click an event, or select several events and double-click one of them (**Figure 3.13**). To return to viewing event thumbnails, click the All Events button or double-click on any blank spot.

◆ When viewing the photos in an event, click the arrows at the top right of the window (shown in **Figure 3.15**) to move to the previous and next events.

◆ In Events view, select an event and choose Open in Separate Window from the Events menu, or Control-click it and choose the same command from the contextual menu, to open a new window showing just the photos in that event (**Figure 3.14**).

To change an event's key photo:

◆ In Events view, scrub over the photos until the desired one is showing, Control-click it, and choose Make Key Photo. Or press Spacebar.

◆ When viewing the photos in an event, select one and choose Make Key Photo from the Events menu, Control-click it and choose Make Key Photo, or drag it to the key photo well (**Figure 3.15**).

Figure 3.12 Anywhere you see an event title, just double-click it to edit it.

Figure 3.13 Select two or more events and double-click one of them to view all their photos together.

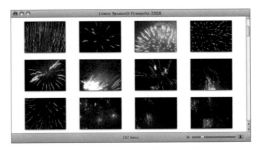

Figure 3.14 Opening an event in its own window can be a good way to focus on just the photos in that event, or to compare it with the contents of another window.

Figure 3.15 Drag a photo to the key photo well to make it the key photo.

Figure 3.16 To split the selected photos into a new event, select some photos and click the Split button at the left of the toolbar.

Figure 3.17 Drag one event onto another to merge the two events.

Figure 3.18 To move photos between events, drag photos from one event to another in Photos view.

Autosplit Preferences

In the Events preference pane, you can set iPhoto's autosplit feature to create one new event per week, one per day, one every 8 hours, or one every 2 hours.

Splitting and Merging Events

It's all too easy to end up with photos that aren't in the right events. You can split events apart, merge events together, and move photos from one event into another.

Ways to split an event:

◆ When you're importing new photos, check Autosplit Events after Importing.

◆ In Events view, select one or more events and choose Autosplit Selected Events from the Events menu.

◆ When viewing an event's photos, select one or more photos and click the Split button (**Figure 3.16**) or choose either Split Event or Create Event from the Events menu.

Ways to merge events:

◆ In Events view, drag one event into another event (**Figure 3.17**) or select two events and click the Merge button.

◆ Select two or more events in Events view, double-click them to view their photos together, select one event, and either drag it to another event, click the Merge button, or choose Merge Events from the Events menu.

Ways to move photos between events:

◆ In Photos view, drag photos from one event into another event (**Figure 3.18**).

◆ Select multiple events in Events view, double-click them to view their photos, and drag photos from one to the other.

◆ In one event, select one or more photos, cut them by choosing Cut from the Edit menu ($\boxed{\text{Cmd}}\boxed{\text{X}}$), switch to another event, and paste them by choosing Paste from the Edit menu ($\boxed{\text{Cmd}}\boxed{\text{V}}$).

Creating and Working with Folders

iPhoto provides folders into which you can organize albums, and, although it may not seem obvious, books, cards, calendars, saved slideshows, and other folders. Folders are a great way to tuck away older items.

To create a folder:

1. From the File menu, choose New Folder (Cmd Shift Option N) or Control-click in an empty spot at the bottom of the source pane and choose New Folder.

   iPhoto creates a new untitled folder with the name selected so you can name it.

2. Enter a name for the folder.

To move items into and out of folders:

◆ Drag one or more items (albums, books, slideshows, etc.) into or out of the folder.

   iPhoto moves the items, giving the folder an expansion triangle if necessary so you can open and close it (**Figure 3.19**).

To duplicate a folder and its contents:

◆ Control-click a folder and choose Duplicate from the contextual menu that appears.

To delete a folder:

◆ Select one or more folders and press Delete, or Control-click a folder and choose Delete Folder from the contextual menu that appears.

   iPhoto prompts you to make sure you know what you're doing; click Delete to delete the folder and all its contents.

◆ Select one or more folders and press Cmd Delete to delete them and their contents (albums, slideshows, books, etc. but not the associated photos) without being prompted for confirmation.

Figure 3.19 Drag items into or out of a folder to add or remove them from the folder.

Facts about Folders

Folders can take a bit of getting used to:

◆ Folders appear only in the Albums list in the source pane, but you can move items from the Keepsakes and Slideshows lists into folders. When you remove such items from a folder, they snap back into the appropriate lists.

◆ Folders cannot contain MobileMe, Facebook, or Flickr galleries.

◆ When you select a folder in the source pane, the display pane shows all the photos from all the albums, slideshows, books, cards, and calendars inside that folder.

◆ When you delete a folder, you delete the items (albums, books, and so on, though not the original photos, of course) inside it as well. Be careful!

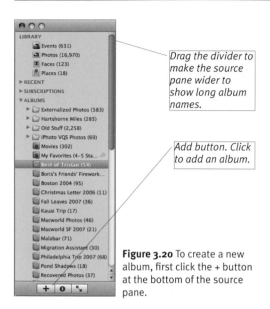

Drag the divider to make the source pane wider to show long album names.

Add button. Click to add an album.

Figure 3.20 To create a new album, first click the + button at the bottom of the source pane.

Figure 3.21 Next, select Album from the icon list, name the album, and click Create.

Figure 3.22 When you drag photos into the source pane to create a new album containing them, notice how the entire source pane gets a thick blue border.

Creating Albums

iPhoto provides *albums* to help us categorize photos—these were from the Fiji trip, those were from Joe's birthday party, and so on. Albums are also useful starting points for saved slideshows, books, and calendars.

To create an album:

1. Click the Add button (+) at the bottom of the source pane (**Figure 3.20**), or choose New Album (Cmd N) from the File menu. iPhoto displays a dialog asking what type of item you want to create, if you want to add any selected photos to it, and what you want to call it (**Figure 3.21**).

2. Choose Album from the item icon list, enter a name, and click Create to add it to the source pane.

Other ways to create an album:

◆ Select some photos, and then follow the steps above or just choose New Album from Selection (Cmd Shift N) from the File menu.

◆ Drag one or more photos, or an entire event, into the source pane, onto the Albums list title (**Figure 3.22**).

◆ Drag one or more photos, or a folder of photos, from the Finder into the source pane, onto the Albums list title.

◆ Control-click an empty spot at the bottom of the source pane and choose New Album or New Album From Selection.

✔ Tip

■ Use albums for categories of pictures that appear once in your photo collection. Use keywords for categories that recur throughout your collection. Albums work well for a specific trip's photos; keywords work better for identifying all pictures of your family members or recurring events.

Creating and Editing Smart Albums

Unlike normal albums, which you must maintain manually, smart albums use a set of rules that you create to maintain their contents automatically.

To create a smart album:

1. Click the Add button (+) below the source pane, select Smart Album from the item icon list, and click Create. Better yet, either Option-click the Add button, choose New Smart Album (Cmd Option N) from the File menu, or Control-click an empty spot at the bottom of the source pane and choose New Album.

   iPhoto displays a dialog for you to name and configure your album (**Figure 3.23**).

2. Enter a name for the new album.

3. From the first pop-up menu, choose a criterion that photos must match to be included (**Figure 3.24**).

4. From the second pop-up menu, choose how that criterion should be evaluated (**Figure 3.25**).

5. Enter a condition against which the criterion is to be evaluated (**Figure 3.26**).

6. If you want your smart album to have multiple criteria, click the + button and repeat steps 3–5.

7. When you're done, click the OK button.

   iPhoto looks at all your photos and adds those that match to the smart album.

To edit a smart album:

1. Control-click an album and choose Edit Smart Album from the contextual menu.

2. Follow steps 2–7 above to change the smart album's name or configuration.

Figure 3.23 Name and configure your smart album in the dialog that appears after choosing New Smart Album from the File menu.

Figure 3.24 Smart albums can match photos based on numerous criteria, shown here. In this case, I'm looking for photos with a specific rating.

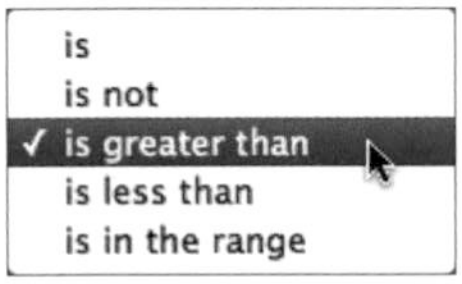

Figure 3.25 Once you've chosen a criterion, you must determine how it should be evaluated. The second pop-up menu changes dynamically to match the selected criterion. Here, since I'm matching on rating, and because I'd like the smart album to find only photos with 4 or 5 stars, I've chosen Is Greater Than.

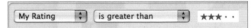

Figure 3.26 Lastly, enter the condition against which your criterion will be evaluated. To finish the smart album that matches my 4- or 5-star photos, I've clicked the field to select 3 stars. Read as a whole, my rule says, "Select all photos whose rating is greater than 3 stars."

Smart Album Ideas

Here are some ideas to help you get started with making useful smart albums.

Smart album ideas:

◆ By matching on ratings, you can easily create a Favorites smart album that contains just your top-rated photos.

◆ Use the new Face criterion to make a smart album that collects all "unnamed" photos to make it easier to train iPhoto's face-recognition feature.

◆ The Photo criterion lets you select specific kinds of photos, including those that are flagged, hidden, or edited, and those that are really movies or in RAW format.

◆ The new Place criterion is useful for finding all the photos from a state or country, even though the individual photos have more specific locations.

◆ With the Camera Model criterion, it's easy to create a smart album that contains photos taken by cameras *other than* yours—likely photos that were taken by other people and sent to you.

◆ To create an album that contains all the photos of a person, use the Any Text criterion matching that person's name. It will also pick up any photos identified by the Faces feature (which you can access directly via the new Name criterion).

✔ Tips

■ You can't remove photos from a smart album manually; the only way to take them out is to change either the photo or the criteria so they no longer match.

■ The fact that you can now find photos that have been edited could be very useful if you were ever exporting all your photos from iPhoto to another program.

Folders Enhance Smart Albums

There's a problem with smart albums. When a smart album has multiple criteria, you must choose whether the smart album should match Any or All of the conditions you specify. So I could have a smart album that finds all the photos containing either Tristan *or* Tonya (Any) or both Tristan *and* Tonya (All). But, if I wanted the smart album to show me all the photos of either Tonya or Tristan that are rated 5 stars, there's no way do define that in the smart album interface.

Reader Charles Jacobs came up with the solution: folders. Since folders by definition combine all the photos from their enclosed items, I could make a folder containing a smart album that collects all the photos of Tonya that I'd rated as 5 stars and another smart album of Tristan's 5-star photos. Selecting the folder in the source pane would display all the desired photos. And once they're collected in that folder, I could easily work with them as a group, perhaps making a slideshow or setting them as my screen saver.

So if you're having trouble figuring out how to bend smart albums to your will, consider the humble folder.

Duplicating Sources

Anything you can create in the source pane—except a MobileMe, Facebook, or Flickr Web album—you can duplicate. Duplicating isn't something you'll use every day, but it can be useful.

Ways to duplicate a source:

◆ Control-click an item in the source pane and choose Duplicate from the contextual menu that appears (**Figure 3.27**).

◆ Select an item in the source pane, and then choose Duplicate from the Photos menu (Cmd D).

iPhoto duplicates the album, appending "2" to its name (**Figure 3.28**).

Reasons to duplicate sources:

◆ If you're making picture books for two sets of grandparents, for instance, you might want to use a very similar set of photos with different text. Lay out one book, then duplicate it to eliminate the effort of arranging photos again.

◆ If you want make differently themed books or calendars with the same set of images, create one, then duplicate it and change the theme of the duplicate.

◆ If you've put quite a lot of work into a book, calendar, or slideshow, and you want to try something without potentially messing up your work, make a duplicate first.

◆ If you've constructed a complex smart album and want to make another that's only slightly different, duplicating the first one and modifying the duplicate is easier than making a new one.

✔ Tip

■ Remember that duplicating a folder also duplicates everything inside it.

Figure 3.27 To duplicate a source, Control-click it and choose Duplicate from the contextual menu.

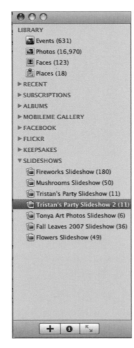

Figure 3.28 iPhoto appends a number to the name of the duplicate.

Figure 3.29 To rename a source (such as one you just duplicated), double-click its name and edit it.

Figure 3.30 To move an item in the Source list, drag it to the desired location.

Renaming and Rearranging Sources

You'll undoubtedly want to rename every-thing in the source pane to give the items descriptive names. Plus, since iPhoto initially lists sources in the order you created them, you'll probably want to move them around in the list.

To rename a source:

◆ Double-click the source's name, and then edit the name (**Figure 3.29**).

To rearrange the source list:

◆ Drag a source to the desired location in the list. Note the blue bar that indicates where the item will appear when you drop it (**Figure 3.30**).

◆ Control-click any item in the source pane and choose Sort Albums from the contex-tual menu that appears.

iPhoto alphabetizes all the items in the source pane, other than folders and their contents. It's a little wacky.

✔ Tips

■ Names need not be unique (but it's a good idea to avoid replicating them).

■ Each type of source—folders, albums, smart albums, books, cards, calendars, and saved slideshows—sorts together (both in the source pane and inside fold-ers), and you can rearrange items only within each type.

■ You can use iPhoto's spelling tools while editing names. For details, see "Checking Spelling as You Type," on page 183.

■ You can Cmd-click or Shift-click to select and move multiple sources at once.

Deleting Sources

It's easy to create items in the source pane, but if you decide you don't want one cluttering your list, they're even easier to delete.

Ways to delete a source:

◆ Select one or more items and press Delete.

iPhoto prompts you to make sure you know what you're doing; click Delete to delete the source (**Figure 3.31**).

◆ Select one or more items and press Cmd Delete.

iPhoto deletes the items instantly, without asking for confirmation.

◆ Control-click an item and choose Delete from the contextual menu that appears (**Figure 3.32**).

iPhoto prompts you to make sure you know what you're doing; click Delete to delete the item (**Figure 3.31**).

✔ Tips

■ You can't Undo the act of deleting something from the source pane.

■ Deleting an album (or anything else in the source pane) doesn't affect the original photos in your library since albums merely contain pointers to the originals.

■ Deleting a folder also deletes all the albums, slideshows, books, etc. (but not their photos) inside it. Be careful!

■ Don't feel that albums must be created carefully and then kept forever. It's totally reasonable to group a bunch of photos in an album, work on them for a little while, and then delete the album.

■ On the other hand, if you think you might want to use an item again, store it away inside a folder for future reference.

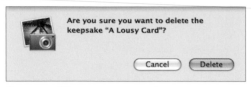

Figure 3.31 iPhoto prompts to make sure you want to delete the selected item. Click Delete if you do.

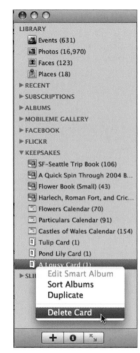

Figure 3.32 You can Control-click an item in the source pane and choose Delete to delete it, though that's harder than just pressing Delete or Command-Delete.

Deleting Web Albums

When you delete a MobileMe, Facebook, or Flickr album from within iPhoto, the photos disappear from the Web as well.

DELETING SOURCES

Figure 3.33 To select multiple pictures by dragging, click in an empty area of the display pane, and then drag a selection rectangle over the desired photos.

Selecting Photos

Throughout the rest of this chapter, I tell you to select photos before performing some task. I'm sure you have figured out the basic ways of selecting and deselecting images, but some others aren't so obvious.

Ways to select photos:

◆ Click a photo to select it.

◆ Click one photo to select it, hold down (Shift), and then click another photo to select it and all the intervening pictures.

◆ Click one photo to select it, hold down (Cmd), and then click additional photos to add them to the selection individually.

◆ Click in an empty area of the display pane, then drag a selection rectangle over the photos you want to select (**Figure 3.33**). If you drag to the top or bottom of the display pane, iPhoto scrolls the pane and keeps selecting additional images.

◆ When viewing photos, choose Select All ((Cmd)(A)) from the Edit menu to select all the images in the current album.

◆ In Photos view, use the View menu to make sure event titles are showing, and then click an event title to select all the images in that event.

Ways to deselect photos:

◆ To deselect one of several selected images, (Cmd)-click it.

◆ To deselect all photos, click in the empty area surrounding the photos or choose Select None from the Edit menu ((Cmd)(Shift)(A)).

✔ Tip

■ iPhoto slows to a crawl if you click Photos and then do a Select All.

Select Multiple Albums

Don't assume you must work with only the photos in a single album at a time. You can select multiple albums at once by (Cmd)- or (Shift)-clicking album names, and when you do that, the photos from all the selected albums show in the display pane.

Similarly, if you select a folder, the display pane shows all the photos in all the items inside that folder.

Adding Photos to Sources

Even after you've made an album, book, calendar, Web album, or saved slideshow, you can add photos to it (remember that smart albums populate themselves).

Ways to add photos to sources:

◆ Select one or more photos in the display pane and drag them onto a source other than a folder, which can hold only other sources. Note the thick, blue border that appears when you drag over a source (**Figure 3.34**).

◆ From the Finder, drag one or more photos, or an entire folder of photos, to a source. iPhoto imports the photos and then adds them to the source. Note that the photos will appear in the library also, not just in the source.

◆ Drag photos from the display pane into the source pane, but not onto a specific source (the easiest drop location is the Albums list title). This technique creates a new album and adds the images to it (**Figure 3.35**).

◆ Select photos, choose Copy ([Cmd][C]) from the Edit menu, click the desired destination album, and choose Paste ([Cmd][V]) from the Edit menu.

◆ [Control]-click one or more selected photos, choose Copy from the contextual menu that appears, switch to the desired album, [Control]-click a blank spot in the display pane, and choose Paste from the contextual menu. It's the same idea as the previous method.

✔ Tip

■ You can add a photo to a source only once. To put a photo in a source twice, you must duplicate it—see "Duplicating Photos," on page 85.

Figure 3.34 To add photos to a source, select them and drag them onto the desired source in the source pane. Note how the destination source gets a thick blue border and how the pointer changes from a plain arrow to one with a + badge. iPhoto also tells you, via a number in a red circle, how many images you're dragging.

Figure 3.35 To create an album and add photos to it in one fell swoop, select the images and drag them to Albums list title in the source pane.

Figure 3.36 To remove the picture from that album, Control-click a photo and choose Delete From Album.

Removing Photos from Sources

As you work with a source, you may decide that you don't want some of the images in the source. Luckily, they're easy to remove.

Ways to remove photos from sources:

◆ Making sure you're in the desired source, select the photos you want to remove and press Delete.

◆ Select the photos you want to remove, and choose Delete From Album from the Photos menu (Cmd Delete) or, for albums only, Cut (Cmd X) from the Edit menu.

◆ Drag the photos you want to remove to the Trash album.

◆ For albums only, Control-click one or more selected photos, and then choose Cut or Delete From Album from the contextual menu (**Figure 3.36**).

◆ To remove a photo from a smart album you must either redefine the smart album or change the photo's information such that the photo no longer matches the smart album's criteria.

✔ Tips

■ Removing a photo from an album, book, card, calendar, or saved slideshow doesn't delete it from your library.

■ Removing a photo from a Web album also removes it from the MobileMe, Facebook, or Flickr Web site.

■ If you make a mistake, either choose Undo from the Edit menu (Cmd Z) or add them again.

■ Dragging a photo to the Trash album from another album does not delete it from your library, nor does it copy the photo to the Trash album.

REMOVING PHOTOS FROM SOURCES

Sorting Photos

iPhoto can perform four sorts, or you can move images around manually, which is useful for arranging photos in albums you can use for books, calendars, and slideshows.

To sort photos automatically:

1. When in any album, choose the desired sort method from the View menu's Sort Photos submenu (**Figure 3.37**).

2. From the Sort Photos submenu, choose either Ascending or Descending to control the direction of the sort (ascending sorts go from oldest to newest, A to Z, 1 to 9, whereas descending sorts go from newest to oldest, Z to A, 9 to 1).

To sort photos manually:

◆ Drag one or more photos to the desired location in the album, as marked by a black line (**Figure 3.38**).

◆ To make iPhoto forget your manual changes, switch to an automatic sort and then choose Reset Manual Sort.

✔ Tips

■ Albums maintain individual sort settings.

■ iPhoto remembers how you've sorted photos manually even if you switch to another sort order and back to Manually.

■ You can't sort photos manually in smart albums, in the Events and Photos views, or in the automatically generated albums like Last Import and Last 12 Months.

■ When you're viewing Events, the Sort Photos submenu changes to Sort Events and lets you sort events the same ways you sort individual photos.

■ It's much easier to sort photos manually in an album than in a book, calendar, or slideshow, so create an album first.

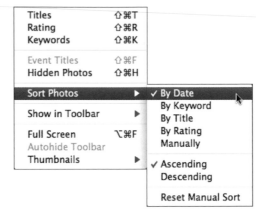

Figure 3.37 To sort photos, choose the desired method from the Sort Photos submenu.

Figure 3.38 To sort photos manually, drag one or more photos to the desired location, as indicated by a black line between photos.

The Liberty Bell

Figure 3.39 To assign a title to a photo, double-click its title and enter a new one.

Figure 3.40 Batch Change enables you to set the titles of multiple selected photos all at once, appending numbers if you so desire.

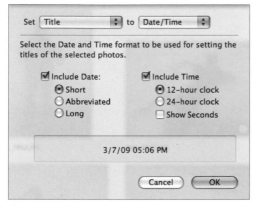

Figure 3.41 When changing the title of a photo to Date/Time, set the format in the dialog before clicking the OK button.

Assigning Titles to Photos

Digital cameras assign sequential numeric names to photos, but iPhoto lets you add your own descriptive titles. Smart albums can look for text in titles, and iPhoto can use the titles when you design books or publish to the Web.

Ways to assign custom titles:

◆ Make sure titles are showing (choose Titles from the View menu; Cmd Shift T), and then anywhere you see a title, click it and enter the new title (**Figure 3.39**).

◆ In either the Information pane or the Information dialog (Cmd I), click the Title field and enter a title for the photo.

To assign titles to multiple photos:

1. Select a number of photos, and choose Batch Change (Cmd Shift B) from either the Photos menu or by Control-clicking the photos.

2. In the dialog that appears, choose Title from the Set pop-up menu, and then choose Empty, Text, Event Name, Filename, or Date/Time from the To pop-up menu (**Figure 3.40**).

3. If you chose Text or Date/Time, select the desired options in the dialog (**Figures 3.40** and **3.41**).

✔ Tips

■ Keep titles short so they're easy to read in the display and Information panes and so they fit when used in Web pages.

■ You can assign a title to multiple selected photos in the Information dialog too.

■ If you don't like the way the batch change works out, just choose Undo Batch Change from the Edit menu.

ASSIGNING TITLES TO PHOTOS

Assigning Descriptions to Photos

It's often helpful to describe a photo briefly so you remember the original scene better. iPhoto also uses descriptions as text in some of the book designs.

To assign a description to a photo:

◆ Select a photo, choose Get Info from the File menu ([Cmd][I]) to display the Information dialog and type your description in the Description field.

◆ With the Information pane showing, select a photo and type your description in the Description field (**Figure 3.42**).

To assign descriptions to multiple photos at once:

1. Select a number of photos, and choose Batch Change ([Cmd][Shift][B]) either from the Photos menu or by [Control]-clicking the photos.

2. In the dialog that appears, choose Description from the Set pop-up menu, and then enter the description to attach to each photo (**Figure 3.43**).

3. If you want to append your text to each description, instead of replacing what's there, select Append to Existing Description and click OK.

   iPhoto changes the descriptions.

✔ Tips

■ If multiple photos are selected, the Information dialog appends what you type in the Description field to the description of each photo.

■ You can use iPhoto's spelling tools in the Description field. See "Checking Spelling as You Type," on page 183.

Drag to make the Information pane taller and wider to show large descriptions.

Description field.

Information button.

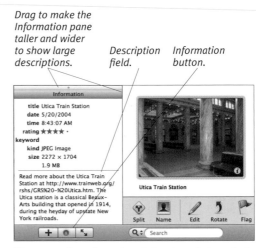

Figure 3.42 To assign a description to a photo, select the photo and enter the description in the Description field in the Information pane.

Figure 3.43 Use the Batch Change command to change or append to the description for a number of photos at once.

✔ More Tips

■ The Description field can hold a very large amount of text. If you need long descriptions, create them in another application and paste them into iPhoto.

■ You can drag or use the arrow keys to scroll through too-long descriptions.

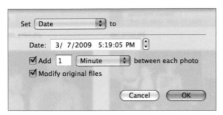

Figure 3.44 Use the Batch Change command to modify the dates of multiple photos at once.

Figure 3.45 Use the Adjust Date and Time command to increase or decrease the dates of multiple photos in relation to the first one in the selected set.

✔ More Tips

■ Modify Original Files always changes the file dates in the Finder to the current date, not the date you set.

■ If iPhoto is set to arrange photos by date, changing a photo's date causes it to be re-sorted according to the new date and it may move to an unexpected place.

■ In the Batch Change dialog, you can type numbers into the date and time fields, use the arrow keys to move the values up and down, or click the up/down arrow controls to adjust the selected number.

■ When using Batch Change to modify a number of photos with a time increment, note that iPhoto changes them in the order (left to right, top to bottom) that they're currently arranged.

■ It's a good idea to use the time increment with Batch Change so you can be sure how photos will sort by date later on.

Editing Photo Dates

You can edit photo dates in iPhoto to correct problems caused by your camera losing track of the correct date and time. Note that Batch Change *sets* each photo's date, whereas Adjust Date and Time *adjusts* each photo's date in relation to how you set the first one.

To edit a photo's date and time:

◆ Make sure the Information pane is showing, and then select a photo and edit its Date and/or Time fields.

To edit multiple dates/times at once:

1. Select a number of photos, and choose Batch Change (Cmd Shift B) from either the Photos menu or by Control-clicking the photos.

2. In the dialog that appears, choose Date from the Set pop-up menu, and then use the controls to set the date and time to attach to each photo, and the amount of increment time (**Figure 3.44**).

 iPhoto changes the dates appropriately.

To adjust photo dates and times:

1. Select an event or a number of photos, and choose Adjust Date and Time from the Photos menu.

2. In the dialog that appears, use the controls to set the new date and/or time for the first photo (**Figure 3.45**).

 iPhoto calculates the offset between the old and new dates for the first photo and adjusts the dates for all the other photos accordingly.

✔ Tip

■ Use the Modify Original Files checkbox to ensure that your changes are saved in the EXIF data for each photo file as well, rather than just being stored in iPhoto.

Assigning Ratings

Just as with iTunes, where you can rate your favorite songs on a scale of 1 to 5 stars, you can rate your photos, which is a great way to identify your favorites easily.

Ways to assign ratings:

◆ With ratings showing (choose Rating from the View menu; Cmd Shift R), click the appropriate star button in the rating field under a photo (**Figure 3.46**).

◆ Select one or more photos, and from the My Rating submenu in the Photos menu, choose the desired rating. Note the Cmd 0 through Cmd 5 keyboard shortcuts—if you're ever going to use keyboard shortcuts, now is the time.

◆ Select one or more photos, Control-click one of the selected photos, and choose the desired rating from the My Rating submenu (**Figure 3.47**).

◆ Select one or more photos, choose Get Info from the File menu (Cmd I), and click the appropriate star button.

◆ With a photo selected, click the appropriate star button in the Information pane.

After you choose a rating, iPhoto applies it to the selected photos, displaying it below each photo if you have Rating turned on in the View menu.

✔ Tips

■ The keyboard shortcuts for rating photos are available when you're editing a photo, but as of iPhoto '09, you can no longer assign ratings while watching a slideshow.

■ You can change the rating for a photo at any time; it's by no means set in stone.

■ iPhoto considers 5 stars better than 1 star, although there's nothing stopping you from assuming the reverse.

Figure 3.46 To assign a rating to a photo, make sure ratings are showing and click the desired star button.

Agate Beach in California
★★★★★

Figure 3.47 Alternatively, Control-click the photo and pick the desired rating from the My Rating submenu.

Consider Using Only High Ratings

Don't assume you must rate all your photos. My feeling is that there's relatively little point in rating anything with 1 or 2 stars, since those ratings basically mean, "I like this photo only enough to keep it." I consider 3 stars an average rating, so I usually don't use that either, reserving my rating effort for the 4- and 5-star photos that are my favorites.

Remember, too, that you can create smart albums that match photos whose ratings are lower than a set number, so you could easily find all the photos that didn't have 4 or 5 stars.

Figure 3.48 In the Edit Keywords window, you can add, remove, and rename keywords, and assign single-key shortcuts to them.

Unexpected Keywords

If you find keywords in the list that you can't remember creating, you're not losing your mind. If a photo sent to you by a friend contains a keyword, iPhoto imports it. There's no reason to save it.

Working with the Checkmark Keyword

iPhoto provides a special checkmark "keyword" that, when applied to a photo, appears on top of the image itself, rather than under it, like all other keywords. Plus, the checkmark appears whether or not other keywords are visible. It can 7be useful as a temporary marker.

However, iPhoto's flagging capability makes the checkmark keyword less useful than it used to be, since it's easier to work with flagged photos thanks to the special Flagged album and other commands related to flagged photos.

Managing Keywords

iPhoto '09 offers an easy interface for working with keywords. Before going further, when you're viewing photos (as opposed to events), make sure keywords are showing by choosing Keywords from the View menu (Cmd Shift K). Also, open the Keywords window by choosing Show Keywords (Cmd K) from the Window menu. Then click the Edit Keywords button.

Ways to create a new keyword:

◆ In the Edit Keywords window, click the + button, type the new keyword, and press Return.

◆ Click in the Keywords field under any photo, type the new keyword, and press Return or ,.

To assign a keyword shortcut:

◆ In the Edit Keywords window, either double-click a keyword shortcut or click Shortcut, type the single letter shortcut, and press Return.

To rename a keyword:

◆ In the Edit Keywords window, either double-click a keyword or select it; then, click Rename, type the new name, and press Return (**Figure 3.48**).

To delete a keyword:

◆ In the Edit Keywords window, select a keyword, and click the – button.

iPhoto deletes the keyword immediately, prompting you first if it's in use, and then deleting it from all photos that use it.

✔ Tip

■ If you rename a keyword, photos with that keyword update to match.

MANAGING KEYWORDS

Assigning and Removing Keywords

Assigning and removing keywords is extremely easy.

To assign keywords to photos:

◆ Click in the Keywords field under any photo, and type the first few letters of the keyword. iPhoto autocompletes the rest of the keyword (**Figure 3.49**). Press ⌐,⌐ or ⌐Return⌐ to enter another keyword.

◆ Select one or more photos, and click a keyword in the Keywords window or press a keyword's single-letter shortcut.

To remove keywords from photos:

◆ Click a keyword in the Keywords field under a photo, and press ⌐Delete⌐.

◆ With photos containing a particular keyword selected, switch to the Keywords window and click the desired keyword (which should be highlighted) to remove it from the selected photos (**Figure 3.50**).

✔ Tips

■ The single-letter shortcuts are really great! I encourage you to use them.

■ If you press ⌐Tab⌐ after entering a keyword, iPhoto automatically jumps to the Keywords field of the next photo.

■ Be careful when selecting photos and keywords to avoid assigning the wrong keywords to the wrong photos. You can always choose Undo (⌐Cmd⌐⌐Z⌐) from the Edit menu if you make a mistake.

■ Keywords are always listed alphabetically in the Keywords window.

Figure 3.49 You can add and remove keywords in the Keywords field under any photo. iPhoto autocompletes as you type, offering suggestions in a menu if there are multiple matches.

Figure 3.50 Remove a keyword from multiple photos at once by selecting them and clicking the highlighted keyword in the Keywords window.

Keywords vs. Albums

Use keywords for categories of pictures that recur throughout your photo collection. In contrast, use albums for unique events or categories.

Keywords Do Export!

iPhoto '08 and '09 include keywords in the IPTC metadata in JPEG or TIFF files when exporting. This means that work you do in applying keywords won't be lost if you switch to another program.

To export keywords with photos, make sure to use the JPEG or TIFF format and select the Include Titles and Keywords checkbox in the File Export dialog. See "Exporting Files," on page 152.

ASSIGNING AND REMOVING KEYWORDS

Click to hide and unhide photos.

The X indicates that a photo is hidden.

Click to hide these hidden photos.

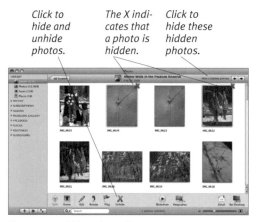

Figure 3.51 Hidden photos have an orange X next to the upper-right corner of their thumbnails, as you can see in the top row.

Figure 3.52 Clicking Hide Hidden Photos at the upper right makes the hidden photos disappear from view and causes "Hide x Hidden Photos" to change to "Show x Hidden Photos," as in this screenshot.

Hiding Multiple Photos

You can, of course, hide and unhide multiple photos at once by selecting more than one photo before you click Hide or Unhide. I wrote the instructions to the right as I did because the names of all the menus change to plural, and the writing became too awkward.

Hiding Photos

iPhoto can hide photos that you don't want to see when working, but which are worth keeping overall.

To hide a photo:

◆ Select a photo and click the Hide button, choose Hide Photo from the Photos menu ([Cmd][L]), or [Control]-click the photo and choose Hide Photo.

iPhoto puts an orange X by the upper-right corner of the selected photo's thumbnail (**Figure 3.51**) and, if Hidden Photos is deselected in the View menu ([Cmd][Shift][H]), makes the photo disappear.

To unhide a hidden photo:

◆ Make sure Hidden Photos is selected in the View menu, select a photo and click the Unhide button, choose Unhide Photo from the Photos menu ([Cmd][L]), or [Control]-click the photo and choose Unhide Photo.

iPhoto removes the orange X from the selected photo's thumbnail, and the photo displays normally.

To hide and show hidden photos:

◆ From the View menu, choose Hidden Photos ([Cmd][Shift][H]). When Hidden Photos is selected, hidden photos are visible, though marked with an X. When it is deselected, hidden photos don't appear.

◆ When the display pane is showing an event that contains hidden photos, click the "Show x Hidden Photos" text that appears in the upper-right corner of iPhoto's window (**Figure 3.52**) or in the event title's line in Photos view.

That text changes to "Hide x Hidden Photos" when they're showing (**Figure 3.51**); click it again to make those photos disappear from view.

Flagging Photos

iPhoto can flag photos that you want to work with temporarily. Flagging is much like using the checkmark keyword, but iPhoto provides a few specific features for flagged photos.

To flag a photo:

◆ Select a photo and click the Flag button on the toolbar or choose Flag Photo from the Photos menu (Cmd .).

iPhoto puts an orange flag icon by the upper-left corner of the selected photo's thumbnail (**Figure 3.53**), and the photo appears in the Flagged album in the Recent list (**Figure 3.54**).

To unflag a flagged photo:

◆ Select a flagged photo and click the Unflag button or choose Unflag Photo from the Photos menu (Cmd .).

iPhoto removes the orange flag icon from the photo's thumbnail, and the photo disappears from the Flagged album.

✔ Tips

■ You can make a new event from your flagged photos. Choose Create Event from Flagged Photos from the Events menu. This removes the photos from their current events and creates a new one.

■ You can also add flagged photos to another event, which could be an easy way to merge photos from widely separated events. Select the event you want to contain the photos and choose Add Flagged Photos to Selected Event from the Events menu.

■ For those of us who remember Cmd . as the universal "stop everything" keyboard shortcut from ancient versions of the Mac OS, having it assigned to Flag Photo feels very odd.

Flagged photos appear in the Flagged album automatically.   *Click to flag and unflag photos.*   *The flag icon indicates a photo has been flagged.*

Figure 3.53 Flagged photos have an orange flag icon next to the upper-left corner of their thumbnails, as you can see above.

Figure 3.54 Flagged photos automatically appear in the Flagged album in the Recent list.

Figure 3.55 Here I've searched for the words "Rick running" and iPhoto has displayed all those photos that have either of those words associated with them.

Display and Select

When you perform any search, iPhoto displays only the results of the search, which is helpful for working with the found photos. But what if you want to see photos in the same event as one of the found photos? Follow these steps:

1. Perform a search or otherwise display a subset of photos.

2. Select a photo in the event you want to see.

3. Click Events in the source pane.

   iPhoto switches back to Events view, scrolled such that the event containing the selected photo is visible and selected.

Note that this works (almost) no matter how you've arrived at a subset of photos, whether from viewing photos associated with a person or place, photos in an album or smart album, and even photos in a calendar. Oddly, it doesn't currently work when viewing photos in a book, card, or slideshow. I've reported it as a bug to Apple.

Searching with the Search Field

For quick searches, use the Search field that's always showing at the bottom of the window in organize mode. The Search field finds matches in photo titles, descriptions, keywords, event titles, face names, and locations. It's not as granular as a keyword search (searching for "Jen" finds not only pictures of my sister, but also pictures she sent me, and pictures of a friend named Jennifer).

To search for photos using the Search field:

◆ Type one or more words into the Search field.

   iPhoto displays all those photos that in some way are associated with **all** the words you typed (**Figure 3.55**).

Ways to clear the Search field:

◆ Click the X button in the Search field.

◆ Switch to any other item in the source pane.

✔ Tips

■ The ways to clear a search and show all photos apply to each of the specific searches discussed next, too.

■ Searches take place in the current event, current album, or the currently selected set of photos. This can cause confusion, since a search you're sure should work will fail if the wrong photos are selected.

■ Searches are not case-sensitive.

■ As you type more words, your search becomes ever more narrow.

■ iPhoto is happy to search for word fragments, so when I search for "Rick", iPhoto also finds pictures of "Jim Derick".

Searching by Date

iPhoto's search-by-date feature makes it easy to display just photos within certain date ranges. The tasks explained below take place in the Date tool; to open it, click the Search field's magnifying glass, which is actually a pop-up menu, and choose Date.

To change the Date tool's view:

◆ To switch to year view, click the view triangle so it points right (**Figure 3.56**).

◆ To switch to month view, click the view triangle so it points left (**Figure 3.57**).

◆ To display earlier or later months or years, click the left or right arrows.

To search for photos using the Date tool:

◆ Select the days or months corresponding to the time period in which you want to find photos. You can [Shift]-click or [Cmd]-click to select multiple contiguous or non-contiguous dates.

◆ Click a month or year heading to select all the days or months within.

✔ Tips

■ Searches take place in the current event, current album, or the currently selected set of photos.

■ Pay attention to whether a month or day is bright white or light gray. White dates contain photos; gray dates do not.

■ The Date tool disappears if you move the pointer out of it. To bring it back, click anywhere in the Search field.

■ Although the selected dates appear in the Search field, you can't type dates there.

Click to toggle between month and year views.

Click to select entire year.

Selected months.

Click to move back and ahead in time.

White shows photos were taken in these months.

Gray indicates that no photos were taken in these months.

Figure 3.56 Here, in year view, I've searched for photos taken in January 2007 and February 2007.

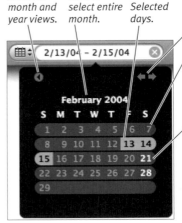

Click to toggle between month and year views.

Click to select entire month.

Selected days.

Click to move back and ahead in time.

Gray indicates that no photos were taken these days.

White shows that photos were taken these days.

Figure 3.57 Here, in month view, I've searched for photos taken over Valentine's Day weekend in 2004.

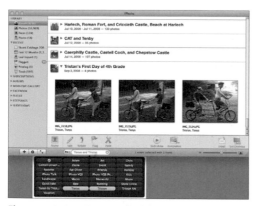

Figure 3.58 Here I've searched for all the photos in my Library that have both the "Tristan" keyword and the "Tonya" keyword.

Figure 3.59 Here I've done a more complex search, asking iPhoto to find those photos with the "Tonya" keyword but not the "Adam" keyword.

Searching by Keyword

If you've assigned keywords to your photos, they can make it easy to find the photos associated with certain keywords.

To search for photos by keyword:

1. In the Search field, open the Keyword tool by clicking the magnifying glass, which is actually a pop-up menu, and choosing Keyword.

2. Click one or more keywords.

   iPhoto displays all those photos that have **all** the selected keywords (**Figure 3.58**). The more keywords you select, the narrower your search becomes, and the fewer photos will match. This is an AND search.

To perform an OR search:

◆ In step 2 above, instead of just clicking keywords, [Shift]-click one or more keywords whose associated photos you want to add to the results.

   iPhoto displays all those photos that contain **any** of the selected keywords.

To perform a NOT search:

◆ In step 2 above, instead of just clicking keywords, [Option]-click one or more keywords whose associated photos you want to avoid finding.

   iPhoto removes from the set of found photos those with the [Option]-clicked keyword(s) (**Figure 3.59**).

✔ Tips

■ Although the selected keywords (and the search logic) appear in the Search field, you can't type search phrases there.

■ Searches take place in the current event, current album, or the currently selected set of photos.

Searching by Rating

You can also search for photos with specific ratings, much as you search for dates and keywords.

To search for photos via rating:

1. In the Search field, click the magnifying glass, which is actually a pop-up menu, and choose Rating.

2. Click the star corresponding to *at least* the rating of photos you wish to find.

   iPhoto displays all those photos that have the selected rating or a higher rating (**Figure 3.60**).

✔ Tips

■ You may find iPhoto's approach of finding photos with at least the selected rating confusing. This means that when you click one star, you're actually finding photos with 1, 2, 3, 4, or 5 stars. If you click 3 stars, you're finding photos with 3, 4, or 5 stars. And if you click 5 stars, you're finding only those photos with 5 stars, since there's nothing higher (**Figure 3.61**). If this bothers you, work around it by creating smart albums that find exactly the number of stars you want.

■ Searches take place in the current event, current album, or the currently selected set of photos.

Figure 3.60 Here I've searched for 4-star photos and iPhoto has displayed all those photos that have 4 or 5 stars.

Figure 3.61 Notice how, in each of these ratings searches, the number of found photos goes up as the minimum number stars a photos must have goes down.

Figure 3.62 The Information dialog provides much the same information as the Information pane, but adds both a location field and a map showing the location.

Information pane, with Title, Date, Time, Rating, Keyword, Kind, Size, and Description fields.

Click to display the Information dialog.

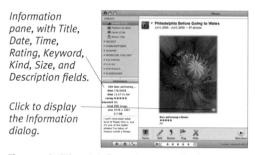

Figure 3.63 iPhoto's Information pane displays some basic information about selected photos.

Using the Information Dialog

As you've noticed throughout this chapter, the Information dialog helps you modify the title, rating, location, and description for one or more photos.

You can also cycle through photos using the left and right arrow keys, or the left and right buttons.

When you're finished viewing or changing photo information, click the Done button to dismiss the pop-up.

Viewing Basic Photo Information

iPhoto presents basic information about photos in two places: the new Information dialog and the old Information pane.

To view info in the Information dialog:

◆ Select one or more photos and choose Get Info ([Cmd][I]) from the File menu.

◆ Move your mouse pointer over a photo and click the little i button that appears in the lower right corner of the photo thumbnail. (See it in **Figure 3.63**.) iPhoto displays the Information dialog (**Figure 3.62**).

To view info in the Information pane:

◆ If the Information pane is hidden, click the Information button underneath the source pane to display the Information pane (**Figure 3.63**).

✔ Tips

■ Both the Information dialog and pane can display information about multiple selected photos as well, but only the Information dialog can change the information for multiple selected photos.

■ The Information pane lacks location information entirely. It's essentially a holdover from iPhoto 1.0.

■ Apple expects users to modify most photo information with the Information dialog, new in iPhoto '09. In particular, it's how you assign location information to photos that lack geotags. See Chapter 5, "Working with Places," which begins on page 71.

■ Oddly, you can't change the time and date of a photo in the Information dialog.

Viewing Extended Photo Information

To see more information than the Information dialog and the Information pane display, use the Extended Photo Info window.

To view information in the Extended Photo Info window:

1. Select a photo and choose Show Extended Photo Info from the Photos menu (⌘ Cmd ⌥ Option I).

   iPhoto displays the Extended Photo Info window (**Figure 3.64**).

2. If necessary, click an expansion triangle to reveal Image, File, Location, Camera, or Exposure information.

✔ Tips

■ When the Extended Photo Info window is showing, you can click another photo to see its information immediately.

■ The Extended Photo Info window, unlike the Information dialog and Information pane, is entirely read-only—you can't change anything in it.

■ Location information in the Extended Photo Info window can come either from a camera or via manual entry. See Chapter 5, "Working with Places," which begins on page 71.

■ The Extended Photo Info window picks up its information from the EXIF (Exchangeable Image File) data stored by most digital cameras. *EXIF* is an industry standard that's designed to help interoperability among cameras, printers, and other imaging devices.

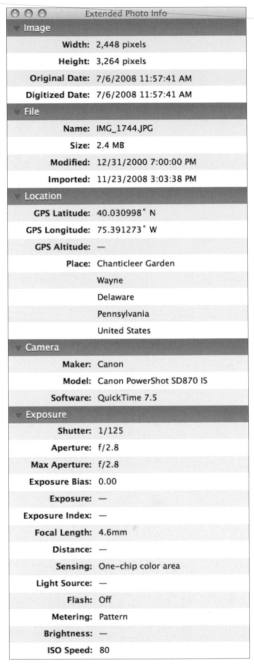

Figure 3.64 The Extended Photo Info window provides detailed information that was recorded about the image by the camera.

VIEWING EXTENDED PHOTO INFORMATION

WORKING WITH FACES

The most important addition to iPhoto '09 is Faces, which can detect faces in photos and, after you've trained it by identifying a person in a number of photos, automatically recognize that person's face in other photos.

Faces is important for two reasons. First, as our digital photo collections grow—I have about 17,000 photos right now, and many people have far more—it becomes ever more difficult to find any given photo. That's not because iPhoto's search tools are bad, but because adding keywords or other metadata takes time many of us don't have. With a little effort spent training Faces, you can reap the benefits of having useful metadata automatically applied to many of your photos.

Second, from a historical standpoint, photos that don't identify at least the people in them (and, ideally, also the place and event at which the photos were taken) are nearly worthless. Just recently, my mother had to ask my grandmother to identify some people in an ancient family photo, since no one had thought to write names on the back. You may know who the people in your photos are, but will your children or grandchildren?

One warning. Many people find training Faces to be addictive, so you may wish to set aside some time to do it when you don't have anything more important to do.

Sad Faces

As much as I find Faces utterly magical and truly addictive, it isn't perfect, as you'll find out. It sometimes doesn't see faces in photos, and it can, particularly before it's fully trained, identify people incorrectly. Faces can recognize some people, like my brother-in-law, after only minimal training, whereas it fails miserably to recognize other people, like my sister, no matter how many times I identify her in a photo.

Although I have no inside information, I fully expect that Apple will be improving iPhoto's face detection and recognition capabilities in future updates to the program. So even if the feature has some quirks now, it will only be improving as time goes by.

The Faces of Faces

Unlike most of iPhoto's other modes, Faces offers a number of different views, depending on whether you're naming faces, browsing through identified faces, or training iPhoto to recognize a face.

Subsequent pages in this chapter explain these features in more detail.

To name faces:

◆ Whenever you're viewing a group of photos (not events!), select a photo and click the Name button at the left side of the toolbar.

iPhoto magnifies the photo and displays a name lozenge under any faces it has detected (**Figure 4.1**).

To browse faces:

◆ Click Faces in the source pane to display the Faces corkboard, which shows a snapshot for each person you've named (**Figure 4.2**).

◆ In the Faces corkboard, double-click a person's snapshot to display all the photos that have been identified as containing that person (**Figure 4.3**).

To train Faces:

◆ Double-click a snapshot in the Faces corkboard, and, if there are any photos shown below the "So-and-so may also be in the photos below" bar, click the Confirm Name button in the toolbar.

iPhoto switches from merely displaying the photos to letting you click them to confirm whether or not the person appears in the photos (**Figure 4.4**).

✔ Tip

■ You can drag snapshots on the corkboard around to rearrange them.

Figure 4.1 In naming view, iPhoto displays a name lozenge under any faces it has identified.

Figure 4.2 Click Faces in the source pane to display the Faces corkboard.

Figure 4.3 Double-click any face in the Faces corkboard to display all of that person's identified photos.

Figure 4.4 Clicking the Confirm Name button switches you into training mode.

Figure 4.5 When iPhoto thinks it recognizes a face, click the checkmark button to accept the suggestion or the X button to reject it.

Figure 4.6 When iPhoto can only identify that a face is unknown face, enter a name in the name balloon.

Figure 4.7 If iPhoto doesn't even identify a face, use the Add Missing Face button to add a face rectangle.

Navigating while Naming

You may find it easiest to assign names to faces in a lot of photos at once. To do this easily, click the arrow buttons to move to the next or previous photo, or just use the arrow keys.

Putting a Name to a Face

iPhoto can *identify* faces, but until you've assigned a name to a face and trained iPhoto to *recognize* that face (see the next page), iPhoto won't be able to recognize that face in the future automatically.

To get started, select a photo containing at least one face and click the Name button in the toolbar. Then use one of the following approaches.

To assign a name to a face:

◆ If iPhoto thinks it recognizes a face in the photo, click the checkmark button to accept the suggestion or the X button to reject it (**Figure 4.5**).

◆ If iPhoto has only identified that an unnamed face exists in the photo, click the name balloon, enter the person's name, and press Return (**Figure 4.6**).

◆ If iPhoto hasn't identified a face, click the Add Missing Face button, center the rectangle on the face and resize it, click Done, and enter the person's name (**Figure 4.7**).

✔ Tips

■ iPhoto attempts to autocomplete as you type, as you can see in **Figure 4.6**. Use the arrow keys and Return or the mouse to select suggested names (which can come from entries in Address Book), or just keep typing to enter a new name.

■ If iPhoto identifies multiple faces in a photo, press Tab to move among them.

■ You can assign names to faces whenever the Name button appears in the toolbar. When you're browsing through faces (and have a Confirm Name button instead), magnify a selected photo by pressing Spacebar or m, at which point the Name button appears again.

Training Face Recognition

Although you can navigate through photos fairly quickly while adding names, iPhoto provides a much faster way of training the face recognition technology.

To train face recognition:

1. Click Faces in the source pane, and then double-click the snapshot of a person for whom you want to improve iPhoto's recognition.

   iPhoto shows photos to which you've already assigned the person's name. If it thinks the person's face is also in other photos, it displays them below the bar and enables the Confirm Name button (**Figure 4.8**).

2. Click the Confirm Name button in the toolbar.

   iPhoto switches into confirmation mode (**Figure 4.9**). Note that iPhoto zooms each photo to focus on the identified face, and adds a Confirm button to each photo.

3. Confirm each photo by clicking it, or reject it by Option-clicking it.

   Confirmed photos receive a green name; rejected photos receive a red name, prefixed with "Not" (**Figure 4.10**).

✔ Tips

■ If you make a mistake, just click the photo again to change your vote.

■ Instead of clicking each photo, drag or Option-drag a selection rectangle around the photos to confirm or reject.

■ It's usually fastest to confirm or reject all the photos with a drag-select, then click the few that are incorrect to reverse them.

■ When browsing, as in **Figure 4.8**, you can switch the view between close-ups and the full photos with the View control.

Figure 4.8 Double-click a face in the Faces corkboard to see all the photos associated with that person.

Figure 4.9 Clicking the Confirm Name button switches you into confirmation mode.

Figure 4.10 Click the photos to confirm the name, or Option-click them to reject the name.

No Photos to Confirm?

If iPhoto doesn't find any photos for you to confirm, you'll have to locate them yourself and assign the name manually, as discussed on the previous page.

Figure 4.11 Control-click a mistaken photo and choose This Is Not "Name" from the contextual menu.

Figure 4.12 In confirmation mode, click already-recognized photos to fix mistaken recognition.

Figure 4.13 When naming photos, you can always enter a new name for an incorrectly recognized face.

Should You Identify Everyone?

If you're a completion freak like me, you'll probably want to identify nearly everyone in your photo collection. Normal people may wish to identify just family and close friends. There's no right way to do it.

Fixing a Mistaken Face

At some point, you're certain to make a mistake and assign an incorrect name to a face, or iPhoto may assign a name to a face incorrectly despite your training (I haven't seen this happen yet, but I assume anything is possible). There are various ways to fix face recognition mistakes.

Ways to fix a misrecognized face:

◆ When browsing through a person's identified photos (double-click a snapshot in the Faces corkboard), [Control]-click an incorrect photo and choose This Is Not "Name" from the contextual menu (**Figure 4.11**).

◆ When browsing through a person's identified photos, select one or more photos and press [Delete].

◆ In confirmation mode, click incorrectly recognized photos *above* the bar to reject them (**Figure 4.12**).

◆ When you're naming faces in photos, if you come across an incorrect one, just enter the correct name (**Figure 4.13**).

✔ Tips

■ When in confirmation mode, you can [Control]-click a suggested face, which displays a contextual menu with Confirm, Reject, and Name items. Choose Name to enter the correct name for the suggested face without leaving confirmation mode.

■ Using [Delete] when browsing through a person's identified photos does not delete the photo, it merely tells iPhoto to disassociate the person's name with the photo.

■ Removing the last identified photo from the collection of photos associated with a person removes their name from the Faces corkboard.

Adding Info to People

There are four pieces of information associated with a person's snapshot in the Faces corkboard: the person's display name, full name, email address, and a key photo.

Ways to set the display name:

◆ In the Faces corkboard, click the person's display name and enter a new one (**Figure 4.14**). *Or...*

1. In the Faces corkboard, mouse over a snapshot and click its i button, or select it and choose Get Info from the File menu (Cmd I) to show the Information dialog (**Figure 4.15**).

2. Click the display name and enter a new one.

3. Click Done to dismiss the dialog.

To set the full name:

◆ In the Information dialog, click "full name" and type the person's full name (**Figure 4.15**). Click Done.

To set the email address:

◆ In the Information dialog, click "email address" and type the person's email address (**Figure 4.15**). Click Done.

Ways to set the key photo:

◆ In the Faces corkboard, scrub over the person's snapshot and when you see a new one you like, press Spacebar.

◆ When browsing through a person's photos, Control-click the desired photo and choose Make Key Photo from the contextual menu.

◆ In the Information dialog, scrub over the person's key photo and when you see one you like, click it. (The change isn't reflected until you click Done.)

Figure 4.14 To change a person's display name, just click it in the Faces corkboard and enter a new name.

Figure 4.15 In the Information dialog, you can change a person's display name, full name, email address, and key photo.

Name and Email for Facebook

If a full name like "Tonya Engst" is present in the Information dialog, iPhoto uses that for the photo's tag in Facebook instead of the "Tonya" display name. More important, Facebook uses the email address in the Information dialog to connect a photo with the profile of the pictured Facebook user. The email address must match the person's email address in Facebook (verify that in the person's profile). This is why it's helpful that iPhoto 8.0.2 and later suggest name and email address information from Address Book. Changes made to the full name and email address aren't reflected in photos already uploaded to Facebook.

Figure 4.16 With the View control at the left side of the toolbar toggled to the left, you see full photos when browsing a person's photos in Faces.

Figure 4.17 Click the View control's right-hand button and you see only close-ups when browsing a person's photos in Faces.

Faces and Organize Mode

Most of your initial time with Faces will be spent teaching iPhoto how to recognize your friends and family. What do you do with Faces after that's done?

The slightly confusing fact about Faces is that when you're browsing a person's photos via the Faces corkboard, you're in organize mode, with only two slight differences.

Differences from organize mode:

◆ When browsing faces, click the View controls to toggle between showing full photos (**Figure 4.16**) and close-ups (**Figure 4.17**).

◆ As you take more photos that may not be recognized automatically, use the Confirm Name button to continue iPhoto's training.

✔ Tips

■ Remember, since you're essentially in organize mode when browsing a person's photos in Faces, you can use those photos as the source for photos for a slideshow, book, calendar, or Web album.

■ Since Faces can't identify people who aren't facing the camera, consider using keywords that are the same as your display names and making smart albums that collect *all* the photos of a person.

Deleting People from Faces

If you've assigned names to people who appear only once or twice in your entire photo library, it may not be worth having them cluttering your Faces corkboard. It's easy to remove a person from Faces.

To delete a face:

◆ From the Faces corkboard, drag a person's snapshot to the Trash in the source pane (**Figure 4.18**), or select a snapshot and press ⌘⌫.

iPhoto prompts to make sure you really want to delete the person from Faces (**Figure 4.19**).

◆ When browsing through a person's identified photos, select all the photos and press ⌫. Alternatively, Control-click the selection and choose This Is Not "Name" from the contextual menu.

✔ Tips

■ When you use the second method above, iPhoto doesn't prompt you at all.

■ Deleting a snapshot from the Faces corkboard removes the name from photos, but does not delete the photos themselves.

■ Remember that you can rearrange the snapshots on the corkboard by dragging them, making it less necessary that you delete little-represented people. I recommend putting your most frequent photo subjects at the top.

Figure 4.18 Drag snapshots you don't want on the corkboard any more to the Trash icon in the source pane.

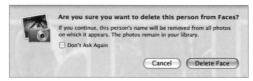

Figure 4.19 Click Delete Face to confirm that you really want to delete the person from the Faces corkboard.

Working with Places

A major addition to iPhoto '09 is Places, which makes it possible to see where your photos were taken, find them by location, and include maps of the locations in books.

Geotagging with Other Programs

For those interested in geotagging their photos automatically right now, two programs, Houdah Software's Houdah Geo and Ovolab's Geophoto, promise to match up a GPS track log (containing locations associated with times) recorded with a special GPS device with the time stamps on the photos you take. They then write the latitude and longitude coordinates into the photos, after which iPhoto can read them.

I haven't used either program personally, nor do I own a GPS track logger, so I can't comment on how easy they are to use with iPhoto. The cost of entry is $25–$30 for the software and about $100 for a GPS track logger that you'd clip on your belt loop or camera bag as you take photos.

For more information about Houdah Geo, including a list of recommended GPS track loggers, visit Houdah Software at www.houdah.com/houdahGeo/. To learn more about Geophoto, check out Ovolab at www.ovolab.com/geophoto/.

Unfortunately, you can't train iPhoto to recognize where a photo was taken. *Geotags*—location information—are either embedded in a photo's metadata automatically by the camera used to take the photo, or they're something you add later in iPhoto. (There is one other way; see the sidebar to the left.)

Right now, apart from Apple's iPhone, only a handful of cameras contain the necessary *GPS* (Global Positioning System) chip necessary for a camera to divine its location from orbiting satellites. So unless you take a lot of photos with an iPhone, assigning location information to photos will largely be a manual effort. Don't worry, it's not hard.

Note that Places, because it relies on maps from Google and Google searches, requires an Internet connection.

How obsessive you wish to be when geotagging your photos is up to you. I'm the sort of person who will carefully find the particular beach at Half Moon Bay where a photo was taken; other people may be happy to say the photo was taken in Half Moon Bay, or even just in California.

The Faces of Places

Unlike most of the other modes in iPhoto, Places offers a number of different views, depending on whether you're viewing a photo's location information, looking at map showing the locations of your photos, browsing a list of places, or making a new place.

To view a photo's location:

◆ Select one or more photos and choose Get Info from the File menu ([Cmd][I]), or click the i button that appears when you mouse over a photo.

iPhoto displays the Information dialog, with a prominent map of the photo's location (**Figure 5.1**).

To view a map of photo locations:

◆ Click Places in the source pane and make sure the World View button (the one with the globe) is selected in the View control at the left side of the toolbar (**Figure 5.2**).

◆ While viewing the Information dialog for photos that have geotags, click the little arrow next to Show in Places to jump to a zoomed-in map view in Places.

To browse through photo locations:

◆ Click Places in the source pane and make sure the Browser View button (it has four little rectangles in it) is selected in the View control in the toolbar.

iPhoto shows the hierarchical location browser (**Figure 5.3**).

To view your custom places:

◆ From the Window menu, choose Manage My Places.

iPhoto displays the Edit My Places dialog, showing the custom places you've created and letting you perform a Google search to find the location for a new custom place (**Figure 5.4**).

Figure 5.1 Photos with geotags show maps of their locations in the Information dialog.

Figure 5.2 Places can display maps (here of Northern Wales) with pins showing the locations where you took photos.

Figure 5.3 Alternatively, you can browse through your photos by selecting from a hierarchical list of places.

Figure 5.4 You can make your own places, with their own names, that you can apply to photos without geotags, and that will be applied automatically to photos taken by GPS-equipped cameras within the radius you set.

Figure 5.5 Terrain map style shows hills and valleys, along with map borders, place names, and roads.

Figure 5.6 Satellite map style shows only satellite imagery, making it useful for extreme close-ups. You can zoom in further in Satellite and Hybrid style than in Terrain style.

Figure 5.7 Hybrid map style uses satellite imagery but also overlays it with place and road names, making it the most useful of the three views. Like Satellite style, the Hybrid style can zoom closer than Terrain.

Select Pin before Zooming

To make sure iPhoto zooms where you're expecting when using the size slider, select a pin before zooming.

Working with Maps

Before we dive into how to use Places, it's important to understand how to work with the maps you see, as in **Figure 5.1**, **Figure 5.2**, and **Figure 5.4**, previous page.

To move the map view in the window:

◆ Click-and-hold anywhere within the map and drag the map view around. Let up and repeat to move it more than a screen.

To zoom in and out:

◆ In the main map view in Places, drag the size slider to the right to zoom in, and to the left to zoom out. Alas, you can't zoom in all the way with the size slider.

◆ In the Information dialog and in the Edit My Places dialog, click the + and – buttons to zoom in and out.

◆ In the main map view in Places and in the Edit My Places dialog, double-click anywhere in the map to zoom in, and (Control)-double-click to zoom out.

To change the view style:

Although the button styles vary slightly, iPhoto's map interfaces provide three ways to view the map: Terrain, Satellite, and Hybrid.

◆ To view the map in traditional terrain map style, with map borders, place names, road names, and other cartographic marks, click the Terrain button (**Figure 5.5**).

◆ To view the map with satellite imagery sufficient to see buildings at the most zoomed level, but without any cartographic marks, click the Satellite button (**Figure 5.6**).

◆ To view the map in with both satellite imagery and cartographic marks, click the Hybrid button (**Figure 5.7**).

Geotagging Photos

Photos you take with an iPhone or other GPS-equipped camera will be geotagged automatically. For all other photos, you must add geotags manually.

To geotag photos:

1. In the Advanced pane of iPhoto's Preferences window, choose Automatically from the Look up Places pop-up menu (**Figure 5.8**).

2. In organize mode, select an event or one or more photos, and either choose Get Info from the File menu (Cmd I) or click the little i button that appears when you mouse over an event or photo.

   iPhoto displays the Information dialog (**Figure 5.9**).

3. Click the location field and enter the place where the photos were taken.

   As you type, iPhoto matches against its internal database of places and any custom places you've created, displaying a list of locations.

4. If iPhoto finds the location you want, click it to select it, and click Done.

5. If you need to make a new custom place, see "Adding New Places," on the next page.

✔ Tips

- You *must* click found locations to select them; simply pressing Tab or Return won't work.

- To remove a location from selected photos, display the Information dialog, click in the location field, and click the X button that appears at its right side. This doesn't remove GPS coordinates stored by a camera, just the connection with a place name that you set previously.

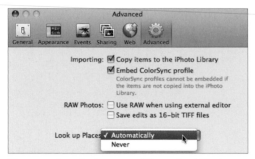

Figure 5.8 Set whether or not iPhoto should look up places based on the GPS coordinates in photos taken with a GPS-equipped camera (like an iPhone).

Figure 5.9 Type a place name into the location field and, if iPhoto suggests an appropriate location, click the name in the drop-down list to select it.

Lost?

In theory, events and their photos should share location information. In practice, the connection seems weak and changing an event location may not change the location of its photos. To increase the chances of this working, first remove location information by clicking the X button at the right side of the location field. Then reassign locations.

I anticipate this behavior improving in future updates beyond iPhoto 8.0.2.

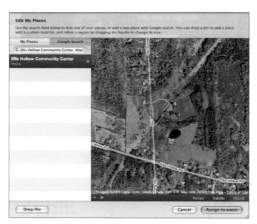

Figure 5.10 Start with a Google search when adding new places. Once you've found a place, select it, position its blue pin as you want, and click Assign.

Working in My Places

What if you want to edit the name of a place or remove it? Click My Places in the Edit My Places dialog to see a list of all your places. Once there, you can double-click a place's name to edit it, or click the – button next to the name to delete the place. iPhoto warns you if there are photos associated with the place before deleting it.

Places Is Buggy

Honestly, giving exact directions on how to create and assign new locations has been difficult, because I've run into a number of odd and incorrect behaviors in iPhoto 8.0.1 and 8.0.2. If I can isolate these, I'll report them as bugs and hopefully Apple will fix them. In the meantime, suffice to say that things may not work exactly as I've described here.

Adding New Places

Although iPhoto knows about thousands of places, you're likely to want to make your own places, if only for places like your house.

To add a new place:

1. Choose Manage My Places from the Window menu, or click New Place when typing a place name in the location field (**Figure 5.8**, previous page).

    iPhoto opens the Edit My Places dialog.

2. Click Google Search if it's not already selected.

3. Perform a Google search for the place you want to find.

    iPhoto displays a list of possible matches.

4. If one of the matches is correct, click it to select it and turn its pin blue.

5. If there are no matches, or if you want to add a completely unsearchable location (like a trailhead), zoom and pan the map to the desired spot and click Drop Pin.

6. If you want the location to be more precise, zoom in, drag the pin to reposition, and adjust the vicinity by dragging the control on the right edge of the blue circle (**Figure 5.10**).

7. If necessary, enter a name for the place.

8. Click the Assign or Done button (depending on your starting point in step 1).

✔ Tips

- When searching, be as precise as you can to get the best results, with a full address if you know it.

- Click the + button next to the selected location's name to add it to the My Places list. Assigning the location to a photo also has this effect.

ADDING NEW PLACES

Displaying Photo Locations on the Map

There are two basic ways of finding photos with geotags: displaying them on iPhoto's zoomable map and browsing through a hierarchical list of places (next page).

To display photo locations on the map:

◆ Click Places in the source pane and, if necessary, click the World View button in the View control in the toolbar.

◆ When in the Information dialog for a photo or event that contains geotags, click the arrow next to Show in Places.

iPhoto displays its map zoomed to display the places in which the selected photo(s) were taken (**Figure 5.11**).

Things you can do on the map:

◆ Zoom in to see more detail or out to see more of the surrounding area.

◆ Switch among terrain, satellite, and hybrid styles by clicking their buttons.

◆ Drag the map to move the view within the window.

◆ Mouse over a pin and click the arrow button in the Name pop-up (**Figure 5.12**) to view the photos taken in that location. Alternatively, click a pin to select it, and then click the Show Photos button.

iPhoto displays the photos from that location in organize mode (**Figure 5.13**). Return to the map view by clicking the Map button at the top of the display pane.

◆ Click the Zoom All button to zoom out to the point where all your photo locations can appear on the map.

◆ Click the Smart Album button to make a smart album of photos from the pins visible on the map at that time.

Figure 5.11 Click Places to see a map zoomed sufficiently to show all the locations in which your photos have been taken.

Figure 5.12 Mouse over a pin, and click the arrow in the Name pop-up to view all the photos from that location.

Figure 5.13 When viewing photos from a location, you're in organize mode, with all its associated tools. To return to the map, click the Map button in the upper left corner.

Browser   Country State   City   Location
View button. column. column. column. column.

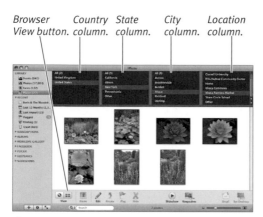

Figure 5.14 Click the Browser View button in Places to use the hierarchical location browser to select photos.

Figure 5.15 As you select places, starting from the left, the columns to the right display only the places within the selected location.

Browsing by Place

It may be easier, particularly after you've added a lot of places, to navigate your photos with iPhoto's hierarchical location browser.

To browse hierarchically:

1. Click Places in the source pane.

2. Click the Browser View button in the View control to display iPhoto's location browser (**Figure 5.14**).

3. Click a place name in any one of the four columns (country, state, city, location). iPhoto displays just those photos whose geotags are within the selected place.

✔ Tips

- When you click a place name in one of the columns, the next column to the right displays only the places within the selected place.

  In **Figure 5.15**, because I selected *United States* in the first column, the second column contains only U.S. states. And because I selected *New York* in the second column, the third column contains only cities in New York. And because I selected *Ithaca* in the third column, the fourth column contains only places in Ithaca. Realistically, this approach to drilling down will be necessary only for people with many different places.

- When you've displayed the photos in a particular place, via either the hierarchical browser or the map, you're in organize mode. See Chapter 3, "Organizing Photos," starting on page 29.

- You can also search for place names, and iPhoto will find all the photos within that place (see "Searching with the Search Field," page 57).

Putting Maps in Books

Places provides a major new book feature. In all book themes, a new map page layout becomes available to show where photos in the book were taken. The Travel theme offers additional map pages and options. To start making a book (where these steps pick up), see "Creating Books Overview," page 172, and "Designing Book Pages," page 173.

To put a map in a Travel book layout:

1. Select a page, and from the Layout pop-up menu, choose one of the Map layouts to insert a map (**Figure 5.16**).

2. Click the map on the book page to display the map editing pop-up (**Figure 5.17**).

3. Use the Zoom slider to adjust the zoom level to show the desired amount of detail, and drag the map within the frame to position it appropriately.

4. Enter a title for the map in the Title field.

5. Deselect places you don't want to appear on this particular map.

   You can also remove places from this map's list by clicking the – button below the list. You can also add a new place that's not currently associated with the photos in the book. Click the + button and follow the instructions on "Adding New Places," page 75.

6. To edit the place names for this map, double-click a name and change it.

7. If the places aren't in the right order, drag them around in the list to rearrange.

8. Click Show Lines to display lines connecting the places, in chronological order.

9. For more options related to lines, titles, and other adornments, Control-click the map and choose the appropriate item from the contextual menu (**Figure 5.18**).

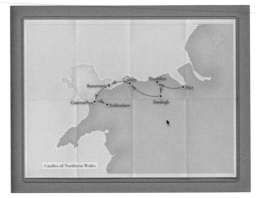

Figure 5.16 You can add map pages to books, complete with dots for the places the photos were taken, and lines showing your path between those places.

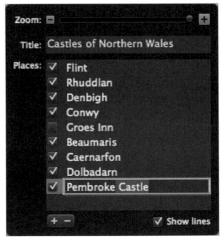

Figure 5.17 The map editing pop-up helps you zoom the map, give it a title, and choose which places appear (and in what order).

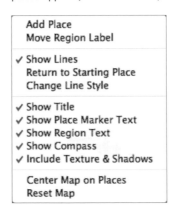

Figure 5.18 Control-click the map to access additional options in the contextual menu.

Editing Photos

Nondestructive Editing

In the first few versions of iPhoto, the program saved each change as you made it, which was a bad idea because the lossy JPEG compression that was applied each time could degrade the image quality. In iPhoto 5, Apple reduced the number of times an edited photo would be recompressed by writing all changes out at once when you clicked Done or moved to another photo.

In iPhoto '08, Apple switched again, this time to the nondestructive editing approach used by Aperture, iPhoto's high-end sibling. Since that version, all changes you make to new photos, or those that have never been edited in an earlier version, are saved in an *edit list* and applied to the original. (Previously edited photos don't use nondestructive editing unless you first revert to the original photo.) So in theory, image degradation due to multiple applications of JPEG compression should be a thing of the past.

iPhoto still maintains the current edited version of each photo in the Modified folder; those files are still necessary for display and export.

If you're anything like me, not all your photos come out perfect. In fact, lots of them are probably pretty bad, and those you can delete after import. No harm, no foul, and you didn't pay for developing.

What about those pictures that are okay, but not great? Much of the time they merely require a little work. Perhaps you need to crop out extraneous background that distracts the eye from the subject of the photo, or maybe you want to remove the red glow from that cute baby's eyes (it's the fault of the camera flash, not necessarily the sign of a demon child). iPhoto can help with those tasks and more.

I'm not suggesting that you whip out an image-editing application, clip your cousin's ex-husband out of the family reunion photo, and use filters that sound like alien death rays (Gaussian blur?) to make it appear as though he was never there. If you can do that, great, and iPhoto will even let you use any other image-editing application, including Photoshop and Photoshop Elements. But for most people, iPhoto provides all the basic editing tools that they need.

The main thing to remember is that there's no shame in editing photos to improve them. All the best photographers do it, and you can do it, too.

Entering Edit Mode

Since you can edit in the main window, in full screen mode, or in another application, it makes sense that you can enter edit mode in several ways.

To choose how to edit photos:

1. From the iPhoto application menu, choose Preferences ([Cmd][,]).

   iPhoto opens the Preferences window. Click the General button.

2. Select whether double-clicking a photo edits it (what I'm used to) or magnifies it.

3. From the Edit Photo pop-up menu, choose how you want iPhoto to edit photos by default (**Figure 6.1**). To use another program, choose In Application, and select a program in the Open dialog (**Figure 6.2**).

4. Close iPhoto's Preferences window.

Ways to enter edit mode:

◆ Double-click a photo in any mode ([Option]-double-click in organize mode if you set double-click to magnify), or double-click a photo *twice* if it's a small photo on a calendar page. In organize mode, you can also just press [Return].

◆ In organize mode, click the Full Screen button or choose Full Screen from the View menu ([Cmd][Option][F]) to edit the selected photos in full screen mode.

◆ [Control]-click a photo in organize mode, and choose an editing command from the contextual menu (**Figure 6.3**). Book mode offers a different contextual menu that also has an Edit Photo command.

✔ Tip

■ The capability to edit a photo in a separate window is no longer in iPhoto '09.

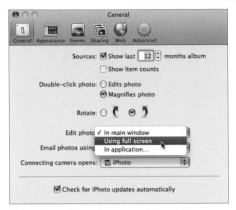

Figure 6.1 In the Preferences window, choose how you want iPhoto to enter edit mode when you click the Edit button or double-click a photo.

Figure 6.2 To use another program, choose In Application, and then find your desired program in the Open dialog.

Figure 6.3 Control-click a photo in organize mode and choose one of the editing commands from the contextual menu. This is a particularly good way to edit in an external application on an occasional basis.

✔ Tips

- Hide or show the Thumbnail list at the top of the window by choosing Hide or Show ([Cmd][Option][T]) from the View menu's Thumbnail submenu.

- When in edit mode, [Control]-click anywhere on a photo to access the commands that appear in the Photos menu.

Edit Tools Overview (Main Window)

Here's a quick look at the tools available when you edit an image in the main window (**Figure 6.4**).

Images around the photo being edited appear in the Thumbnail list. Click one to edit it.

The selected image appears in the display pane for editing.

Click Done to save your changes to the photo (and return to the previous mode).

Click to switch to full screen mode.

Click to hide or show the Information pane (now hidden).

Click to add an item to the source pane.

Size slider. Adjust this slider to zoom in and out of the picture in the display pane.

Use the previous and next buttons to navigate to the previous or next photo in the current album.

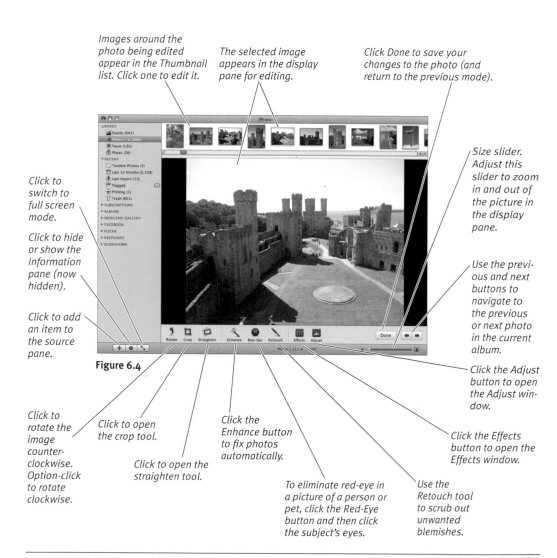

Figure 6.4

Click to rotate the image counterclockwise. Option-click to rotate clockwise.

Click to open the crop tool.

Click to open the straighten tool.

Click the Enhance button to fix photos automatically.

To eliminate red-eye in a picture of a person or pet, click the Red-Eye button and then click the subject's eyes.

Use the Retouch tool to scrub out unwanted blemishes.

Click the Adjust button to open the Adjust window.

Click the Effects button to open the Effects window.

Edit Tools Overview (Full Screen)

When you edit a photo in full screen mode, the editing tools and thumbnails are the same as in the main window, but they automatically appear and disappear at the bottom and top of the screen when you move your pointer to those locations, and there are several other buttons that provide necessary features (**Figure 6.5**).

✔ Tips

- Choose Always Show from the Thumbnails submenu in the View menu to display thumbnails all the time. You can also set the thumbnail column position and number of columns in the Thumbnails submenu.

- Choose Show Toolbar from the View menu to display the toolbar all the time.

Effects window. Click an effect to apply it to the image.

The selected image takes over the entire screen for editing.

Images around the photo being edited appear in the thumbnail list. Click one to edit it.

Adjust window. Use the controls here to modify the image.

Information window. Use it to view information, and change titles, date, and time.

Use the previous and next buttons to navigate to the previous or next photo in the current album.

Navigation window. Drag the selection rectangle to scroll around in the image.

Close button. Click to leave full screen mode.

Size slider. Use this slider to zoom in and out of the picture. Opens the Navigation window.

Figure 6.5

Click to open the Information window.

Click to open the crop tool.

Click to open the straighten tool.

Use the Retouch tool to scrub out unwanted blemishes.

Click the Effects button to open the Effects window.

Click the Adjust button to open the Adjust window.

Click to compare this image with the next one to the right.

Click to rotate the current image counter-clockwise. Option-click to rotate clockwise.

Click the Enhance button to fix photos automatically.

To eliminate red-eye in a picture of a person or pet, click the Red-Eye button and then click the subject's eyes.

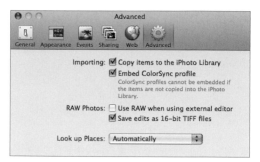

Figure 6.6 Set your RAW preferences in the Advanced pane of the iPhoto Preferences window.

Lossy vs. Lossless Compression

There are two basic ways of compressing a file so it takes up less space on disk: lossy and lossless.

With *lossy* compression, some data is deleted from the file, usually in ways that aren't particularly noticeable but that always reduce the overall quality. Files compressed with lossy compression methods are usually much smaller than their originals. Lossy compression methods work well with pictures and sound where data that most people can't see or hear can be eliminated.

In contrast, *lossless* compression methods preserve all the data in the original file perfectly when compressing it. That's best for retaining quality, but means that the file isn't nearly as small as it would be with a lossy method.

The basic difference then, is the trade-off between size and quality. For higher quality, choose file formats such as TIFF that use lossless methods of compression; for smaller files, stick with file formats such as JPEG that use lossy compression.

Editing RAW Files

Some digital cameras offer the option of shooting in *RAW format*, in which the image isn't compressed at all. RAW is considered a "digital negative" format that isn't to be modified, which has some implications when you want to edit a RAW photo in iPhoto.

Useful facts about working with RAW:

◆ When you edit a RAW file in iPhoto, a small RAW badge appears either at the bottom of the display pane or in the toolbar in full screen view.

◆ iPhoto offers you the option to save edited RAW files in TIFF format, which uses lossless compression to preserve all the original detail in the RAW file. Normally, iPhoto saves edited files in JPEG format, which uses lossy compression, meaning that some detail is lost on save. You can change this behavior in the Advanced pane of iPhoto's Preferences window by selecting Save Edits as 16-Bit TIFF Files (**Figure 6.6**).

◆ If you prefer to edit RAW files in an external editor like Adobe Photoshop, you can select Use RAW When Using External Editor in the Advanced pane of iPhoto's Preferences window (**Figure 6.6**). That setting overrides iPhoto's normal preferences for how you edit photos.

◆ If you select an edited RAW photo, the normal Revert to Original command in the Photos menu changes to Reprocess RAW. However, the end result is the same—all your changes are thrown away and you start again with the original RAW file.

Zooming Photos

It can be helpful to zoom in and out while editing, particularly when using the Retouch tool or clicking eyes for red-eye reduction.

To zoom in the main window:

◆ With an image showing in the display pane in edit mode, drag the size slider to the right to zoom in (**Figure 6.7**). The Navigation window appears to help you scroll in the photo. To zoom out, drag the slider to the left (**Figure 6.8**).

To zoom in full screen mode:

◆ Drag the size slider to the right to zoom in and to the left to zoom out. The Navigation window appears to help you scroll around in the photo (**Figure 6.9**).

✔ Tips

■ On Mac laptops introduced in late 2008, you can use the pinch open and close gestures to zoom in and out. Check the Trackpad pane of System Preferences for little demo movies of how this works.

■ iPhoto '09 removes the scroll bars when zoomed in while editing in the display pane. To navigate in both the display pane and in full screen view, drag the view rectangle around in the Navigation window.

■ If your mouse or trackball has a scroll wheel, you can use it to scroll vertically within a zoomed photo, even in full screen mode. Press [Shift] while moving the scroll wheel to scroll horizontally.

■ On Mac laptops from the last few years, you can scroll by dragging two fingers on the trackpad. It's a great way to scroll around in photos.

Figure 6.7 To zoom in on a photo, drag the size slider to the right. Here I've zoomed in all the way. Move around in the photo using the Navigation window that appears (lower right).

Figure 6.8 To zoom back out, drag the slider to the left. Here I've zoomed back out to the size that matches the display pane's size.

Figure 6.9 In full screen mode, use the size slider to zoom in and out, and navigate around with the tiny Navigation window that appears (lower right).

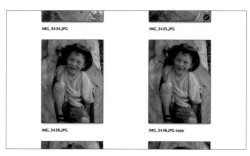

Figure 6.10 Notice how the duplicated photo appears next to its original and how it has "copy" appended to its title.

Duplicating Photos

iPhoto lets you duplicate photos, which can be useful in a variety of situations.

Reasons to duplicate a photo:

◆ If you want a photo to appear twice in a saved slideshow, you must duplicate the photo and add it to the slideshow separately.

◆ If you want to crop a head shot out of a photo, for instance, while keeping the original photo intact, duplicate the photo and crop the copy.

Ways to duplicate photos:

◆ In any mode, select one or more photos (not thumbnails!) and from the Photos menu, choose Duplicate (Cmd D).

◆ Control-click a photo and choose Duplicate from the contextual menu.

iPhoto duplicates the photo, appending "copy" to the title of the duplicate (**Figure 6.10**).

✔ Tips

■ The duplicate image shows up next to the original in the Library, and iPhoto does not create a new event.

■ The Last Import album does not show the duplicated photo.

■ If a specific source (calendar, slideshow, book, etc.) is selected when you duplicate a photo, the duplicate is added to that source too. However the photo won't be duplicated in any other sources that contain it. Also, as of iPhoto 8.0.2, you must switch out of a source and back in to see the duplicate. It's a bug.

■ iPhoto duplicates everything about the original, including keywords and ratings.

About Copies

iPhoto is consistent about where it places duplicates; they are always "newer" than the originals, so they sort to the left of the originals if Descending is selected in the View menu's Sort Photos submenu, or to the right if Ascending is selected (assuming you're sorting by date, of course).

iPhoto is also consistent about appending "copy" to the title of duplicate photos, making them easy to select by searching for the word "copy" in the Search field (for details, see "Searching with the Search Field," on page 57).

If the photo has been edited, iPhoto duplicates both the original and modified files, appending "_2" to their filenames. See "iPhoto Directory Structure," on page 19.

Rotating Photos

If you've turned your camera to switch from landscape view (horizontal) to portrait view (vertical), you may need to rotate the image in iPhoto to view it right side up.

Ways to rotate photos:

◆ In organize or edit mode, to rotate one or more photos clockwise, select them and click the Rotate button (**Figure 6.11** and **Figure 6.12**). To rotate the selected photos counter-clockwise, hold down Option and click the Rotate button.

◆ In organize or edit mode, select one or more photos, Control-click one, and choose the desired rotation direction from the contextual menu that appears.

◆ In organize, edit, or slideshow mode (but not book mode), select one or more photos and choose either Rotate Clockwise (Cmd R) or Rotate Counter Clockwise (Cmd Option R) from the Photos menu.

✔ Tips

■ Most cameras automatically rotate the image, eliminating the need for Rotate.

■ You can change the direction used by the Rotate button in iPhoto's Preferences window; Option-clicking always reverses the default direction (**Figure 6.13**).

■ It may be easiest to rotate photos in batches in organize mode. Shrink the thumbnail size so you can see a number of photos at once, Cmd-click the ones that need rotating clockwise, and click Rotate. Repeat with any images that need counter-clockwise rotation, holding down Option when you click Rotate.

■ On recent MacBooks, you can also rotate photos with a two-fingered twirl.

Figure 6.11 Here I'm showing a "before" photo in the main window; note the Rotate button in the lower left that I'm clicking.

Figure 6.12 Here's the "after" picture that resulted from clicking the Rotate button.

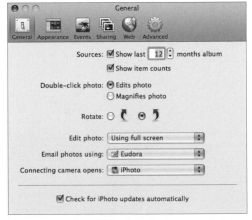

Figure 6.13 In the middle of the Preferences window, select which direction you want iPhoto to rotate photos by default.

Figure 6.14 To select a portion of a photo, drag to create a selection rectangle. Move it by dragging it; resize it by dragging an edge or corner. Here I've created a selection rectangle with no specific proportion to focus on the peach.

Figure 6.15 To constrain an image to specific proportions, choose an aspect ratio from the Constrain pop-up menu in the constrain tool (in this screenshot I've chosen 4 x 6, which will make a good print). You can move and resize the selection rectangle while maintaining the selected aspect ratio.

Figure 6.16 To constrain an image to custom proportions, choose Custom from the Constrain pop-up menu, and then enter your proportions in the fields to the right.

Selecting Portions of Photos for Cropping

In iPhoto '09, you must click the Crop button before you can select a portion of the picture to crop. Before proceeding with the rest of this page, click the Crop button.

To select part of a photo:

◆ Click outside the default selection rectangle and drag to create a new rectangle. iPhoto darkens the photo outside your selection rectangle to help you focus on what you have selected (**Figure 6.14**).

◆ To resize a selection rectangle, drag one of the rectangle's edges or corners.

◆ To move your selection rectangle around, drag it. You may need to move the rectangle to align it to the edges of a picture.

◆ To constrain the selection rectangle to specific proportions, choose an aspect ratio from the Constrain pop-up menu in the constrain tool. If you haven't created a selection rectangle, it will be constrained when you do; if you have one already, iPhoto resizes it (**Figure 6.15**). To remove a constraint, deselect the checkbox in the constrain tool or press (Shift) as you resize the rectangle.

◆ To constrain the selection rectangle to custom proportions, choose Custom from the Constrain pop-up menu, and enter the desired aspect ratio before you start selecting (**Figure 6.16**).

◆ To switch the orientation of the selection rectangle, choose Constrain as Landscape or Constrain as Portrait from the Constrain pop-up menu.

The next two pages have more details about aspect ratios and cropping.

Specific Aspect Ratios

If you want to order prints of a photo, you first should crop it to the appropriate aspect ratio (**Figure 6.17**). See the next page to learn about cropping photos and see "Understanding Aspect Ratios," on pages 186 and 187, for more details about aspect ratios.

Uses for specific aspect ratios:

◆ Use 1920 x 1200 (Display) before you crop the image for use as a Desktop picture. These numbers are specific to your monitor's resolution.

◆ Use 4 x 3 (DVD) or 16 x 9 (HD) for a landscape image for a DVD slideshow created with iDVD.

◆ Use Square when you want a square selection; I've found it helpful for making headshot images for use on the Web.

◆ Use a custom ratio if some external use, such as a Web page, calls for a specific aspect ratio.

✔ Tips

■ iPhoto assumes you want to crop in the same orientation as the photo, but you can change that by choosing Constrain as Landscape or Constrain as Portrait from the Constrain pop-up menu.

■ iPhoto has some duplicate aspect ratios, presumably for people who don't realize that aspect ratios are ratios between numbers and multiplying those numbers by some value doesn't change the ratio.

■ Don't bother cropping for books, cards, calendars, and printing on your own printer; it's better to use the zoom and center feature instead because it doesn't modify the original image the way cropping does. See "Editing Photos on Pages," on page 176.

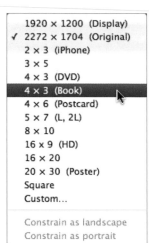

Figure 6.17 Before cropping, choose the aspect ratio that matches your intended use.

Figure 6.18 To crop an image, click the Crop button, select the desired portion, and then click the Apply button in the constrain tool. Here I've cropped out all the irrelevant background around the insect.

Figure 6.19 As you can see, cropping this image improves it immensely.

Adjust Shooting Style

When taking pictures, you usually want to fill the frame with the scene, but if you plan to order prints of all your photos, you might want to include a little extra space on the edges to allow for cropping to a print aspect ratio. For more tips, see Appendix B, "Taking Better Photos," starting on page 209.

Cropping Photos

If you plan to order a print of a photo or display it on your Desktop, you should crop it using an appropriate aspect ratio. Even if you don't plan to print a photo, cropping extraneous detail can improve an image. For more information, see "Understanding Aspect Ratios," starting on page 202.

To crop a photo:

1. Click the Crop button or press [c] to display the crop tool and a selection rectangle.

2. Select the desired portion of the image, using a constrain setting if you plan to use the image for display or printing. See the previous two pages for more details.

3. Click the Apply button in the constrain tool.

   iPhoto deletes the darkened area of the picture (**Figure 6.18** and **Figure 6.19**).

✔ Tips

- Press and release [Shift] to toggle between the "before" and "after" views.

- If your selection rectangle is very close to one of the standard aspect ratios, it's best to use the standard aspect ratio in case you want to print the image later.

- When you crop a photo, you remove pixels from it. So if you were to crop a 1600 x 1200 pixel photo (1,920,000 pixels) down to 1200 x 900 (1,080,000 pixels), you've removed almost half the image. Thus, if you print the original and the cropped version at the same size, the original will be of a much higher quality. Heavy cropping is one reason why iPhoto may show a low-resolution warning icon when you're creating books or prints. For details, see "Understanding Resolution," starting on page 204.

Straightening Photos

Most of the time, we're pretty good at keeping the horizon level in photos, but every now and then we mess up, as in the picture of a glacier in **Figure 6.20**. Since iPhoto can straighten images, it was easy to rotate the angle by 1.6 degrees to make it straight, as you can see in **Figure 6.21**.

To adjust the angle of a photo:

1. Click the Straighten button or press ⓢ to display the straighten tool.

2. Drag the slider to the right to rotate the image clockwise or to the left to rotate the image counter-clockwise, using the yellow grid lines as a reference for true vertical and horizontal.

3. When you're done, click the X button, press [Esc], or switch to any other editing feature to save your changes.

✔ Tips

- The straighten slider actually zooms in on your photo and crops it slightly to keep the edges straight.

- You can use the straighten slider to tweak the angle of a photo up to 10 degrees in either direction.

- If 10 degrees isn't enough (and remember that the greater the angle, the more iPhoto is cropping), save your changes, edit the photo again, and use the straighten slider one more time.

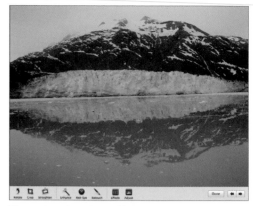

Figure 6.20 I'm going to blame my inability to take a straight photo of a glacier on the rocking boat.

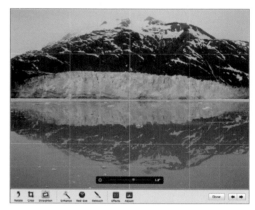

Figure 6.21 Luckily, iPhoto's straighten slider lets me eliminate the need for the lame excuse.

Figure 6.22 The original photo. It's too dark.

Figure 6.23 The photo after clicking Enhance. It's a lot better.

Enhancing Photos

Traditional photo processors learned long ago that fiddling with brightness and contrast and messing with the colors could turn a plebeian picture into a luminescent photo. iPhoto aims to help you do the same for your photos with its one-click Enhance feature.

To enhance a photo:

1. In edit mode, click the Enhance button.

iPhoto adjusts several aspects of your photo, including color levels, color saturation, and exposure.

2. Press and release Shift to toggle between the "before" (**Figure 6.22**—too dark) and "after" (**Figure 6.23**—much better) views of your photo.

3. If you like what Enhance has done to your photo, continue working. If not, choose Undo Enhance Photo (Cmd Z) from the Edit menu.

✔ Tips

■ A welcome new feature in iPhoto '09 is that changes made by the Enhance button are reflected in the Adjust window, so you can use Enhance as a starting point for improving photos further.

■ In my testing, it appears that Apple has significantly improved the algorithms behind the Enhance button, so it does a better job than in previous versions.

■ Use Enhance *before* any other adjustments, since other changes can result in Enhance thoroughly mucking up a photo.

■ Don't assume Enhance will always improve your photo. It's usually worth trying, especially as a starting point for additional work in the Adjust window, but only you can decide if its results are better or worse than the original.

Reducing Red-Eye

Perhaps the most annoying thing that can go wrong in a photograph is *red-eye*, a red glow in subjects' eyes that plagues flash photography. Thanks to iPhoto's face-detection technology, reducing red-eye is usually easy.

To reduce red-eye in a photo:

1. Click the Red-Eye button or press ⟨r⟩ to open the red-eye tool.

2. Click the Auto button.

   This often fixes red-eye accurately, converting the red shades to dark gray. If not, choose Undo Reduce Red-Eye (⟨Cmd⟩⟨Z⟩) from the Edit menu and continue.

3. Adjust the slider so the mouse pointer's size matches the subject's pupils.

4. Position the circle over each pupil, and click (**Figure 6.24**).

5. When you're done, click the X button or switch to any other editing feature to save your changes.

✔ Tips

- The Auto button fixes red-eye for all the faces it can identify in a photo.

- Press and release ⟨Shift⟩ to toggle between the "before" and "after" views.

- The Auto button works best when the subject is facing the camera directly so iPhoto can identify a face.

- It's easier to click the subject's eyes accurately if you zoom in first.

- iPhoto's technique makes people look as though they have black eyes, and it won't work on green-eye in dogs. You may be able to achieve better results in other image-editing programs. Also consider converting the photo to black-and-white.

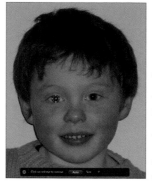

Figure 6.24 If the Auto button in the red-eye tool doesn't work, adjust the slider to match the mouse pointer's size to the size of the pupil, position the circle over the pupil, and click.

What Is Red-Eye?

Red-eye is a phenomenon that occurs in photographs when light from the camera's flash reflects off the blood vessels in the retina of the subject's eyes. It's worse when the flash is close to the lens, with young children, with blue or gray eyes (which reflect more light than darker eyes), and in dim settings.

You can reduce the likelihood of red-eye occurring in the first place:

◆ Try to cause the subject's pupils to contract by increasing the room light, asking the person to look at a bright light right before taking the picture, or using a red-eye reduction feature in your camera (which pulses the flash before taking the picture).

◆ Have the subject look slightly away from the camera lens rather than directly toward it.

◆ If your camera supports an external flash unit, use it to increase the distance between the flash and the camera lens.

Figure 6.25 The original photo. Note the jelly smudge on the left side of Tristan's lips.

Figure 6.26 You can see how I'm drawing over the jelly smudge with the retouch circle.

Figure 6.27 Much better!

Retouching Photos

Cindy Crawford's famous mole notwithstanding, many otherwise great photos are marred by small blemishes. Perhaps it's a smear of jelly on your toddler's face, or someone's chapped lips. Either way, iPhoto's Retouch tool can help.

To retouch a photo:

1. Click the Retouch button or press t to open the retouch tool (**Figure 6.25**).

2. Adjust the slider to make the mouse pointer a size that's a bit smaller than the blemish you're trying to remove.

3. Click and scrub over the blemish, using short strokes (**Figure 6.26**).

   iPhoto blurs the area under the circle pointer, blending it with the surrounding colors and textures.

4. Press and release Shift to toggle between the "before" (**Figure 6.25**) and "after" (**Figure 6.27**) views of your photo.

5. When you're done, click the X button or switch to any other editing feature to save your changes.

✔ Tips

- For additional accuracy, zoom in first.

- Retouch is not a panacea. It can fix small blemishes but will make large ones look like dust bunnies. It works best on skin.

- Avoid the Retouch tool on sharp color edges, such as between Tristan's hands and his blue shirt. When the Retouch tool hits edges, it smears the sharp lines. Luckily, you can always undo mistakes.

- Retouch can be good for taking the flash shine off eyes or other reflective surfaces.

Using the Effects Window

iPhoto's Effects window provides single-click access to a variety of different effects.

To use the Effects window:

1. Click the Effects button or press ⓔ to open the Effects window (**Figure 6.28**; next page).

2. Click a button in the Effects window to apply the associated effect to the current photo (**Figure 6.29**; next page).

✔ Tips

- Click the Original button to revert to the original look of the photo; this is a fast way to undo a number of changes in the Effects window.

- For all the buttons other than B & W and Sepia, clicking the button multiple times applies the effect again and again. I recommend you do this because you can achieve some really interesting results with multiple applications of an effect.

- iPhoto adds a number at the bottom of the button to remind you how many times you've clicked, and provides arrows so you can reduce the number of applications of an effect.

- When you click B & W or Sepia, iPhoto puts a small ON badge underneath so you know it's on. Click again to remove the effect.

- You can combine effects simply by clicking multiple buttons. For instance, make a photo look old by clicking Antique and Vignette a few times.

- Edge Blur, combined with cropping, can be a good way to focus attention on the subject of the photo.

Effect Descriptions

Since the Effects window does a good job of showing what the result of clicking its buttons will be, refer to **Figure 6.28** on the next page for examples.

- **B & W:** Makes the photo black-and-white. Click once to apply, again to remove.

- **Sepia:** Makes the photo sepia-toned. Click once to apply, again to remove.

- **Antique:** Desaturates the color in the photo and gives it a sepia tint for that old-time look. Click it multiple times to reduce the color saturation and replace more of the color with sepia.

- **Fade Color:** Fades the color in the photo, exactly like moving to the Saturation slider in the Adjust window to the left. Click it repeatedly to remove all color.

- **Original:** Returns the photo to its original look with a single click.

- **Boost Color:** Increases the color saturation in the photo, exactly like moving to the Saturation slider in the Adjust window to the right. Click it multiple times to make the photo's color truly shocking.

- **Matte:** Applies a white oval mask around the photo. Click it multiple times to increase the size of the mask, obscuring more of the picture.

- **Vignette:** Exactly like Matte, except its mask is black, instead of white.

- **Edge Blur:** Exactly like Matte, except its mask consists of blurred pixels in the photo, instead of plain white.

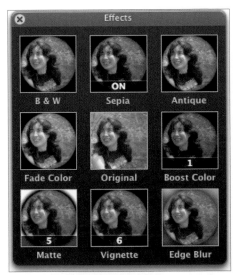

Figure 6.28 To achieve the effects in the photo below, I turned on Sepia, boosted the color by 1 level, and applied 5 and 6 levels of Matte and Vignette.

Figure 6.29 You can apply more than one effect at a time, and some of the effects can be applied multiple times to achieve unusual effects.

Using the Adjust Window

The Adjust window enables you to modify photos in all sorts of useful ways. Although using the Adjust window can be a fair amount of effort, it's usually worth the results.

To use the Adjust window:

1. Click the Adjust button or press a to open the Adjust window (**Figure 6.30**).

2. Drag the various sliders until the photo looks the way you want (see the following pages in this chapter for details).

3. To apply the same slider settings to another image, click the Copy button, switch to the other image, and click Paste.

✔ Tips

■ There is no "right" way to adjust a given photo other than what looks good to you!

■ Pressing Shift to toggle between the "before" and "after" views shows you the view before you started working with the Adjust window, not in between the use of each individual slider, so it doesn't help discern the effect of a given slider.

■ It's difficult to center a slider, so if you decide you don't like the effect of one, use Undo (Cmd Z) immediately rather than trying to reset it to the middle manually.

■ Click Reset to reset all the sliders to the middle.

■ Click the X button in the upper left of the Adjust window to close it, but note that there's no need to do so unless you want to avoid the screen clutter.

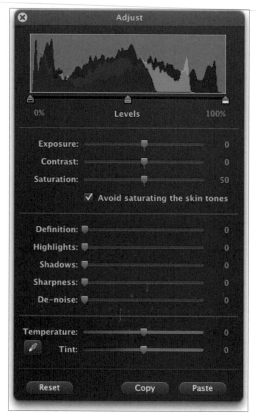

Figure 6.30 Use the sliders in the Adjust window to modify the exposure, color levels, sharpness, noise levels, and more.

Color Reproduction

I can't be certain of how the colors in the example photos in the rest of this chapter will reproduce onto paper, so if my comments about what a photo looks like and how I adjusted it seem off, rest assured that I'm describing what I see on my screen! For more details, see "Understanding Color Management," starting on page 206.

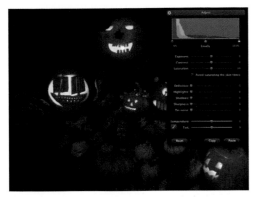

Figure 6.31 The histogram tends toward the left in dark photos like this one of Halloween pumpkins.

Figure 6.32 In light photos, the histogram moves to the right, as in this Golden Gate Bridge picture.

Figure 6.33 In this well-balanced photo, the histogram is fairly balanced, neither too far right nor left.

Understanding the Levels Histogram

Since all the sliders affect the Levels histogram at the top of the Adjust window, it's helpful to understand what it's telling you.

A histogram is a bar chart with each value on the horizontal axis representing a brightness value (0 equals black, and 100 equals white) and the height of each bar representing the proportionate distribution of pixels with that brightness value. iPhoto's Levels histogram contains three separate graphs, one each for red, blue, and green. I like to think of them as mountain ranges.

So, if a picture has a lot of blue in it, the blue mountain range will probably be large, and will likely be on the right side (since it's the brightest color). The red and green mountain ranges may also be large, but will likely be further to the left, since they're being used combinatorially to provide the exact shade of blue that you see.

The histogram for a too-dark photo will be pushed over to the left (**Figure 6.31**) and one that's too light will be pushed to the right (**Figure 6.32**). In general, a good photo has a balanced histogram, with roughly equal areas shown on either side of the midpoint (**Figure 6.33**). Balancing the histogram is a suggestion, not a rule, but keep it in mind when you're editing.

Every photo's histogram looks different, and every change you make to the contents of the image will change the histogram in some way, since it's merely another way of representing the content of the photo.

As we look at each of the Adjust controls, I'll explain what each does to the histogram so you can use them effectively to create balanced, attractive photos.

Adjusting Exposure

Exposure is the most fundamental aspect of photography, since it refers to the amount of light that strikes the camera's sensor. Most cameras control exposure automatically and do a good job, but they can be fooled or set wrong, producing an *underexposed* (too dark) or *overexposed* (too light) image. If that happens, you'll want to use iPhoto's Exposure slider and its Levels (next page) sliders.

To adjust the exposure of a photo:

◆ In the Adjust window, drag the Exposure slider to the left to make it seem as though less light hit the camera sensor or to the right to make it seem as though more light hit the camera sensor.

What the Exposure slider does:

This photo of the waterfall in **Figure 6.34** is rather underexposed, thanks to incorrect camera settings. By increasing the exposure in **Figure 6.35**, I've lightened the photo and brought out more detail.

Increasing exposure generally squishes the mountain ranges and slides them to the right, and decreasing exposure makes them taller and moves them left.

✔ Tip

■ You may be able to achieve slightly better (or at least different) effects by using the white point (left) and midtone (center) Levels sliders, along with the Shadows slider to boost detail in the darker areas of the image, as I've done in **Figure 6.36**.

Figure 6.34 This photo, taken with incorrect camera settings, is rather underexposed, and thus too dark.

Figure 6.35 By increasing the exposure to lighten the scene, I brought out some of the detail.

Figure 6.36 You can use the Levels controls to do much of what the Exposure slider does, possibly with better results.

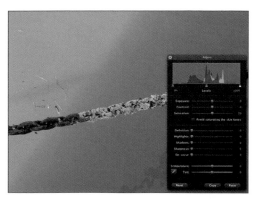

Figure 6.37 All the pixels in this image are huddled together in the middle of the histogram.

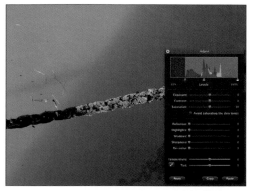

Figure 6.38 By redefining the black point, I give the picture a little more depth and darkness.

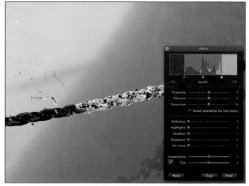

Figure 6.39 Then, resetting the white point brings up the luminosity a bit.

Adjusting Levels

The Levels slider under the histogram gives you independent controls for adjusting the black and white points, which define the pixels that should be considered pure black and those that should be considered pure white. Also useful is the midtone control for adjusting the overall brightness within the new range.

To adjust the levels of a photo:

◆ In the Adjust window, drag the left Levels slider to the right to set the black point.

◆ Drag the right Levels slider to the left to set the white point.

◆ Drag the midtone slider (the center control) left to lighten the photo or right to darken it.

What the Levels sliders do:

If, when you look at a photo's histogram, you see a blank space between the end of the mountain ranges and the black or white points (**Figure 6.37**), it's often safe to move those sliders toward the middle of the histogram, which is conceptually the same as grabbing the edges of the mountain ranges and pulling them out to the edges of the histogram. In **Figure 6.38**, I've moved the black point to the right to deepen the shadows; it's redefining what was a dark gray as total black. In **Figure 6.39**, I've moved the white point to the left to set a new value for what should be considered white, thus making the water glow a bit.

Moving the midtone slider moves the entire mountain range left or right, thus brightening or darkening the entire image but without going (much) beyond the new black and white points. Play with it to get a feel for how it might help your photos.

Adjusting Contrast

The *contrast* of a photo is the difference between its darkest and lightest areas. With too much contrast, you end up with overly dark and bright areas; with too little contrast, your photo appears flat.

To adjust the contrast of a photo:

◆ In the Adjust window, drag the Contrast slider to the left to decrease the contrast or the right to increase the contrast.

What the Contrast slider does:

In **Figure 6.40**, I set the Contrast slider at zero to show how it makes the reflected trees indistinct, with little difference between the light and dark areas. In **Figure 6.41**, I've maxed out the contrast to bring out the blackness of the tree trunks in the white pond.

Most photos won't need significant contrast adjustments; usually a little nudge will be all that's necessary.

Note how the mountain ranges in the histogram have been flattened and spread out by the increase in contrast. If I had reduced contrast, the mountain ranges would have been squished in and up instead. Put another way, increasing contrast distributes the pixels in the photo over a greater range of brightness values, whereas reducing the contrast increases the number of pixels within a small range.

✔ Tip

■ The Contrast slider is a relatively unsophisticated tool. You're better off using the black and white point sliders in the Levels histogram to set which colors should be considered pure black and pure white. Also play with the Definition, Highlights, and Shadows sliders.

Figure 6.40 With the Contrast slider all the way at zero, this black-and white photo of trees reflected in an ice-covered pond becomes flat and indistinct.

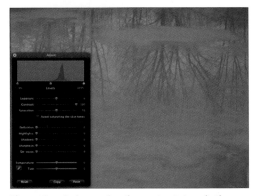

Figure 6.41 By increasing the contrast, I made the black trees stand out significantly more.

What Else Would I Do?

To sharpen the tree trunks and increase the difference between white and black even more, I'd bring the black and white points in, and move the Definition slider far to the right.

Figure 6.42 The bright green of the background leaves distracts a bit from Tonya's face (especially when the Adjust window is closed).

Figure 6.43 Reducing the color saturation of the photo causes it to become almost black-and-white, but that's not the effect I want either.

Figure 6.44 By protecting skin tones while decreasing saturation, I focus on Tonya's face while making the photo look as though it's from the 1970s.

Adjusting Saturation

The *saturation* of a photo is a measure of how intense the colors are. Highly saturated colors are said to be deep, vivid, or rich, whereas desaturated colors (think pastels) are often thought of as being dull, weak, or washed out. That's not to say that one is better than other; it depends on what you want.

To adjust the saturation of a photo:

◆ In the Adjust window, drag the Saturation slider to the left to make the colors weaker or the right to make them more intense.

What the Saturation slider does:

In **Figure 6.42**, Tonya has bright green leaves in sunshine behind her, and they distract a bit from her face. So I decreased the color saturation quite a lot in **Figure 6.43**. But since I wanted to decrease the saturation of only the background, in **Figure 6.44** I selected the "Avoid saturating the skin tones" checkbox, which returns Tonya to her original color and makes her face stand out.

This checkbox, which is new in iPhoto '09, is absolutely brilliant, and it lets you use the Saturation slider in many more situations than before, when iPhoto would have made skin overly gray or shockingly ruddy.

When you increase saturation, the mountain ranges move to the left (the picture gets a little darker) and they tend to separate, since each color has more independent brightness values (the reds are redder, the greens are greener, and the blues are bluer).

If you decrease saturation, the mountain ranges move to the right (the picture gets lighter) and overlap more. Decreasing the saturation entirely causes the mountain ranges to overlap entirely, giving you a monochrome image.

Adjusting Definition

New to iPhoto '09 is the Definition slider, which helps you bring out details and increase contrast in automatically selected portions of a photo. Its effect is often worthwhile, but almost always fairly subtle.

To increase the definition of a photo:

◆ In the Adjust window, drag the Definition slider to the right to increase contrast and pull out details.

What the Definition slider does:

The photo of milkweed fluff in **Figure 6.45** is interesting largely because of the detail of each individual seed pod. By moving the Definition to the right, I was able to make the edges of the hairs more distinct, as in **Figure 6.46**. I'm not sure how much of this you'll be able to see in the print book, but the effect is definitely noticeable in iPhoto when I press and release the Shift key to compare versions.

What I like about the Definition slider is that it almost always helps photos that would benefit from additional detail. The main place I've found the Definition slider to be unhelpful is with faces, particularly close-ups. In that situation, the additional detail tends to emphasize skin blemishes. Nonetheless, I encourage you to try the Definition slider when you're working in the Adjust window, just to see if it will help.

Moving the Definition slider to the right slightly flattens and spreads out the histogram's mountain ranges, but, as you'll see if you try it, not by a huge amount.

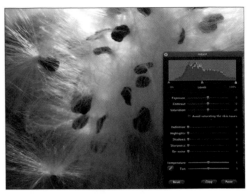

Figure 6.45 This photo of milkweed fluff is a little fuzzy, but there are details that could be pulled out.

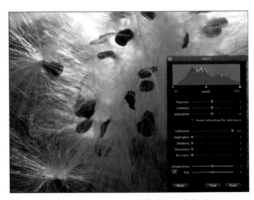

Figure 6.46 Maxing out the Definition slider increases the detail a bit, without causing any other problems.

What Else Would I Do?

If I wanted to increase detail even further, I could increase the sharpness for the entire photo. Plus, raising the Shadows slider would bring out more detail in the darker portion of the photo.

Figure 6.47 The whitecaps on the ocean waves are overexposed and washed out in this photo.

Figure 6.48 By dragging the Highlights slider to the right, I can darken the waves enough so that their details become visible, all without affecting the rest of the photo.

Adjusting Highlight Detail

Adjusting the exposure of a photo lightens or darkens the entire photo. But when you have just a portion of the photo that's overexposed, you can use the Highlights slider to darken just those too-bright spots, increasing the detail in those areas.

To adjust the highlight detail of a photo:

◆ In the Adjust window, drag the Highlights slider to the right to darken the brightest spots while leaving the darker spots alone.

What the Highlights slider does:

If you look at the ocean waves at the top of **Figure 6.47**, you can see that the bright sunlight caused them to be overexposed, as the camera tried to keep the exposure correct for the foreground. By dragging the Highlights slider to the right, I darkened just the overexposed parts, as you can see in **Figure 6.48**.

Try using the Highlights slider whenever you have a photo where only parts of it are overexposed, or where adjusting the exposure would mess up dark areas.

When you increase the highlight detail, you're flattening the higher mountain peaks at the right (light) end of the histogram while largely leaving the left (dark) end alone.

What Else Would I Do?

Using the Shadows slider will bring out a bit more of the detail in Tonya's and Tristan's faces, bumping up the Definition slider adds a bit more contrast in appropriate spots, and since this is actually a cropped portion of a larger photo, using the Reduce Noise slider smooths out the red in Tonya's shirt.

Adjusting Shadow Detail

Whereas increasing the highlight detail helps photos that are overexposed in places, increasing the shadow detail improves pictures that have too-dark areas mixed with properly exposed sections. Again, simply increasing the exposure won't work because that would blow out the already-light areas.

To adjust the shadow detail of a photo:

◆ In the Adjust window, drag the Shadows slider to the right to lighten the too-dark areas while leaving brighter portions of the photo alone.

What the Shadows slider does:

The problem with **Figure 6.49** is obvious—the hillside is bathed in shadow, but because the camera set its exposure based on the sunlit buildings, the hillside is too dark.

By dragging the Shadows slider to the right a fair amount, I can throw some more light on the darker areas of the image, increasing the detail significantly, as you can see in **Figure 6.50**.

The lesson to take away from this is that the Shadows slider can rescue photos that lose detail in the dark areas while still having some bright spots.

When you increase the shadow detail, you're moving the mountain peaks on the left (dark) side of the histogram toward the right (light) side while leaving the right end alone.

Figure 6.49 Because the low sun has been blocked from the right, the hillside is bathed in deep shadow.

Figure 6.50 By dragging the Shadows slider to the right, I can increase the exposure on just the shadowed hillside, without blowing out the properly exposed buildings or sky.

What Else Would I Do?

Using the Definition slider would bring out a bit more detail on the hillside, and increasing the saturation would make the green grass and bushes a bit more vivid.

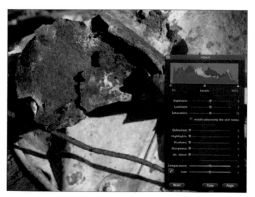

Figure 6.51 The fine detail in the rusted metal and the wire suffers a bit from too much blur.

Figure 6.52 Radically increasing the sharpness brought out the fine edge detail in the rusted metal.

What Else Would I Do?

A small increase in saturation might help a little, and using the Definition slider would bring out even more of the texture in the metal. Raising the Shadows slider would also reveal a bit more detail in the darker areas.

Adjusting Sharpness

Many photos are slightly blurry due to motion of the subject or the camera. You can use the Sharpen slider to increase the *sharpness*—the contrast between adjacent pixels—and thus sharpen the perceived focus of the photo (sharpening the actual focus can be done only with the camera lens, and it's too late for that).

To adjust the sharpness of a photo:

◆ In the Adjust window, drag the Sharpness slider to the right to increase the sharpness of the image.

What the Sharpness slider does:

The photo in **Figure 6.51** is a picture of an old, rusted pail next to some rusty wire. I had good light and managed to hold the camera still, but there was still a little more fuzziness than I would have liked. So I increased the sharpness quite a lot in **Figure 6.52**, and I hope you can see that the result is more sharply defined edges and textures on the rusted metal. I find that many photos are similarly improved by increased sharpness.

It's a little hard to predict exactly what changes to the sharpness will do to the histogram's mountain ranges, but in general, increasing the sharpness tends to "erode" them away, making them shorter and wider, whereas decreasing the sharpness makes them taller and narrower.

✔ Tips

■ Be careful when increasing the sharpness on photos that contain a lot of mostly solid colors, since the increased contrast between adjacent pixels will make those previously solid colors appear blotchy.

■ In earlier versions of iPhoto, you could reduce the sharpness of a photo. Use the Reduce Noise slider for that now.

Reducing Noise

Photos taken in low light conditions can suffer from *noise,* which most commonly appears as spots or blotches within areas of solid color. Since we expect areas of solid color to be, well, solid, the blotching is quite off-putting.

To reduce the noise of a photo:

◆ In the Adjust window, drag the Reduce Noise slider to the right to reduce the noise and smooth out blotches.

What the Reduce Noise slider does:

Figure 6.53 is a photo of the indoor track in Barton Hall, at Cornell University. Because of the high ceilings and poor lighting (for photography), there is quite a lot of noise in the solid colored areas of the track, even though I was able to avoid blur by resting the camera on a railing in the stands.

With the Reduce Noise slider, I was able to smooth out the blotches in the red of the track and the green of the infield, as I hope you can see in **Figure 6.54**.

You'll know if you need to use Reduce Noise by the blotches in large areas of solid color, but expect it most commonly in pictures taken in low light conditions.

Reducing the noise in a photo causes the mountain ranges to adopt a picket fence look, trading their relatively smooth lines for a jagged, up-down, up-down display.

Figure 6.53 The red of the track and the green of the infield show quite a bit of noise thanks to the low light conditions.

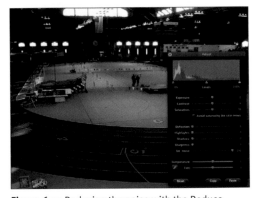

Figure 6.54 Reducing the noise with the Reduce Noise slider blurs the noisy bits to make the end result smoother. It will be hard to see the difference in photos that are so heavily reduced.

What Else Would I Do?

The lighting conditions in this photo are extremely odd, so I would bump up the shadow detail, and increase saturation a bit too. Note that I would not use the Definition slider, since it will make the solid colors blotchier, as it attempts to create more detail.

REDUCING NOISE

Figure 6.55 There's nothing really wrong with this photo, but I got the idea that I could make it more striking by increasing the blue in the sky.

Figure 6.56 Lowering the temperature caused the slight oranges and pinks from the sunset to be cooled down with the addition of blue, making for a more interesting photo.

What Else Would I Do?

About the only thing that would be helpful for this photo would be to increase the saturation a bit to make the remaining sunset colors in the center pop.

Adjusting Temperature

The *temperature* of a photo refers to your perception of which wavelengths of light illuminate the scene in a photo. That's a roundabout way of saying that the Temperature slider lets you adjust the colors of a photo from cool (bluish) to warm (yellowish).

To adjust the temperature of a photo:

◆ In the Adjust window, drag the Temperature slider to the left to make the colors cooler and bluer or the right to make them warmer and more yellow.

What the Temperature slider does:

Figure 6.55 is a picture of a sunset, with plenty of warm pinks and oranges, and while there's nothing wrong with the photo, I wondered if cooling it down would make it more interesting. By decreasing the temperature a lot in **Figure 6.56**, I've turned the entire sky a deep blue, making more of a contrast with the black trees in the foreground.

Although I'm seeing color problems less frequently with modern cameras, it's most likely that you'll need to adjust the temperature of artificially lit photos. Indoor lighting may give a yellow cast whereas flash lighting may provide a bluish cast.

When you decrease the temperature, as I've done here, the green mountain range stays put, the blue mountain range moves to the right to increase the amount of blue in the photo, and the red mountain range moves to the left to decrease the amount of red. If you increase temperature, the red mountain range moves to the right to increase the amount of yellow in the photo, and the blue mountain range moves to the left to decrease the amount of blue in the photo.

Adjusting Tint

Whereas the Temperature slider helps you adjust the blue and yellow colors in a photo, the Tint slider modifies the magenta and green colors. I seldom need to use either one.

To adjust the tint of a photo:

◆ In the Adjust window, drag the Tint slider to the left to add magenta to the photo or to the right to add green.

What the Tint slider does:

Check out **Figure 6.57**, a picture of my friend Oliver at his daughter's birthday party. The light from the birthday candles causes the colors to be far too yellow and magenta. By moving the Tint slider all the way to the green (right) in **Figure 6.58**, I've restored the green to Oliver's shirt, although pushing the Temperature slider most of the way to blue (left) is also necessary to get the colors right.

As you would expect, moving the Tint slider toward the right moves the green mountain to the right as well, and slides both the red and blue mountain ranges to the left, increasing the amount of green and decreasing the amount of magenta (since magenta is composed of both red and blue). Moving the Tint slider to the left has the opposite effect. Also, note that the mountain ranges also change in size and shape somewhat.

✔ Tip

■ To adjust tint and temperature simultaneously by setting the white balance, click the eyedropper button next to the Tint slider, and then click on a portion of the photo that should be white or light gray (a white shirt, or the white of an eye), but which is not overexposed. I find this method of controlling white balance to be tricky, due to the necessity of finding some white or light gray.

Figure 6.57 The lack of a flash in this photo means that all the light comes from the birthday candles, throwing the colors seriously out of whack.

Figure 6.58 Slamming the Tint slider all the way to green restores Oliver's green shirt, but it's also necessary to drop the Temperature slider most of the way to blue to get the particular hue of green correct.

What Else Would I Do?

Realistically, this just isn't a very good photo, technically speaking. Increasing the shadow detail would help, as would moving the midtone slider most of the way to the left to lighten it up, but neither will rescue the photo from the Trash.

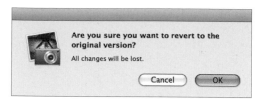

Figure 6.59 When you choose Revert to Original, iPhoto warns you that you'll lose all your changes.

Recovering Originals

It turns out that Revert to Original isn't doing anything complicated. When you edit a photo, iPhoto makes a copy of the original in a folder named for the photo's event, stored in the Modified folder. As long as this happens, you can recover the original image no matter what edits you make to it.

In fact, this is why Revert to Original works even if you edit a photo in another program—iPhoto starts tracking the original as soon as you double-click the photo. However, don't drag a photo from iPhoto to the Dock icon of another program to edit it; if you do so, iPhoto can't track the changes.

You can locate an original image in the Finder by Control-clicking it in iPhoto and choosing Show File (to find the original if unedited, or the modified version if it has been edited) or Show Original File (to find the original file if the photo has been edited).

Undoing Changes

We all make mistakes, and that's certain to happen on occasion when you're working with your photos too. With iPhoto, though, your changes aren't irrevocable.

Ways to undo changes to a photo:

◆ After you've performed an action, to undo just that action, choose Undo from the Edit menu (Cmd Z). Keep choosing Undo to undo earlier actions.

◆ To remove all the changes to a photo in a particular editing session, but *not* changes made in a previous session, choose Revert to Previous from the Photos menu or its contextual menu. You can also press Esc when editing in the main window or in full screen mode.

◆ To remove all changes from a photo, select it and choose Revert to Original from the Photos menu or its contextual menu.

 iPhoto warns that you'll lose all changes to the photo, and swaps in the original image (**Figure 6.59**).

◆ To revert to the original look of a photo while working in the Effects window, click its Original button.

◆ To throw away changes while working in the Adjust window, click its Reset button.

✔ Tips

■ You can undo individual changes made in edit mode *only* until changes are saved by clicking Done or moving to the next one.

■ To see what the photo would look like if you were to undo a change, press Shift. You must still choose Undo if desired.

■ Anything you can undo via the Undo command, you can redo via the Redo command in the Edit menu.

Using an External Editor

iPhoto's editing tools are sufficient for most tasks, but for more-involved changes to photos, iPhoto lets you turn to another image-editing program.

To set a default external editor:

1. From the iPhoto menu, choose Preferences ([Cmd][,]) to open the Preferences window. If necessary, click the General button.

2. From the Edit Photos pop-up menu, choose In Application (**Figure 6.60**).

3. In the Open dialog that appears, choose the desired program.

To edit in an external editor (I):

1. If you set the Double-Click Photo option to Edits Photo in the General preference pane, double-click one or more photos. iPhoto launches your selected editing program and opens the photos in it.

2. Make your changes, and when you're done, save and close the photos.

To edit in an external editor (II):

1. Set a default external editor, but don't set iPhoto to open photos in it by default.

2. [Control]-click one or more photos and choose Edit in External Editor from the contextual menu (**Figure 6.61**).

✔ Tips

■ Revert to Original works on photos edited in another program as long as you open them from within iPhoto (*don't* drag them to the other application to open).

■ Use the contextual menu or click the Full Screen button to avoid opening a photo in an external editor when that's the default option.

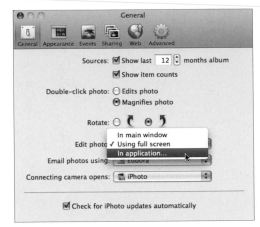

Figure 6.60 To configure iPhoto to use another program for editing photos, choose In Application from the Edit Photos pop-up menu in the General pane of iPhoto's Preferences window.

Figure 6.61 To edit a photo in an external editor without switching iPhoto's preferences, Control-click the image and choose Edit in External Editor from the contextual menu.

Reasons to Use an External Editor

iPhoto, good as it is, lacks some common editing capabilities because they require a lot of knowledge and skill to use effectively. You might want to look beyond iPhoto for the following reasons:

◆ Some of iPhoto's tools, like Red-Eye, are quite primitive and inflexible. Other programs have better tools for fixing red-eye.

◆ If you want to put text on top of an image in iPhoto, you'll need to use another image editor.

◆ With the exception of the Retouch tool, all of iPhoto's color-correction and image adjustment tools apply to the entire image. They may affect only a portion (such as the Shadows and Highlights sliders), but you can't avoid applying them to the entire photo. In contrast, other image editing programs let you select a portion of the photo before color-correcting it or otherwise modifying it.

◆ Other image editing programs include a bevy of filters and effects that you can apply to normal photos to turn them into amazing images that look like they were painted, embossed, photocopied, or drawn with charcoal.

◆ Most image editing programs support *layers* (imagine a sheet of clear plastic over the image) and enable you to make changes on the layer, thus making it easy to experiment without hurting the original image.

◆ Once you have layers, it becomes easier to paint or draw on top of an image, or to cut out portions of a photo.

External Editors to Try

Although iPhoto's editing tools have become more sophisticated over the years, other applications offer even more capabilities. It's beyond the scope of this book to talk about them in any depth, but if you want more editing power, check out these applications.

Acorn

Flying Meat's $49.95 Acorn lets you put text and graphics on top of your photos, apply sophisticated filters, and more, all with what may be the simplest interface of any of these programs. Although Acorn has layer support, iPhoto can't import a layered Acorn document. www.flyingmeat.com/acorn/

GraphicConverter

Lemkesoft's GraphicConverter provides useful tools for adding text to images, working on non-rectangular selections, applying filters, and more. The $34.95 app is also extremely useful if you need to import and export unusual formats. www.lemkesoft.com

Photoshop Elements

Adobe's $89.99 Photoshop Elements offers a subset of the capabilities in Photoshop, with lots of attention paid to making difficult tasks (like merging photos and making panoramas) easy. Photoshop Elements can save layered Photoshop files that iPhoto can use. www.adobe.com/products/photoshopelmac/

Pixelmator

The $59 Pixelmator, from Pixelmator Team, is one of the most capable of these apps, with all the usual features plus a photo browser that can look into your iPhoto Library, support for pressure-sensitive graphics tablets, and a plug-in architecture for filters. It can even save layered Photoshop files that iPhoto can import and use. www.pixelmator.com

Working with Layers

Layers in image editing programs are great, since they let you work on a photo without changing the base image. However, you can't save layers in a JPEG file (likely the original format of your photo), and if you save a photo as a layered Photoshop file, the change in filename extension prevents iPhoto from seeing the edited photo. There are two solutions to this problem.

First, you can "flatten" the image, squishing the layers together into one. In Photoshop Elements, when you're done editing, choose Flatten Image from the Layers menu, and then save the photo with its original name and location. That way iPhoto sees your changes to the photo, though you lose access to the separate layers for future editing. (There's no need to flatten an image specially in Pixelmator; you can just save.)

Second, if you want to retain layers for multiple editing sessions in either Photoshop Elements or Pixelmator, follow these steps:

1. Drag a photo from iPhoto to the Photoshop Elements or Pixelmator icon in the Dock.

2. Add a layer, but don't make any other changes, so you retain a clean original.

3. Use Save As to save a copy in Photoshop format on your Desktop. Close the file.

4. Drag the Photoshop file from your Desktop back into iPhoto to re-import it. Delete the copy on your Desktop.

5. From then on, use iPhoto to edit the photo *only* in the external editor. Editing in iPhoto flattens the layers silently.

✔ Tip

- Use a keyword to identify photos that should not be edited in iPhoto.

MAKING
SLIDESHOWS

Although some people feel that a photo isn't real unless it appears on a piece of paper (and iPhoto can satisfy those people too), one of iPhoto's coolest features is its capability to present photos on screen in a wide variety of ways—including slideshows on your Mac; ever-changing Desktop pictures; and slideshows on an iPod, iPhone, or Apple TV.

Gone are the days of the carousel projector and a darkened room; now a slideshow involves high-resolution photographs slipping on and off a computer screen, complete with elegant transitions between pictures. But that's only the beginning with iPhoto. iPhoto '09 adds a number of elegant slideshow themes that turn your photos from still images to scenes in a movie.

iPhoto's various onscreen presentation tools are not only the best way to display your photographs to friends and relatives, but also the best way for you to experience your own photos, whether through a constantly changing Desktop picture or a slideshow-based screen saver that kicks in whenever your Mac is idle.

Slideshows aren't limited to your Mac, either. You can copy both individual photos and slideshows to your iPod or iPhone, and the Apple TV turns out to be a wonderful way to display photos on your large screen TV.

Web-Based Slideshows

This chapter looks at slideshows you make within iPhoto and—for the most part—display on your Mac or on devices you own, like an iPhone or Apple TV. If you want to know how to make a Web-based slideshow that anyone can view in their Web browser, flip ahead to Chapter 8, "Publishing Photos on the Web," starting on page 135. That chapter discusses various different ways you can upload photos to a Web site—MobileMe, Facebook, and Flickr being the easiest ones—after which visitors can use the tools on that Web site to play a slideshow of your photos.

Types of Slideshows

iPhoto offers two types of slideshows, which I call "basic" slideshows and "saved" slideshows.

About basic slideshows:

Basic slideshows are quick to start from a selection of photos and offer a basic set of options that apply equally to all slides.

Use basic slideshows when you want to show someone a set of photos quickly, without any fuss or bother. Basic slideshows can also be useful for reviewing just-taken photos.

Lastly, you can use *only* basic slideshows when viewing images from a shared iPhoto Library over a network.

About saved slideshows:

Saved slideshows appear in the source pane like albums, books, cards, and calendars, and any changes you make to them are saved for the future. You can organize saved slideshows in folders, duplicate them to experiment with different approaches, and export them for display on a computer, on an iPod, on an iPhone, on an Apple TV, and on MobileMe.

Use saved slideshows when you want to put some effort into making a slideshow as visually impressive as possible. You can add and remove individual photos from the slideshow, apply temporary effects to photos during the slideshow, change the time each slide appears on screen, adjust the Ken Burns Effect for each slide, set the transition between any two slides, and more.

What's particularly neat about saved slideshows is that they're created with default settings, so you can customize them as much or as little as you like.

Arranging Basic Slideshows

Basic slideshows start with the image in the upper-left position of the selection or the album. So if you want to display the pictures in the reverse order, choose either Ascending or Descending (whichever one isn't currently selected) from the Sort Photos submenu of the View menu. Of course, whatever sort is in effect applies, so you can change the order by changing to a different sort, too.

Book Slideshows

iPhoto also offers "book slideshows" that are almost identical to basic slideshows. When in book mode, click the Slideshow button in the toolbar to run a slideshow of each page in the book at full size.

The main difference between a book slideshow and a basic slideshow is that you can't pick any of the slideshow themes or use the Ken Burns Effect. Other settings, such as showing photo titles and scaling photos to the screen, either aren't available or don't work, since the book page display preempts them.

Book slideshows are a great way to gain extra benefit from the work of putting together a book.

✔ Tip

■ iPhoto '09 shuffled the slideshow controls, such that the Slideshow button in the toolbar plays a basic slideshow instead of starting a saved slideshow.

Slideshow Tools Overview

When you select a saved slideshow in the source pane, iPhoto displays a new set of tools for customizing your slideshow (**Figure 7.1**).

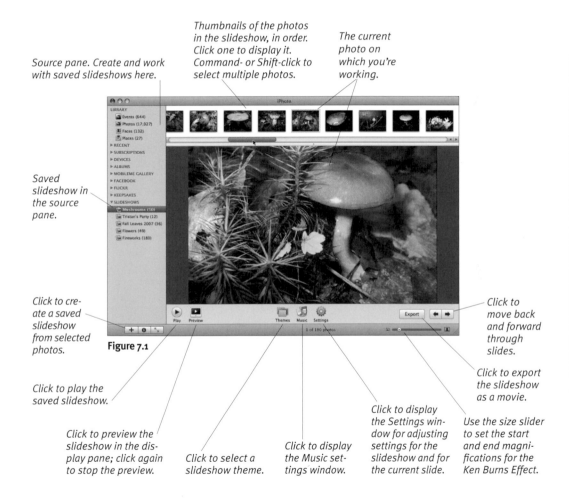

Thumbnails of the photos in the slideshow, in order. Click one to display it. Command- or Shift-click to select multiple photos.

The current photo on which you're working.

Source pane. Create and work with saved slideshows here.

Saved slideshow in the source pane.

Click to create a saved slideshow from selected photos.

Figure 7.1

Click to move back and forward through slides.

Click to play the saved slideshow.

Click to export the slideshow as a movie.

Click to preview the slideshow in the display pane; click again to stop the preview.

Click to select a slideshow theme.

Click to display the Music settings window.

Click to display the Settings window for adjusting settings for the slideshow and for the current slide.

Use the size slider to set the start and end magnifications for the Ken Burns Effect.

Creating and Deleting Saved Slideshows

For total control over a slideshow's presentation, create a saved slideshow. Saved slideshows are also ideal if you plan to show the same slideshow on multiple occasions.

To create a saved slideshow:

1. Select one or more photos or albums, and click the + button under the source pane.

2. In the dialog that appears, click Slideshow in the item icon list and enter a name for the slideshow in the Name field (**Figure 7.2**); then click Create.

   iPhoto creates a new saved slideshow in the source pane and displays the slideshow tools under the display pane (**Figure 7.3**).

To delete a saved slideshow:

◆ Select the saved slideshow in the source pane, press [Delete], and click Delete when iPhoto asks if you're sure. Or just press [Cmd][Delete] to avoid the warning dialog.

◆ Select the slideshow in the source pane, and then either choose Delete Slideshow from the Photos menu or [Control]-click it and choose Delete Slideshow from the contextual menu.

✔ Tips

■ iPhoto won't let you create a saved slideshow if you select a book, card, calendar, or another saved slideshow instead of an event, album, or individual photos.

■ You can also create a slideshow by duplicating an existing one, which is helpful for experimenting with different settings. With the slideshow selected in the source pane, choose Duplicate from the Photos menu or [Control]-click it and choose Duplicate from the contextual menu.

Figure 7.2 When creating a saved slideshow via the + button, iPhoto gives you a chance to change the automatic name it creates based on the currently selected album or event.

Figure 7.3 iPhoto provides slideshow tools under the display pane only when you select a saved slideshow in the source pane.

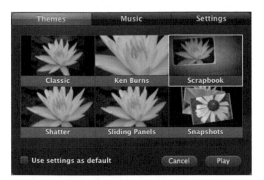

Figure 7.4 Select a theme for your slideshow. This is the settings dialog for basic slideshows; saved slideshows have exactly the same options in a slightly different presentation.

Figure 7.5 Configure settings for the entire slideshow. The precise controls here vary by theme.

Setting up Slideshows

In iPhoto '09, there isn't much difference between configuring basic and saved slideshows. Follow these basic steps after clicking the Slideshow button for a basic slideshow or creating a saved slideshow; subsequent pages provide more details.

To set up a slideshow:

1. Select a theme. For basic slideshows, click the Themes button in the settings dialog; for saved slideshows, click the Themes button in the toolbar. Click the desired theme to select it (**Figure 7.4**).

2. Select the music you want to play, if any. For basic slideshows, click the Music button in the settings dialog; for saved slideshows, click the Music button in the toolbar to display the Music window (see "Assigning Music to Slideshows," on page 119). Select a song or playlist, or make a custom playlist.

3. Configure the overall slideshow settings. For basic slideshows, click the Settings button in the settings dialog; for saved slideshows, click the Settings button in the toolbar to display the Slideshow Settings window (**Figure 7.5**).

4. For saved slideshows, configure each slide individually by clicking the This Slide button in the Slideshow Settings window.

5. Click Play or press Return.

✔ Tips

- In basic slideshows, select Use Settings as Default in **Figure 7.4** to use the same settings for future basic slideshows.

- The options in the Slideshow Settings window change with the theme; only Classic and Ken Burns have the controls shown in **Figure 7.5**.

Selecting a Slideshow Theme

Slideshow themes are new to iPhoto '09, but they're easy to work with and make slideshows even more visually compelling.

To select a slideshow theme:

1. For basic slideshows, click the Themes button in the settings dialog; for saved slideshows, click the Themes button in the toolbar to open the themes dialog.

2. Click the desired theme to select it (**Figure 7.4**, previous page).

3. For saved slideshows, either double-click the desired them or click the Choose button.

✔ Tips

■ You can change themes at any time by clicking the Theme button in the slideshow controls for basic slideshows, or the Themes button in the toolbar for saved slideshows.

■ Changing themes in a saved slideshow resets your settings for music and other options, which is a bit annoying.

■ All the themes can display a "title slide" that displays the name of the slideshow on the first slide. Turn it on and off in the Slideshow Settings window.

About Slideshow Themes

The Classic and Ken Burns themes provide the same functionality as previous versions of iPhoto did; the others are new.

◆ Use the Classic theme to show one picture per slide, with transitions and captions (titles, descriptions, places, and dates). The Scale Photos to Fill Screen option causes a slideshow to display only the center of portrait-orientation photos, but eliminates black bands on the sides.

◆ The Ken Burns theme offers the same options as the Classic theme, and, in saved slideshows, lets you configure zooming and panning for each slide individually.

◆ The Scrapbook theme builds pages containing one to three photos in scrapbook-style frames, and it flips between the pages or layers photos on top of one another on the pages. It's a bit like a book slideshow, but doesn't require that you make a book first.

◆ The Shatter theme shows one photo at a time much like Classic, but with an animated transition effect that "shatters" one photo and displays fragments of the next before filling in the rest of the next photo.

◆ The Sliding Panels theme shows one to three photos on a page, sliding one or more of them in and out as the transition effect. You can set the background color.

◆ The Snapshots theme shows a stack of photos, slowly scrolling them up the screen and overlapping a new photo on top of the stack every few seconds.

Figure 7.6 Pick a song or playlist to play during your slideshow.

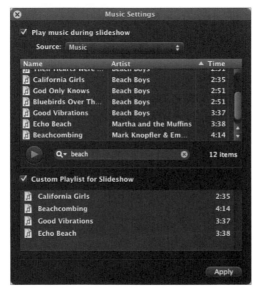

Figure 7.7 You can search for songs by entering a search term in the search field, and you can drag multiple songs to the custom playlist pane to make a custom playlist for just this slideshow.

Assigning Music to Slideshows

Unless you plan to narrate your slideshow in person, playing carefully selected songs from your iTunes Library during the slideshow can enhance the presentation.

To select music:

1. For basic slideshows, click the Music button in the settings dialog; for saved slideshows, click the Music button in the toolbar to display the Music Settings window.

2. Select Play Music During Slideshow.

3. From the Source pop-up menu, choose a collection of music: iPhoto's Sample Music or Theme Music, songs you've made in GarageBand, or playlists from iTunes.

4. Select a song or playlist from the list (**Figure 7.6**), or Cmd-click to select multiple songs to create a custom playlist.

5. Click Apply.

✔ Tips

■ To search for a song, enter a search term in the Search field. iPhoto narrows the list as you type. Click the X button to reset it.

■ To make a custom playlist, you can also click the Custom Playlist for Slideshow checkbox and then drag (first to the side, then down) selected songs to the custom playlist pane (**Figure 7.7**).

■ To sort the list of songs, click the header of the Name, Artist, or Time column; sorting by time makes it easier to match the music to your slideshow's length.

■ Click the triangular Play button to play the selected song; click it again to stop playing. Or double-click a song to play it.

Selecting Default Settings

For basic and saved slideshows alike, it's important to set the default settings that apply to each slide. You can then change the settings for each slide in a saved slideshow, but it's best to start with the right defaults.

To adjust default settings:

1. For basic slideshows, click the Settings button in the settings dialog; for saved slideshows, click the Settings button in the toolbar to display the Slideshow Settings window (**Figure 7.8**).

2. Either set the length of time you want each slide to play or select Fit Slideshow to Music so it plays as long as the selected music.

3. For Classic and Ken Burns slideshows, choose a default transition, and set the transition speed and direction, if available, by clicking the appropriate arrow in the round direction controller. iPhoto offers numerous transitions (**Figure 7.9**).

4. Select the desired checkboxes to display captions (title, description, title and description, place, or date) and a title slide containing the slideshow's name.

5. Select Repeat Slideshow if you want the slideshow to repeat indefinitely.

6. For saved slideshows, choose the screen dimensions (This Screen, 16:9 for HDTV, 4:3 for iDVD and TV, or 3:2 for iPhone) from the Aspect Ratio pop-up menu.

7. For basic slideshows, click Play.

✔ Tip

- When you select Fit Slideshow to Music, iPhoto complains at you if you have too many photos to show for the length of music selected. Select either fewer photos or more music.

Figure 7.8 Set the defaults for a saved slideshow in the Slideshow Settings window. The options are very similar for basic slideshows, which lose the Aspect Ratio pop-up menu and gain Play and Cancel buttons.

Figure 7.9 iPhoto provides a wide variety of transitions, but I recommend using relatively few per slideshow to avoid visual over-stimulation.

SELECTING DEFAULT SETTINGS

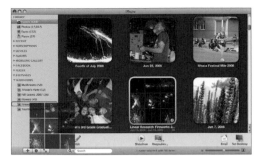

Figure 7.10 Drag photos to a saved slideshow in the source pane to add them to the slideshow.

Manipulating Saved Slideshow Photos

Whereas basic slideshows merely present the selected photos in the current sort order, saved slideshows give you more control. Use these instructions to add, remove, and rearrange photos in saved slideshows.

To add photos to a slideshow:

◆ Select one or more events, albums, or photos and drag them onto the saved slideshow in the source pane (**Figure 7.10**).

To remove photos from a slideshow:

◆ Select one or more photos in the scrolling list of photos above the display pane, and press [Delete].

To arrange photos in a slideshow:

◆ Before you create the slideshow, make an album and drag the photos into the order you want. iPhoto retains that manual sort order in the saved slideshow.

◆ After you've created a slideshow, drag photos around in the scrolling photo list above the display pane.

✔ Tips

■ Alas, there's no way to see multiple rows of thumbnails in the scrolling photo list; those controls in the View menu apply only to full-screen editing view.

■ Pay attention to the sort order of the album from which you create a slideshow. There's no shame in deleting a saved slideshow and re-creating it after sorting the source album properly.

■ If you're sorting by date, you'll probably want to choose Ascending from the View menu's Sort Photos submenu to ensure that your slideshow goes forward in time.

Customizing Slides

The last few pages have helped you get ready; now it's time to customize individual slides in a saved slideshow. Remember that each of these actions is optional, and each theme offers only those options that make sense for that theme!

To customize slides:

1. Click the Settings button to open the Slideshow Settings window. Click This Slide to switch to individual slide settings.

2. Select the first slide in the scrolling list above the display pane to set its options in the Slideshow Settings window (**Figure 7.11**).

3. Choose one of the three effects to apply to the photo. See "Editing Slide Photos," on the next page, for more information.

4. In Classic and Ken Burns, to override the default slide duration, select Play This Slide For, and click the up or down triangle buttons to increase or decrease the slide duration.

5. In Classic and Ken Burns, to override the default transition, choose a different transition from the Transition pop-up menu. You can also override the default transition direction and speed here.

6. To see how your changes look, click the Preview graphic to preview the current and next slides.

7. In the Ken Burns theme, use the Start/End switch along with the display pane's size slider to control the effect. See "Configuring the Ken Burns Effect," on page 124.

8. Select the next photo by clicking it in the scrolling list. Then repeat steps 3–8 until you've customized each slide as desired.

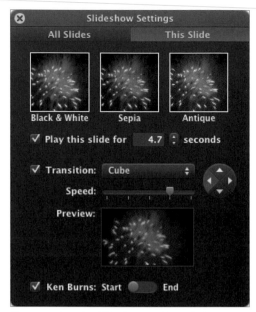

Figure 7.11 Use the Slideshow Settings window's controls to override default settings for slide duration and transition type, direction, and speed. You can also select effects and configure the Ken Burns Effect here.

Duration Locked?

If you find yourself unable to change the amount of time a slide will stay on screen, the reason is likely that you selected Fit Slideshow to Music in the All Slides pane of the Slideshow Settings window. Since iPhoto has to calculate the length of time to display each photo when that checkbox is selected, it prevents you from changing the slide durations.

Editing Slide Photos

You will most likely have edited your photos before you create a slideshow, but if not, you can do so while customizing your slides. Some edits must be permanent; others don't have to be.

To edit slide photos permanently:

1. Double-click the photo that's showing in the display pane to switch to edit mode.

2. Make whatever changes you wish, and when you're done, click the Done button to return to your slideshow.

To edit slide photos temporarily:

You can make several types of temporary edits that iPhoto applies to the photo only in the saved slideshow. These changes do not affect the original photo in any way.

◆ Click Black & White, Sepia, or Antique in the Slideshow Settings window (**Figure 7.11**, previous page) to apply the related effect to the photo.

◆ Use the display pane's size slider to zoom in on the photo.

◆ If you zoom in on a slide or are using a theme like Sliding Panels that doesn't always have enough room for the full photo, drag the photo to set what portion of it appears.

✔ Tips

■ If the photo is rotated incorrectly, you can fix it without entering edit mode by choosing Rotate Clockwise (Cmd R) or Rotate Counter Clockwise (Cmd Option R) from the Photos menu.

■ Use temporary edits unless you want the changes to apply everywhere.

Configuring the Ken Burns Effect

In most cases, Apple's defaults for the Ken Burns theme provide a completely acceptable result, even focusing on faces thanks to iPhoto's face detection capabilities. However, if you wish to zoom further, choose whether to zoom in or out, or even turn off the Ken Burns Effect for a slide, you can do so.

To configure the Ken Burns Effect:

1. In a saved slideshow using the Ken Burns theme, click the Settings button to open the Slideshow Settings window and click This Slide to switch to individual slide settings.

2. Select the Ken Burns checkbox.

3. Click the Start end of the Ken Burns toggle switch.

4. Using the size slider, zoom to the size at which you want the photo to appear first (**Figure 7.12**).

5. Drag the photo in the display pane so the starting view is showing.

6. Click the End side of the toggle switch.

7. Using the size slider, zoom to the size at which you want the photo to fade out.

8. Drag the photo in the display pane so the appropriate part is showing (**Figure 7.13**).

9. Click the Preview button in the toolbar to see if your settings work as desired.

10. Select the next photo and repeat steps 2–8.

Figure 7.12 For my starting point on this slide, I've zoomed in all the way and dragged the photo to focus on the center of this flower.

Figure 7.13 For the ending point, I zoomed out most of the way, and dragged the flower to a pleasing position.

Manual Configuration for Exported Slideshows

The default Ken Burns settings generally work very well, but note that they are random, which means that the effect won't necessarily be the same on any two playings of the same slideshow. As a result, if you're particular about the final slideshow, and particularly if you're exporting the slideshow, you should set Ken Burns manually for each slide. Otherwise, you won't know how it will work on any given playing.

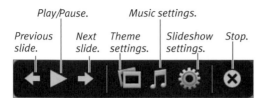

Play/Pause.   *Music settings.*

Previous *Next* *Theme* *Slideshow* *Stop.*
slide. *slide.* *settings.* *settings.*

Figure 7.14 Move the pointer while a slideshow is playing to reveal the slideshow controls.

Slideshow Advice

Although setting up and playing slideshows is easy, you can produce better results by keeping these tips in mind:

◆ To avoid black edges (primarily with portrait-orientation photos) in Classic and Ken Burns themed slideshows, either zoom in on photos or set the Scale Photos to Fill Screen option.

◆ Avoid using images smaller than your screen (in pixels), since they will look jaggy when iPhoto scales them to fit.

◆ Remember that Macs can drive TVs via an S-video cable (you may have to buy an adapter). If you have a huge television, why not use that for a slideshow? The Apple TV and iPod can also display photos on TVs easily.

◆ If you're playing the same slideshow continuously (at a party, for instance), select a large iTunes playlist to avoid repeating music.

◆ If you have two monitors, slideshows appear on the one containing the iPhoto window.

Controlling Slideshows

To controlling a slideshow while t runs is easy: move the pointer during a slideshow to show the slideshow controls (**Figure 7.14**).

To run a slideshow:

◆ For basic slideshows, select some photos and click the Slideshow button.

◆ For saved slideshows, select the slideshow in the source pane and click Play.

To control a slideshow:

◆ To pause and restart a slideshow, click the Play/Pause button in the slideshow controls or press Spacebar.

◆ To move back and forth between slides, click the left or right arrow button in the slideshow controls or press ← or →.

◆ To display thumbnails of photos, move the pointer to the bottom of the screen. Drag the selection box to jump around in the slideshow.

◆ To change the theme, music, or other slideshow settings, click the associated button in the slideshow controls.

◆ To stop the slideshow, click the X button in the slideshow controls or press Esc.

✔ Tips

■ Moving between slides manually causes music to stutter in iPhoto 8.0.2. It's a bug.

■ You can no longer rotate photos, delete photos, or rate photos during a slideshow. Nor can you change the duration of slides while a slideshow is playing.

■ If you are in Photos and have a lot of photos, don't click the Slideshow button without selecting photos first or iPhoto will lock up for many minutes while it builds a multi-thousand photo slideshow.

Exporting Slideshows

iPhoto slideshows are great if people can gather at your computer, but you're not limited by the location of your Mac, now that you can export slideshows to an iPod, iPhone, Apple TV, or QuickTime movie.

To export a slideshow:

1. Select the saved slideshow you wish to export.

2. Click the Export button in the toolbar. iPhoto displays the Export Your Slideshow dialog.

3. Select the checkboxes for the dimensions you want to export, based on where the movie will be viewed (**Figure 7.15**).

4. Particularly if you plan to sync your slideshow to an iPod, iPhone, or Apple TV, select Automatically Send Slideshow to iTunes.

5. Click Export and navigate to the desired location for the file(s); iPhoto defaults to a new iPhoto Slideshows folder it creates in your Pictures folder.

6. Locate your movie in the Finder and double-click it to see the results in either iTunes or QuickTime Player.

✔ Tips

- Mouse over the i button at the right of each size line for an often-inaccurate estimate of the size of the slideshow files.

- For more control, click Custom Export and choose a type of movie to export from the Export pop-up menu in the Save dialog that appears (**Figure 7.16**). For the 3G, MPEG-4, and QuickTime Movie choices, click the Options button to view and change the low-level settings. Most people won't ever need to do this.

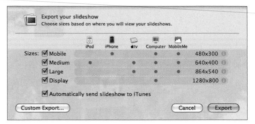

Figure 7.15 In the Export Your Slideshow dialog, select the size of the movie(s) you want iPhoto to create, based on where the movie will be viewed.

Figure 7.16 Click Custom Export and choose a format type for additional control over the movie dimensions and compression settings.

Exporting Photos to QuickTime

There's another quick and dirty way to create a simple QuickTime movie.

1. Select the photos you wish to export, choose Export from the File menu (Cmd Shift E), and click the QuickTime button.

2. Enter the maximum width and height for the images, a slide duration, and select a background color.

3. To include the music associated with basic slideshows, select Add Currently Selected Slideshow Music to Movie.

4. Click Export, name your movie in the Save dialog, choose a destination for it, and click OK to build the movie.

Figure 7.17 Select slideshows to sync to an iPhone or iPod under Movies in the Video tab of the device settings screen.

Figure 7.18 Slideshows synced to an iPhone or iPod touch appear in the Videos list in the iPod app.

QuickTime for Windows

One of the nice things about QuickTime is that it's available for both the Mac and Windows. Some Windows users don't have QuickTime installed, however, so you may need to tell them how to get it. Send them to www.apple.com/quicktime/download/for a free copy.

Syncing and Distributing Slideshows

Once you've exported a slideshow, what do you do with it?

Ways to use exported slideshows:

◆ To sync a slideshow to an iPhone or video-capable iPod, select the device in the iTunes sidebar, click the Video (iPhone) or Movies (iPod) tab, and select the slideshow in the Movies list (**Figure 7.17**). Slideshows appear in the iPod app's Video list on the iPhone (**Figure 7.18**), in the iPod touch's Video app, and in a normal iPod's Video list.

◆ To view a slideshow on an Apple TV, make sure the Apple TV is connected to iTunes, and then find the slideshow in the Shared Movies list in Movies.

◆ Exported slideshows play in QuickTime Player, and you can copy them to a writable CD or DVD disc for friends and family with computers.

◆ If you use Custom Export to make an MPEG-4 or QuickTime Movie file, you can drag it into iPhoto to import it, and then add it to a MobileMe Web album to upload it for viewing on the Web.

◆ Most slideshows will be too large (over 5 MB) to send via email, so use a service like Dropbox (www.getdropbox.com) to send a link to the file via email instead.

◆ If you have FTP or Web space available with your Internet account, upload the movie (perhaps using iWeb) and send people the link.

◆ Upload to YouTube at www.youtube.com. YouTube can take most formats, and it wants the highest quality, but videos must be less than 1 GB and 10 minutes.

Creating an iMovie Slideshow

What if you want to add narration or captions to a slideshow? Turn to Apple's iMovie video editor. These instructions are a brief overview; refer to iMovie's help or Jeff Carlson's *iMovie '09 & iDVD for Mac OS X: Visual QuickStart Guide* for more details.

To create an iMovie slideshow:

1. In iMovie, click the Photos button, select an album, and then drag the desired photos into the Project Browser in the order you want (**Figure 7.19**).

2. Double-click a photo to display the clip inspector. Enter a duration longer than you expect to speak and click Done.

3. To record audio, click the Voiceover button to open the Voiceover window, click the left edge of the photo you just tweaked, and record your narration, clicking anywhere in the project to stop recording (**Figure 7.20**).

4. Double-click the purple audio clip under the photo to see its duration. Then double-click the photo and set its duration to match the length of the voiceover.

5. To adjust the Ken Burns Effect zoom and position, double-click the tiny crop button in the photo and adjust the starting and ending positions in the Viewer pane to the right. You can also click Fit to display the entire photo (with black bars) or Crop to crop it to fit.

6. To add a title, click the Titles button and drag a title style to a photo. Type your text in the Viewer pane (**Figure 7.21**). Drag the edges of the blue title balloon to match the photo clip length.

7. Repeat for each photo.

Drag photos to the Project Browser to add them; you work with them here too.

Photos appear in the Event Browser when you select an album.

Drag and expand to set title length.

Determine clip length here.

Titles button.

Voiceover button.

Photos button.

Viewer pane.

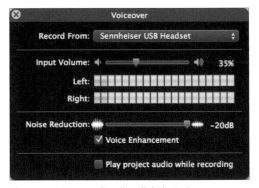

Figure 7.19 Use iMovie to produce and distribute slideshows that are significantly more complex than is possible in iPhoto alone.

Figure 7.20 To record audio, click the Voiceover button, click the left edge of the photo you want to describe, and speak. Click anywhere else to stop.

Figure 7.21 To add a title, click the Titles button and drag a title style to a photo. Then type your title in the Viewer pane.

Drop photos in
the drop zones.
Burn
button.
Theme pane. Click to
choose a theme.

Figure 7.22 Select a theme for your DVD slideshow in the Themes pane; switch to the Media pane to drop photos or movies into the drop zones.

Photo list. Drag to
rearrange; press
Delete to remove.
Media pane. Click to
switch between audio,
photos, and movies.

Click to
return to
the main
screen.
Click to
preview.
Drag photos to
the photo list
to add them.

Figure 7.23 Customize your slideshow in iDVD using the Media pane.

Figure 7.24 Drag photo albums from the Photos pane into iDVD's Magic iDVD screen to create slideshows of them. Switch to the Audio pane and drag songs or playlists onto the same spots to add music to your slideshows.

Creating a DVD Slideshow with iDVD

iPhoto can send a set of photos to iDVD to create a DVD slideshow that can be viewed on any TV with a DVD player. You must have a Macintosh with a SuperDrive to burn such a slideshow to disc.

To create a DVD slideshow with iDVD:

1. Select one or more albums or slideshows (Shift- or Cmd-click to select multiple items), and choose Send to iDVD from the Share menu.

   iPhoto works for a bit, launches iDVD, and shows the iDVD main screen with pre-built iDVD slideshows.

2. Click the Themes button in the lower right, choose a theme, and customize it with text and images (**Figure 7.22**).

3. To add audio, photos, or video to the main title screen; click the Media button; click Audio, Photos, or Movies in the upper right; and drag items to drop zones.

4. Double-click a slideshow icon in the main screen to switch to a screen where you can add, delete, and rearrange photos (only for the album-based slideshows), plus set a slide transition, select music, and set other options (**Figure 7.23**).

5. As you work, use the Preview button to verify that your slideshow plays as you desire. A small player window simulates a DVD remote control.

6. When you're ready, click the Burn button to start burning your DVD.

✔ Tip

- For even easier DVD slideshow creation, launch iDVD, choose Magic iDVD from the File menu, and drag albums and music into the Photos area (**Figure 7.24**).

iDVD Slideshow Tips

Look to other sources for full instructions on how to use iDVD, such as Jeff Carlson's *iMovie '09 & iDVD for Mac OS X: Visual QuickStart Guide* or Jim Heid's *The Macintosh iLife '09*, both from Peachpit Press. That said, these tips should help you use iDVD more effectively.

Tips for using iDVD:

◆ iPhoto sends saved slideshows to iDVD as QuickTime movies, which you can't edit inside iDVD. Remember to choose an aspect ratio for your slideshow that matches the TV screen where it will be shown!

◆ The 99-photo per slideshow limitation in previous versions of iDVD is now gone.

◆ Save your iDVD project with a good name; it's the disc name in the Finder.

◆ Turn on Show TV Safe Area in the View menu to verify that everything you're doing will fit on a TV screen.

◆ If you select Always Add Original Photos to DVD-ROM Contents in iDVD's Slideshow preferences pane, iDVD also makes the photos available as files on the DVD for use with computers. These are stored as normal files and not in an iPhoto Library folder.

◆ Quit all unnecessary applications when burning; if anything interrupts the burn process, it can ruin your DVD-R disc.

◆ DVD-R discs hold 4.7 GB, so you probably won't be able to fill one with slideshows. To use all the space, add video.

Making Good DVD Slideshows

It's easy to work with iPhoto and iDVD, but you must still expend a fair amount of effort when creating a DVD-based slideshow if you want good results. Keep in mind that TV quality will always be lower than the computer screen quality.

◆ Use iDVD's Preview heavily, and run through all your slideshows from start to end before burning.

◆ Landscape photos work better than portrait photos, which have large black borders.

◆ Make sure Always Scale Slides to TV Safe Area is set in iDVD's Slideshow preferences pane (choose Preferences from the iDVD menu and click the Slideshow button).

◆ Resist the temptation to put as many photos in each slideshow as possible; instead, whittle down the slideshow to the most relevant photos. Very similar photos are boring when seen one after another.

◆ You can choose the duration between slides, but it's generally best to fit the slideshow length to the audio length. But don't pick so much music that individual slides appear for too long.

◆ Be forewarned; it can be hard to find good music for slideshows. Think about the subject and the mood of the photos, and then browse through your iTunes collection to see what songs might fit. It's easier to browse quickly in iTunes than in iDVD.

◆ Click the Motion button (it has curved arrows in the middle) to turn off the theme's motion while you work.

Figure 7.25 Click the Set Desktop button to set the selected photo as your Desktop picture.

Figure 7.26 With a single click, you can put the photo you have selected in iPhoto on your Desktop.

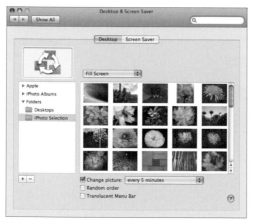

Figure 7.27 In the Desktop view of your Desktop & Screen Saver preferences, configure how you want your Desktop pictures to appear, and how often they should rotate.

Setting the Desktop Picture

In Mac OS X, you can display a picture on your Desktop, and with iPhoto, putting one (or more, in rotation) of your photos on your Desktop is a matter of just clicking a button.

To set the Desktop picture:

1. In iPhoto, select one or more photos, and click the Set Desktop button or choose Set Desktop from the Share menu (**Figure 7.25**).

   If you selected only one photo, iPhoto immediately changes the picture on your Desktop (**Figure 7.26**).

   If you selected multiple photos, iPhoto opens the Desktop & Screen Saver preference pane (**Figure 7.27**).

2. If you selected multiple photos, choose how you want the images to appear on the Desktop.

✔ Tips

- You can also display the photos in an iPhoto event or album on your Desktop by selecting it in the iPhoto Albums list in the Desktop & Screen Saver preference pane's Desktop view.

- If the picture is in landscape orientation, iPhoto scales the photo to make it fit.

- If the photo is in portrait orientation, iPhoto takes a landscape chunk out of the middle to display on the Desktop. Stick with photos in landscape orientation, or crop them appropriately first.

- iPhoto can put a picture on only one monitor. To put a picture on a secondary monitor, open the Desktop & Screen Saver preference pane and drag a photo from iPhoto into the photo well for the second monitor's Desktop picture.

Using Photos as a Screen Saver

Alas, the Set Desktop button in iPhoto no longer sets selected photos as a screen saver, but it's no great loss.

To use photos as a screen saver:

1. Open the Desktop & Screen Saver pane of System Preferences (**Figure 7.28**).

2. If necessary, click the Screen Saver button to switch to the Screen Saver view.

3. In the Screen Savers list, scroll down in the Pictures collection and click an iPhoto event, folder, album, smart album, Web album, or photo feed whose photos you want to cycle through as your screen saver.

4. Select a display style: Slideshow, Collage, or Mosaic.

5. Adjust the Start Screen Saver slider to set how long the screen saver should wait for activity before kicking in. If you want to set a hot corner, click the Hot Corners button and pick a hot corner in the dialog that appears.

6. To configure options for how the screen saver slideshow looks, click Options and then adjust the settings in the Options dialog. (**Figure 7.29** shows the Slideshow options; the Collage and Mosaic settings are different.) Click OK when you're done.

   Mac OS X's screen saver is now set to use the selected photos. The next time your screen saver kicks in, you'll see it display-ing those photos.

✔ Tip

- To make the screen saver use all your photos, create a smart album that con-tains all photos taken after 1904 (or some other equally early date).

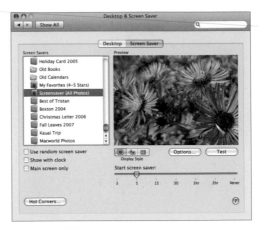

Figure 7.28 Select an event, folder, album, or smart album in the Screen Savers list to use those photos as your screen saver.

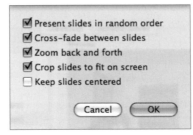

Figure 7.29 Configure how the screen saver displays your photos in the Options dialog. Play with these settings to see how they interact with the photos you're using—I've found varying results with different types and sizes of photos.

Screen Saver Styles

Mac OS X 10.5 Leopard's screen saver provides three styles:

- Slideshow uses the Ken Burns Effect and displays a single photo at a time.

- Collage has a single large photo fade in, shrink, and then remain on screen as subsequent photos overlap it.

- Mosaic picks one photo as the master and then uses other photos to make a mosaic of the master image. It needs a lot of images and a fast Mac.

USING PHOTOS AS A SCREEN SAVER

Figure 7.30 Choose which photos will be copied to your iPod or iPhone in the Photos screen in iTunes.

Viewing Photos on an iPod or iPhone

It's easy to view the photos once you've copied them to your iPod or iPhone.

◆ On an iPod with a clickwheel, select Photos at the top level and press the center button to list albums. Continue pressing the center button to see thumbnails and then full-size photos. Use the Forward and Back buttons to navigate through the photos, or press the Play button to switch into slideshow mode.

◆ On an iPhone or iPod touch, tap the Photos app, tap an album to see its thumbnails, and then tap a photo to see it full size. Swipe right and left to move through the photos, or tap the bottom of the screen and tap the triangular play button to switch into slideshow mode. Remember that you can rotate the iPhone or iPod touch between landscape and portrait modes to avoid black bars on the sides. You can also pinch to zoom in and out, and drag a zoomed photo to navigate around in it.

Syncing Photos to an iPod or iPhone

The best way to carry photos with you is in your color-screen iPod or iPhone, which can display them in their full glory. Though the photos come from iPhoto, you must use iTunes to copy them to your iPod or iPhone.

To copy photos to an iPod or iPhone:

1. In iTunes, select your iPod or iPhone in the Devices list.

2. Click the Photos tab to display the photo-syncing preferences (**Figure 7.30**).

3. Click the Sync Photos From checkbox and select All Photos and Albums, Most Recent Events, or Selected Albums.

4. If you selected Most Recent Events, choose how many from the pop-up menu, and if you chose Selected Albums, select specific albums in the list.

5. Click Apply to save your preferences and start the synchronization process.

✔ Tips

■ To save space, iTunes shrinks the photos for display on the tiny screen.

■ If you want to use a capacious iPod (not iPhone) to move photos to another Mac, select the Include Full-Resolution Photos checkbox in the Photos tab in iTunes.

■ If you have limited space on your iPod or iPhone, it's best to copy individual events or albums rather than everything. Smart albums and the Last 12 Months album are especially useful here.

■ iTunes shows you how many photos are in each album, which can give you a rough approximation of which albums will fit.

Syncing Photos to an Apple TV

A great way to display a slideshow from iPhoto is on a large-screen TV connected to an Apple TV. The Apple TV is easy to connect to iPhoto, although, as with the iPod and iPhone, syncing works via iTunes. The following instructions assume that you've already paired your Apple TV to iTunes.

Figure 7.31 Choose which photos will be copied to your Apple TV in the Photos tab in iTunes.

To copy photos to an Apple TV:

1. In iTunes, select your Apple TV in the Devices list.

2. Click the Photos tab to display the photo-syncing preferences (**Figure 7.31**).

3. Click the Sync Photos From checkbox and select All Photos and Albums or Selected Albums.

4. If you chose Selected Albums, select specific albums in the list.

5. Click Apply to save your preferences and start the synchronization process.

✔ Tips

■ You can also set the Apple TV to stream photos from a different shared iTunes Library, which doesn't copy the photos from the Mac to the Apple TV. Use the Apple Remote to connect the Apple TV to the shared iTunes Library in the Settings > Computers menu. Once that's done, use the Photos tab in iTunes to select albums to stream via Photos > Shared Photos on the Apple TV.

■ Photos originally saved with iPhoto 4 or earlier may be rotated incorrectly on the Apple TV. To fix such photos, select them and choose Revert to Original from the Photos menu, and then rotate each photo again.

Viewing Photos on an Apple TV

The Apple TV can display random photos from your synced collection as a screen saver, and you can also display them manually as a slideshow. Use the Apple Remote to navigate the menus on your Apple TV for these instructions.

◆ Select Settings > Screen Saver to select the screen saver style and set options such as how quickly it comes on and whether or not it runs when music is played through the Apple TV. Select Settings > Screen Saver > Photos to pick an album to use with the Photos screen saver, which scrolls multiple photos up the screen. And select Settings > Screen Saver > Slideshow to run a standard screen saver with the Ken Burns Effect. (The Album option displays album artwork from iTunes.)

◆ Select Photos > My Photos to pick a synced album and either display photos manually using the buttons on the Apple Remote or start a slideshow. You can configure slideshow settings in Photos > Settings.

PUBLISHING PHOTOS ON THE WEB

8

MobileMe, Facebook, and Flickr Accounts

To publish photos to one of these Web-based services, you must first have an account on the service you wish to use.

◆ MobileMe costs $99 per year, although you can sign up for a free trial. To start the process, go to www.me.com and look for a "Sign up for a free trial" link.

◆ Facebook is free, but it's more than just a photo sharing site, so be aware that you're getting into a social networking system. Sign up at www.facebook.com.

◆ Flickr, owned by Yahoo, can be used for free, or you can upgrade to a Pro account to remove the free-account limitations of 100 MB of photo uploads per month, 200 photos in your photostream, and the capability to display only smaller images. Pro accounts cost $24.95 per year. Start signing up at www.flickr.com.

Which you choose is entirely up to you. My feeling is that MobileMe is best for sharing with groups of people you already know, Facebook is best for sharing with friends on Facebook, and Flickr is best for sharing with the world at large.

One of the greatest changes in photography has been the rise of the Web. Before the appearance of sites like MobileMe, Facebook, and Flickr, it was difficult or impossible for the average person to publish a photo such that it could be seen by many others, but that's no longer true. As of early 2009, Facebook contains upwards of 13 billion photos, and Flickr has another 3 billion (Apple hasn't released numbers for MobileMe). People love Web publishing.

Those growth trends are just going to continue for the foreseeable future, since it's becoming ever easier to post photos to the Web, thanks in part to new features in iPhoto. Previously, it was a pain to upload to anywhere but .Mac (the previous name for MobileMe), but with iPhoto '09, putting photos on Facebook and Flickr is just as easy.

Although it's easy, serious Flickr users should note that iPhoto doesn't offer as many options as third-party plug-ins do. So if you get started uploading to Flickr with iPhoto and find yourself wanting more than it provides, don't hesitate to check out other utilities.

That said, let's look at how to publish photos to the Web, and in the next chapter, we'll turn our attention to how to share photos with a small set of people in other ways.

Setting up Facebook

Before you can upload to your Facebook account, you must make a connection between iPhoto and Facebook, so Facebook will accept uploads from iPhoto. This needs to be done only once, the first time you attempt to upload to Facebook.

To connect iPhoto with Facebook:

1. Select one or more photos, albums, or events (including movies!), and either click the Facebook button or choose Facebook from the Share menu.

   iPhoto asks if you want to set up iPhoto to publish to Facebook (**Figure 8.1**).

2. Click Set Up.

   iPhoto presents a dialog with which you can log in to Facebook (**Figure 8.2**).

3. Enter the email address you used for Facebook and your Facebook password, and select the Keep Me Logged In To iPhoto Uploader checkbox, unless you're working on someone else's computer. Then click the Login button.

   iPhoto may show another dialog asking you to allow iPhoto access to your Facebook account (**Figure 8.3**).

4. If you get the Allow Access dialog, click the Allow button to finish the setup process.

Figure 8.1 On the first attempted connection to Facebook, iPhoto asks if you want to connect iPhoto to your Facebook account.

Figure 8.2 Enter your Facebook login information and click the Login button.

Figure 8.3 Click the Allow button to let iPhoto access your Facebook account.

Figure 8.4 On the first attempted connection to Flickr, iPhoto asks if you want to connect iPhoto to your Flickr account.

Figure 8.5 The first step in connecting iPhoto and Flickr is to sign in to your Yahoo account.

Figure 8.6 After signing in, you must allow iPhoto to link to your Flickr account.

Figure 8.7 When you're done, Flickr confirms that you've authorized iPhoto to upload photos.

Setting up Flickr

Before you can upload to Flickr from iPhoto, you must link iPhoto to your Flickr account. This needs to be done only once, the first time you attempt to upload to Flickr.

To connect iPhoto with Flickr:

1. Select one or more photos, albums, or events (including movies!), and either click the Flickr button or choose Flickr from the Share menu.

   iPhoto asks if you want to set up iPhoto to publish to Flickr (**Figure 8.4**).

2. Click Set Up.

   iPhoto opens a Web page in your default Web browser, from which you can log in to your Yahoo account, which provides access to Flickr (**Figure 8.5**).

3. Enter your Yahoo ID and password, and click the Sign In button.

   Another Web page loads, asking you to authorize the link between iPhoto and your Flickr account (**Figure 8.6**).

4. Click the OK, I'll Allow It button to finish the setup process.

   Your Web browser displays a confirmation page (**Figure 8.7**), after which you can return to iPhoto to continue publishing photos.

✔ Tip

■ For geotags to be uploaded to Flickr and for your photos to be mapped automatically, select Include Location Information for Published Photos in iPhoto's Advanced preferences. You may also need to set your account to import geotags at www.flickr.com/account/geo/exif/.

Publishing to MobileMe

Your MobileMe Gallery lets you link photos in iPhoto with a Web page on MobileMe. Albums on MobileMe can be viewable by anyone, by just you, or by a set of people with whom you share a user name and password.

To create an album on MobileMe:

1. Select one or more photos, albums, or events (including movies!), and either click the MobileMe button or choose MobileMe Gallery from the Share menu.

   iPhoto asks who can see your album and how it will appear (**Figure 8.8**).

2. From the Album Viewable By pop-up menu, choose Everyone, Only Me, or a user if you've created any.

3. Select the desired display, download-ing, and uploading options from the checkboxes, and click Publish.

   iPhoto creates a new album in the MobileMe Gallery list in the source pane and starts processing and uploading your photos (it's slow!). When it's done, it shows the URL to your album at the top of the screen (**Figure 8.9**).

To create user names and passwords:

1. From the Album Viewable By pop-up menu in the MobileMe Gallery dialog, choose Edit Names and Passwords.

2. In the dialog that appears, click the + but-ton, enter a name and password (click or press Tab to switch fields), and click OK (**Figure 8.10**).

✔ Tips

- The URL to your album appears at the top of the screen; click it to visit the page.

- The Settings button in the toolbar dis-plays the dialog shown in **Figure 8.8** for after-the-fact changes.

Figure 8.8 iPhoto presents you with choices about who can see your album and how it will be displayed.

Figure 8.9 When you click Publish, iPhoto creates an item in the MobileMe Gallery list for the new album.

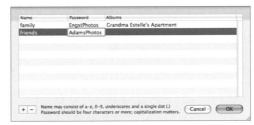

Figure 8.10 Enter names and passwords to create login credentials for people you want to be able to see your photos.

✔ More Tips

- The Advanced settings let you hide the album on your MobileMe Gallery page, and, if you allow downloading of photos, set the quality of the downloaded photos.

- Click the Tell A Friend button to create an email message with login information.

Figure 8.11 iPhoto presents you with choices about who can see your album on Facebook.

Figure 8.12 When you click Publish, iPhoto creates an item in the Facebook list for the new album.

Figure 8.13 You can find your photos in your profile in Facebook; note that faces you've identified in iPhoto appear as tags, and mousing over a person's face displays his or her name.

Publishing to Facebook

Facebook is great for publishing photos that can be viewed by groups of your Facebook friends. What's cool about Facebook is the way faces in your photos can (theoretically) link to your friends' accounts.

To create an album on Facebook:

1. Select one or more photos, albums, or events (but not movies!), and either click the Facebook button in the toolbar or choose Facebook from the Share menu.

   iPhoto presents options as to who can see your album (**Figure 8.11**).

2. From the Photos Viewable By pop-up menu, choose Everyone, Friends of Friends, or Only Friends.

3. Click Publish.

   iPhoto creates a new album in the Facebook list in the source pane and starts processing and uploading your photos (a slow process). When it's done, it shows the URL to your album at the top of the screen (**Figure 8.12**).

✔ Tips

- For a person you've identified in a photo to be tagged (with a link to his Facebook account—see **Figure 8.13**), his Facebook email address must be entered in the Information dialog for his snapshot on the Faces corkboard. As of iPhoto 8.0.2, this is still a little flaky.

- Photos added to the album on Facebook, along with tags added to your photos on Facebook will sync back to iPhoto.

- The Settings button that appears in the toolbar when you're in a Facebook album displays the dialog similar to the one shown in **Figure 8.11** to let you change who can see your photos or remove the current Facebook account from iPhoto.

Publishing to Flickr

Whereas Facebook is a social networking site, Flickr is a more generalized photo-sharing service. Geotagged photos uploaded to Flickr can retain their geotags, allowing them to be associated with other geotagged photos on maps and location pages in Flickr.

To create an album on Flickr:

1. Select one or more photos, albums, or events (but not movies!), and either click the Flickr button in the toolbar or choose Flickr from the Share menu.

   iPhoto gives you options as to who can see your album and how large the largest size photo on Flickr will be (**Figure 8.14**).

2. From the Photos Viewable By pop-up menu, choose Only You, Your Friends, Your Family, Your Friends and Family, or Anyone.

3. From the Photos Size pup-up menu, choose Web, Optimized, or Actual Size.

4. Click Publish.

   iPhoto creates a new album in the Flickr list in the source pane and starts processing and uploading your photos (a slow process). When it's done, it shows the URL to your album at the top of the screen (**Figure 8.15**).

✔ Tips

- The Settings button that appears in the toolbar when you're in a Flickr album displays the dialog similar to the one shown in **Figure 8.14** to let you change who can see your photos or remove the current Flickr account from iPhoto.

- Photos you add to linked photo sets on Flickr are synced to your Flickr Web album, as are tag and name changes you make on Flickr.

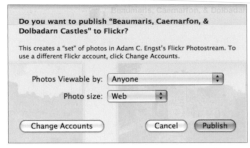

Figure 8.14 iPhoto presents you with choices about who can see your album on Flickr, and how large the maximum photo size should be.

Figure 8.15 When you click Publish, iPhoto creates an item in the Flickr list for the new album.

✔ More Tips

- If you edit a photo published to a free Flickr account, changes won't be reflected in Flickr automatically, at least in iPhoto 8.0.2. To get the image to be updated on Flickr, delete it from the Flickr Web album in iPhoto and add it back again.

- Keywords you add in iPhoto are automatically uploaded to Flickr as tags. There's no way to prevent that in iPhoto.

- Contacts on Flickr can be identified as "friends" or "family" for interaction with the Photos Viewable By pop-up menu.

- Each Flickr Web album corresponds with a photo set on Flickr; you cannot upload loose photos to your photostream in Flickr.

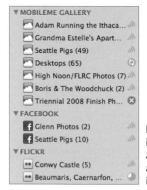

Figure 8.16 iPhoto provides feedback on what it's doing in the upper right corner of the screen.

Figure 8.17 When iPhoto is synchronizing a Web album, it shows a spinning progress icon.

Figure 8.18 When you delete a Web album, iPhoto warns you if it contains any photos downloaded from the Web side and gives you a chance to import them. If the Web album contains only photos that originated in iPhoto, the dialog reassures you that deleting the Web album won't affect your original photos.

Facebook and Flickr Flakiness

As of iPhoto 8.0.2, I've experienced flaky behavior in a number of areas.

◆ Most annoyingly, Facebook tags often failed to link to my friends' accounts reliably, even when I knew the appropriate email address to enter.

◆ Changed names and keywords in one location sometimes failed to be reflected on the other.

◆ Although both Facebook and Flickr support movies, you can neither upload nor download movies in Web albums. Instead, you just get an image placeholder.

Managing Web Albums

The beauty of Web albums, whether uploaded to MobileMe, Facebook, or Flickr, is that they aren't static. You can modify their contents in iPhoto, or you or others can add photos to them or change names and tags on the Web side. Either way, iPhoto keeps both versions in sync.

To add photos to a Web album:

◆ Select one or more photos, and drag them to the desired Web album.

iPhoto processes and uploads the photos, providing the status in the upper-right corner of the screen (**Figure 8.16**).

To remove photos from a Web album:

◆ Select one or more photos in the Web album and press (Delete).

iPhoto removes the photos, updating the files on the Web version and showing a spinning progress icon next to the album while that's happening (**Figure 8.17**).

To start or stop synchronization:

◆ Click the little status icon next to the Web album name in the source pane.

If the icon shows radio waves, iPhoto starts synchronizing.

If synchronization was interrupted, the icon changes to an exclamation point. Click it again to resume updates.

To delete a Web album:

◆ Select a Web album in the source pane and press (Delete).

iPhoto asks for confirmation and then deletes the Web album and the photos on the Web, leaving the originals in iPhoto alone and offering to import any photos that were added on the Web side of MobileMe, Facebook, or Flickr and downloaded to iPhoto (**Figure 8.18**).

Publishing Photo Pages with iWeb

iPhoto's integration with iWeb is similar to its integration with iDVD: it just hands off selected photos. You can create two types of pages when starting from within iPhoto: photo pages and blog pages.

To publish a photo page:

1. Select an event, album, or the individual photos you wish to publish.

2. From the Share menu's Send to iWeb submenu or the iWeb pop-up menu in the toolbar, choose Photo Page.

   iPhoto launches iWeb, creates a new page, and asks you to select a template.

3. Select a template and click Choose.

   iWeb imports the photos and presents you with a page that simulates your eventual photo Web page (**Figure 8.19**).

4. Edit the various text blocks for the page name, description, and photo titles as desired (click a block twice to edit it).

5. Click any photo to show the Photo Grid window, from which you can choose a variety of display options.

6. Click the site's top icon in the sidebar to view the site's Site Publishing Settings pane. From the Publish To pop-up menu choose MobileMe, FTP Server, or Local Folder (**Figure 8.20**). Enter connection details and click the Publish Site button.

✔ Tips

- For full details about iWeb, see Steve Sande's *Take Control of iWeb '09* at www.takecontrolbooks.com/iweb.

- It's best to give your photos titles in iPhoto, rather than in iWeb, to avoid duplicating effort later in iPhoto.

Figure 8.19 In iWeb, edit the text blocks that name and describe your page, and choose styles for the photos from the Photo Grid window.

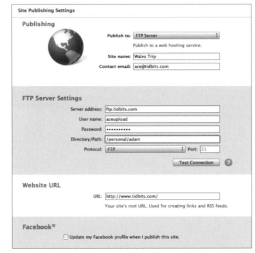

Figure 8.20 In the Site Publishing Settings pane, enter the connection details for the site to which you're uploading your photos.

iWeb Upload Choices

You have three site publishing choices:

- ◆ MobileMe is the easiest and most full-featured, but does cost $99 per year.

- ◆ FTP Server lets you work with almost any other Web server that allows uploads via FTP or one of its variants.

- ◆ Local Folder is available if you can't use one of the other methods.

Figure 8.21 When you send a photo to an iWeb blog, iWeb creates a new entry for the photo.

Figure 8.22 iWeb automatically updates the main page for your blog once you've entered details for a specific blog entry.

More Features in iWeb

Documenting all that iWeb can do is way beyond the scope of this book, but note that there are many other things it can do:

◆ You can put a Google Map widget on the page, showing exactly where photos were taken.

◆ If you've uploaded albums to your MobileMe Gallery, another widget lets you display a clickable thumbnail for that album on your Web site.

◆ By default, iWeb adds an RSS feed and a search field to your blog, though you can remove those if you wish.

Publishing Blog Photos with iWeb

Whereas a photo page looks much as you'd expect a Web photo album to look, a photo blog features a single photo per chronological entry.

To publish a photo to an iWeb blog:

1. Select a photo, and from the Share menu's Send to iWeb submenu or the iWeb pop-up menu in the toolbar, choose Blog.

   iPhoto launches iWeb and creates a new blog entry (**Figure 8.21**).

2. Edit the various text blocks for the blog post title and description as desired (click a block twice to edit it).

   iWeb automatically updates the main page for your blog as well (**Figure 8.22**). Note that you can change the listing style in the Blog Summary window.

3. Click the site's top icon in the sidebar to view the site's Site Publishing Settings pane. From the Publish To pop-up menu choose MobileMe, FTP Server, or Local Folder (**Figure 8.20**, previous page). Enter connection details and click the Publish Site button.

✔ Tips

■ Your iWeb blog can be on the same site as your photo pages or another site.

■ You can drag photos from iPhoto into various spots in iWeb, either into a page for free placement of the photo, or into one of iWeb's image placeholders. This may be easier than using iWeb's media browser pane.

■ Double-click any photo in iWeb to resize it within its placeholder.

Exporting to Web Pages

Although iWeb can create Web pages you can upload to your own server, iPhoto has a built-in way of doing this that's simple and effective, even if its results aren't as visually interesting. (Honestly, use iWeb; it's better.)

To export photos to Web pages:

1. Select an album or the individual photos you wish to publish via the Web.

2. Choose Export from the File menu ([Cmd][Shift][E]).
   iPhoto shows the Export Photos dialog.

3. If it's not selected, click the Web Page button (**Figure 8.23**).

4. Enter the title for your Web page.

5. Enter the desired number of columns and rows of photo thumbnails.

6. If desired, choose a template and select background and text colors.

7. Enter the maximum width and height for the thumbnails and the full-size images.

8. Select the Show Title, Show Description, Show Metadata, and Include Location checkboxes as desired.

9. Click Export, navigate to the desired destination folder (it's best to create a new folder inside your user directory's Sites folder), and click OK.
   iPhoto exports the photos and builds the appropriate HTML files.

10. Switch to the Finder, open the folder in which you saved your Web page, and double-click the index.html file to open it in your Web browser (**Figure 8.24**).

11. If necessary, upload the folder to your Web site using an FTP program like Fetch (www.fetchsoftworks.com).

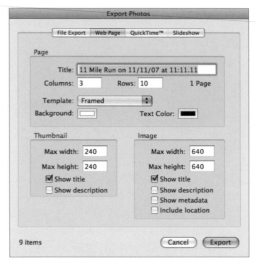

Figure 8.23 Use the options in the Web Page pane of the Export Photos dialog to set how your photos will appear on the Web page.

Figure 8.24 To see your Web page, open the destination folder in the Finder and double-click the .html file in it. To expand a photo, click its thumbnail.

Managing Plug-ins

To manage plug-ins, select iPhoto in the Finder, choose Get Info ([Cmd][I]) from the File menu, and use the checkboxes and buttons in the Plug-ins section to enable, disable, install, and uninstall the plug-ins.

- Picasa Web Albums Uploader for Mac by Google; free. Helps you upload to Picasa Web albums. `http://picasa.google.com/mac_tools.html`

- Kodak Gallery Upload Plug-in by Kodak; free. Provides access to the Kodak Gallery photo-sharing site. `www.kodak.com/eknec/PageQuerier.jhtml?pq-path=150`

- SmugMugExport by Aaron Evans; free. Uploader for the SmugMug photo site. `www.aarone.org/smugmugexport/`

- locr for iPhoto by Norbert Doerner; free. Uploads geotagged photos to locr, a location-based photo-sharing site. `www.locr.com/downloads#iphoto`

- ÜberUpload for iPhoto by Übermind; $19.95. Uploads to FTP and SFTP servers, with many options. `www.ubermind.com/products/uberuploadforiphoto.php`

- PhotoUpLink for iPhoto by Mark Morris; $12.99. Uploads to FTP sites, databases, and Office 2004. `www.photouplink.com`

- Flash Album Exporter from Ken Welch; free. Creates album pages using freeware Flash and JavaScript apps. `http://home.comcast.net/~flashalbumexporter/`

- BetterHTMLExport from Geeks R Us; $20. Makes better static Web pages than iPhoto's built-in export. `www.geeksrus.com/software/betterhtmlexport/`

- iPhotoToGallery by Zach Wily; free. Makes it easier to export to Gallery-driven Web sites. `www.zwily.com/iphoto/`

- PictureSync by Holocore; $10. Standalone application that uploads to many Web services. `www.picturesync.net`

- iPhotoWebShare by bitpatterns; $5. Easy to use preference pane that serves iPhoto albums directly. `www.bitpatterns.com/site/iPhotoWebShare/`

Other Web Export Tools

Developers can build iPhoto export plug-ins for other photo-sharing sites and for generating Web-based albums. I can't list them all, but this collection will get you started.

For more utilities, search for "iPhoto" on VersionTracker at `www.versiontracker.com` and check the iPhoto Plugins News blog at `http://wheezersociety.blogs.com/iphoto_plugins/`.

Make sure any plug-in you download has been updated for iPhoto '09 before installing; not all of these have been updated yet!

Useful Web export tools for iPhoto:

- FlickrExport by Fraser Speirs; £12. Full-featured export plug-in for uploading to Flickr. Try it if iPhoto's Flickr support isn't sufficient. `http://connectedflow.com/flickrexport/iphoto/`

- iP2F by Tagtraum Industries; $14.95. Another export plug-in for uploading to Flickr. `www.tagtraum.com/ip2f.html`

- Facebook Exporter for iPhoto; free. Predates iPhoto's Facebook support, but may be worth trying. `http://developers.facebook.com/iphoto/`

- PixelPipe for iPhoto by PixelPipe; free. An export plug-in for sending photos to the PixelPipe media distribution service. `http://pixelpipe.com/`

- Shutterfly Export Assistant for iPhoto by Shutterfly; free. Simplifies uploading to Shutterfly. `www.shutterfly.com/downloads/features_mac.jsp`

- iPhoto to Picasa Web Albums by Übermind; $19.95. Uploader for Picasa Web albums with support for geotagged photos and more. `www.ubermind.com/products/iphototopicasawebalbums.php`

Subscribing to Web Photo Feeds

Although this chapter has been about *publishing* photos to the Web, you can also *subscribe* to photos that have been published on either MobileMe or any other Web site with an RSS feed. This displays the photos in iPhoto, where you can do anything with them other than edit, burn to disc, or add to a Web album.

To subscribe to a MobileMe Gallery:

1. In your Web browser, navigate to the MobileMe Gallery that you want to subscribe to and, if you want to subscribe only to a particular album, go into that album (**Figure 8.25**).

2. Click the Subscribe button at the top of the screen, and in the dialog that appears, select iPhoto and click OK (**Figure 8.26**).

   iPhoto comes to the front and the Web album is added in your Subscriptions list in the source pane (**Figure 8.27**).

To subscribe to other Web albums:

1. On the Web site containing the photos you want to subscribe to, look for an RSS button or link, [Control]-click it, and choose Copy Link.

2. In iPhoto, choose Subscribe to Photo Feed ([Cmd][U]) from the File menu.

   iPhoto shows the photo feed address dialog.

3. Paste your previously copied URL and click the Subscribe button.

   iPhoto adds the album to the Subscriptions list in the source pane.

✔ Tip

- To unsubscribe from a photo feed, delete its album from the Subscriptions list.

Figure 8.25 To subscribe to a MobileMe Gallery album in iPhoto, click the Subscribe button.

Figure 8.26 Select iPhoto to subscribe to the feed in iPhoto, as opposed to another RSS reader.

Figure 8.27 Subscribed photo feeds appear in the Subscriptions list in the source pane.

✔ More Tips

- If iPhoto doesn't download photos from a new feed right away, quit and relaunch.

- If you delete a photo feed, iPhoto prompts you to import the subscribed photos.

- To subscribe to a better Flickr feed with more, larger photos, use Photocastr at http://photocastr.quantumfoam.org/.

SHARING PHOTOS

Although iPhoto provides numerous ways of presenting your photos to others—slideshows, publishing to the Web, and (coming up in the next chapter), creating books, calendars, and cards—there's an additional way in which you can share photos in iPhoto that's also important.

I'm talking about the sharing of the actual photo files. For instance, you might want to share photos with a family member who also uses your Mac, or a roommate whose Mac is on your network. Or maybe you want to send photos to friends via email or on a CD or DVD. iPhoto can help in all of these situations and more. I've organized this chapter in roughly that order; think of it as near (sharing on your Mac) to far (sending a CD to a Windows-using relative or using email).

Keep in mind that although Apple has provided various different tools for sharing these original photos, there are usually trade-offs. For instance, it's trickier to burn a CD of photos for someone who uses Windows than for someone who uses iPhoto on the Mac. And although iPhoto has one built-in way for people on the same Mac or multiple Macs to share photos in their iPhoto libraries, Apple still hasn't done anything in iPhoto's interface to make it easy for people to share the same iPhoto Library package.

Sharing a Library on the Same Mac

Mac OS X is a multiuser operating system, so it's common for people who share a Mac each to have an account. But what if you want to share the same iPhoto Library among multiple users on the same Mac?

To share your library among users:

1. With iPhoto *not* running, rename your iPhoto Library to iPhoto Shared Library (to avoid confusion) and move it from the Pictures folder to the Shared folder at the same level as your user folder (**Figure 9.1**). The Shared folder may or may not contain other items.

2. Double-click the iPhoto Shared Library to open it in iPhoto and verify that it's OK. Quit iPhoto.

   iPhoto may display a dialog asking you to select the library; the one you double-clicked will be selected, so click Choose (**Figure 9.2**).

3. Switch to the other user via Fast User Switching and double-click the iPhoto Shared Library to open it and make it the default.

   iPhoto may display the dialog asking you to select the library again; the one you double-clicked will be selected, so click Choose (**Figure 9.2**).

   iPhoto displays a dialog asking you to repair permissions (**Figure 9.3**).

4. Click the Repair button.

5. For each additional account, repeat steps 3 and 4.

6. From now on, each user on your Mac should launch iPhoto normally by clicking iPhoto in the Dock or by double-clicking the iPhoto Shared Library package.

Figure 9.1 Store your iPhoto Shared Library in the Shared folder at the same level as your user folder.

Figure 9.2 The first time you double-click the iPhoto Shared Library in the Shared folder from each account, iPhoto may prompt you to select it (it should be selected by default). Click the Choose button to proceed.

Figure 9.3 The first time you open the iPhoto Shared Library in the second account, iPhoto prompts you to repair the permissions. Click Repair.

Figure 9.4 If you don't want to give everyone your user name and password to connect to your Mac, use the Sharing preferences pane to share the Pictures folder and set up login accounts for everyone.

Figure 9.5 Select the host Mac in the sidebar and then click Connect As to connect to the shared Pictures folder.

Network Sharing Decisions

Use the network sharing method on this page to share an entire iPhoto Library and have each person make changes that are seen by every other person. This method let you share the work of editing photos, making albums, and assigning keywords.

Use iPhoto's photo-sharing approach, discussed on the next page, to let other people see and potentially copy your photos without making any other changes. This approach works best when each person has his or her own primary collection of photos but wants to access a few photos from other people.

Sharing a Library among Multiple Macs

You can also share an iPhoto Library across a network from a Mac with file sharing turned on, or via an external hard drive. If you're using a network, the faster the better (ideally wired gigabit Ethernet or 802.11n AirPort Extreme).

To share your library over a network:

1. In the System Preferences Sharing pane on the host Mac, turn on File Sharing. Either give the other people your user name and password, or add the Pictures folder to the Shared Folders list, set up user names and passwords for them using the + buttons, and give them Read & Write access (**Figure 9.4**).

2. From each remote Mac, connect to the host Mac by clicking it in the sidebar, clicking Connect As, and entering the user name and password (**Figure 9.5**).

3. For each user, double-click the iPhoto Library in the shared Pictures folder.

To share your library on a drive:

1. Select the drive in the Finder, choose Get Info ([Cmd][I]) from the File menu, and, in the Ownership & Permissions area at the bottom of the Get Info window, select Ignore Ownership on This Volume.

2. With iPhoto *not* running, copy your iPhoto Library from the Pictures folder to where you want it on the shared volume and rename it iPhoto Shared Library.

3. For each user, double-click the iPhoto Shared Library on the shared volume.

✔ Tip

■ Only one person may use the shared iPhoto Library at a time.

Sharing Photos via iPhoto Sharing

iPhoto enables you to share all your photos, or just individual albums, with other iPhoto users on your Mac or on your network.

To share photos via iPhoto Sharing:

1. From the iPhoto menu, choose Preferences (Cmd,) and click the Sharing button.

   iPhoto displays the Sharing preferences (**Figure 9.6**).

2. Select Share My Photos, and then select either Share Entire Library or Share Selected Albums.

3. If you selected Share Selected Albums, select the albums you want to share in the list below (**Figure 9.7**).

4. In the Shared Name field, enter a name for the shared folder under which your photos will appear for other users on your Mac and network.

5. If you want to restrict access to your shared photos, enter a password in the Require Password field. You'll then have to give that password to approved users (**Figure 9.7**).

6. Close the Preferences window.

✔ Tips

■ Amazingly, iPhoto 8.0.2 cannot share movies in an iPhoto library via network sharing. They simply don't appear.

■ iPhoto sharing also works between users of the same Mac, when both are logged in via Fast User Switching; leave iPhoto running when switching accounts.

■ iPhoto automatically selects the Require Password checkbox when you type the password for the first time.

Figure 9.6 Turn on photo sharing in the Sharing pane of iPhoto's Preferences window.

Figure 9.7 You can restrict shared photos to specific albums, and you can require that users enter a password to access your shared photos.

Turning off Sharing

To turn off photo sharing, simply deselect the Share My Photos checkbox in the Sharing pane of iPhoto's Preferences window. If anyone is currently connected to your photos, iPhoto asks if you're sure you want to turn off photo sharing first.

I recommend you either do this or set a password before taking a laptop on a trip, or anyone with iPhoto on a hotel or hotspot network will be able to see and copy your photos!

Figure 9.8 You access shared photos in the Shares list in the source pane; click the shared photo library to load it, and click the expansion triangle to the left to display its albums.

Actions Allowed for Shared Photos

Just because you can see shared albums in your source pane doesn't mean you can do everything with their contents that you can do with your own photos.

You *can* copy shared photos and albums to your library or albums, play a basic slideshow with shared photos, and send shared photos to others via email.

You *cannot* edit shared photos in any way, assign keywords and ratings, get much photo info, make a new album, use a shared album to create a book, print photos, put shared photos on your Desktop or use them as your screen saver, make an iDVD slideshow, burn them to disc, send them to iWeb, or export them in any way.

Basically, you can only view shared photos; for any action that requires making changes, you must first copy the photos to your Mac.

Accessing Shared Photos

Working with shared photos is similar to using an iPhoto disc (see "Importing from an iPhoto Disc," on page 17).

To access shared photos:

1. Make sure the Mac with the shared photos has iPhoto launched and photo sharing turned on.

2. On the Mac or in the account from which you want to access the shared photos, launch iPhoto, and from the iPhoto menu, choose Preferences (Cmd ,) and click the Sharing button.

    iPhoto displays the Sharing preferences.

3. Make sure Look for Shared Photos is selected (**Figure 9.6**, previous page).

4. Close the Preferences window.

    In the source pane, iPhoto displays the shared library in the Shares list.

5. Click the shared library to load it. If the shared photos are protected by a password, enter it when prompted.

    iPhoto loads the shared photos, displaying individual albums underneath the shared library when you click its expansion triangle (**Figure 9.8**).

✔ Tips

- If more than one copy of iPhoto on your network is sharing photos, iPhoto creates a Shared Photos folder and puts all the shared libraries inside it.

- To disconnect from a shared photo album, click the little eject button next to its name in the source pane.

- To import all the photos in a shared album, drag it to another spot in the source pane.

Exporting Files

iPhoto's export capabilities offer the features most people need.

To export files:

1. Select one or more photos, and choose Export from the File menu ([Cmd][Shift][E]). iPhoto displays the Export Photos dialog (**Figure 9.9**).

2. Click the File Export button.

3. Choose the format for the exported photos from the Kind pop-up menu, set JPEG compression if necessary, choose an image size, and set up how you want them named. Then click Export.

4. iPhoto displays a Save dialog. Navigate to your desired folder and click OK.

✔ Tips

- iPhoto can export into only JPEG, TIFF, and PNG formats. For other formats, use GraphicConverter (www.lemkesoft.com).

- For JPEG format, you can set the quality. The higher the quality, the larger the file.

- Select the Title and Keywords checkbox to export that information to the file's IPTC tags, enabling other applications to read photo titles and keywords from iPhoto. It works only with JPEG and TIFF.

- When iPhoto scales an image, it does so proportionally with the limits you set.

- Use Original in the Kind pop-up menu to export a RAW file, GIF file, or other file format that iPhoto converts to JPEG when edited. Current exports the current format of such photos, without any options to scale them.

- Select the Location Information checkbox to export geotags with the file's EXIF tags, in JPEG or TIFF format.

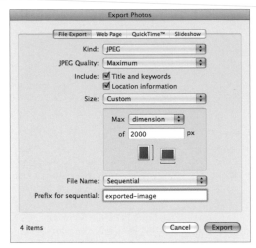

Figure 9.9 Use the File Export pane in the Export Photos dialog to set various options for your exported images.

File Naming Choices

When naming exported files, you can use the title, filename, the album name (with a sequential number automatically appended), or your own name with sequential numbers appended. When exporting files for use on other platforms, it's best to avoid title and album names that could include spaces or other troublesome characters.

Size Names and Numbers

Annoyingly, iPhoto doesn't provide the actual numbers that correspond to the items in the Size menu. Here they are:

- Small = 320 x 240

- Medium = 640 x 480

- Large = 1280 x 960

Figure 9.10 For a quick export without any chance to reformat, rename, or resize the exported photos, just drag one or more to the Finder.

Figure 9.11 iPhoto copies the files from its Modified folder (or the Originals folder if the files haven't been edited in any way) to the destination folder in the Finder.

Exporting Files by Dragging

If you just want copies of a couple of photos and don't need to reformat or resize them, you can just drag the files to the Finder.

To export multiple files:

◆ Select one or more photos and drag the selection to a folder in the Finder (**Figure 9.10**).

iPhoto saves the files where you drop them, using each file's original name (**Figure 9.11**).

✔ Tips

■ With a drag-export, iPhoto is literally copying the files from its Modified (for edited photos) and Originals (for photos you haven't touched) folders to the destination folder in the Finder. See "iPhoto Directory Structure," on page 19.

■ Option-drag a photo from iPhoto to the Finder to export the original file rather than the edited version.

■ When you drag photos to export them, you aren't given the opportunity to change their scale or image format.

■ You can also drag photos to other photo-related programs. This is not actually exporting, since the other program is working with the same file as iPhoto. Because of this, don't drag files to image-editing programs and make changes, because iPhoto won't be able to track those changes (see "Using an External Editor," on page 110). And definitely don't delete photos from those other programs!

■ Unfortunately, you can't drag an album to the Finder to create a new folder that contains the album's photos.

Sharing Photos on Disc with iPhoto Users

If you want to share a lot of photos with a friend or family member, burning a CD or DVD to send to your recipient works best.

To burn an iPhoto disc:

1. Select the items you want to burn, which is best done by selecting entire events, folders, albums, books, or slideshows (**Figure 9.12**).

2. From the Share menu, choose Burn (or click the toolbar's Burn button), insert a blank disc if prompted, and click OK.

   Below the display pane, iPhoto shows the name of the disc and information about how much data will be burned to the disc (**Figure 9.13**). The disc icon will be red if it can't hold the selected photos.

3. Select fewer or more photos to use the space on your destination disc as desired.

4. Change the name of the disc if you want.

5. When everything looks right, click the Burn button (on the far-right side of **Figure 9.13**) to start the burn, and when iPhoto asks you to confirm one last time and lets you set additional burning options, click Burn (**Figure 9.14**).

   iPhoto creates a disk image, copies the selected photos to it, and burns the disc.

✔ Tips

■ If you select albums to burn, the iPhoto disc retains those album references. Event information is lost, however.

■ Your disc name appears in both iPhoto and the Finder.

■ On the disc, your photos are stored in an iPhoto Library *folder,* not an iPhoto Library *package.*

Figure 9.12 To get started, select the items you want to burn in the source pane, choose Burn from the Share menu, and then insert a blank disc.

Figure 9.13 Once you've inserted the disc, iPhoto lets you name your disc and gives you information about how much data will be burned to it.

Figure 9.14 iPhoto verifies that you really want to burn a disc with one last dialog that also provides additional burn options if you click the triangle button in the upper-right corner.

Receiving an iPhoto Disc

If someone sends you an iPhoto disc, you can browse the photos on it directly; to import them see "Importing from an iPhoto Disc," on page 17.

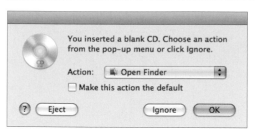

Figure 9.15 Choose Open Finder from the Action pop-up menu after you insert the blank disc.

Figure 9.16 Export your photos to the disc, at the bottom of the Save dialog's sidebar.

Figure 9.17 Click the Burn button in the disc's Finder window to start the burn.

Figure 9.18 The Finder verifies the name and burn speed before burning.

Sharing Photos on Disc with Windows Users

Alas, not everyone uses a Mac or iPhoto, and for these people you need to burn a normal disc, rather than one with an iPhoto Library folder on it.

To burn a disc for use by non-iPhoto users:

1. Insert a blank CD or DVD, choose Open Finder from the Action pop-up menu (**Figure 9.15**), and then give your disc a name like any other volume.

2. In iPhoto, select a group of photos you want to burn and export them directly to the just-inserted disc, which appears at the bottom of the sidebar in the Save dialog (see "Exporting Files," on page 152). If you wish, when saving the exported photos, click the New Folder button to create a new folder for photos (**Figure 9.16**).

3. Repeat step 2 until you've exported all the photos you wish to burn.

4. In the Finder, open the disc's window to verify it contains what you expect, click the Burn button (**Figure 9.17**), and verify the disc name and burn speed before clicking Burn (**Figure 9.18**).

   The Finder proceeds to burn the disc.

✔ Tips

- Choose Use Title from the File Name pop-up menu when exporting so your photos end up with the best possible filenames.

- Choose JPEG from the Kind pop-up menu when exporting, unless you have a good reason for choosing another format.

- If necessary, open the CDs & DVDs System Preferences pane and choose Ask What to Do from the pop-up menus related to inserting blank discs.

Emailing Photos

For many people, email is the preferred method of receiving photos from friends.

To configure iPhoto for email:

◆ In the General pane of iPhoto's Preferences window, choose your email program from the Email Photos Using pop-up menu (**Figure 9.19**).

iPhoto changes the toolbar's Email button to match the icon of your email program.

To send photos via email:

1. Select the photos you want to send.

2. Choose Email from the Share menu, or click the Email button in the toolbar.

   iPhoto displays a dialog with options for your photos (**Figure 9.20**).

3. Choose the maximum size you want the photos to appear from the Size pop-up menu, and, if you want to include titles, descriptions, and location information, select their checkboxes.

4. Click the Compose Message button.

   iPhoto exports the pictures (converting them to JPEG), creates a new message, and attaches the photos, which appear inline only in Apple Mail (**Figure 9.21**).

✔ Tips

■ If you send too many photos, or don't shrink their sizes enough, your message may be too large to be delivered. Try to keep the total amount under 4 MB.

■ You can also drag photos from iPhoto into some email programs, but that sends the photos at full size.

■ To send a lot of photos via email, check out the YouSendIt iPhoto plug-in, which works with the YouSendIt service. www.yousendit.com/cms/plugin-iphoto.

Figure 9.19 In the General pane of iPhoto's Preferences, choose your email program from the Email Photos Using pop-up menu.

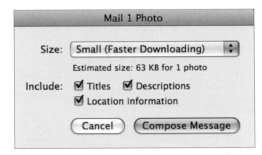

Figure 9.20 Make sure to set a reasonable size for your photos before sending them via email or they'll take too long to transfer for you and your recipient.

Figure 9.21 Here's what the message looks like in Mail. You don't get much control over the layout, but don't worry, because there's no way of telling what it will look like on the receiving end anyway.

PRINTING PHOTOS

Gutenprint/Gimp-Print Drivers

What your printer can do is determined by its *driver,* system-level software provided by Apple or the manufacturer. There's also Gutenprint (formerly called Gimp-Print), an open source set of drivers for over 700 printers, which supports options that the manufacturers may not expose, such as printing on roll paper or other unusual paper sizes. Learn more at: `http://gimp-print.sourceforge.net/MacOSX.php`.

How to Find Info in This Chapter

The iPhoto printing interface borrows heavily from the interface used to create books, cards, and calendars. As a result, if you've created any of those items, you'll be at home with creating prints. To avoid duplication in this chapter, I first give an overview of creating each type of keepsake, followed by details that are specific to each (such as adding photos to dates on a calendar), and then I finish up with general instructions (such as how to enter and edit text) that are common to all of them.

If I had to pick a single feature that sets iPhoto apart from most photo management programs, I'd choose the way iPhoto enables you to create professional-looking prints, cards, calendars, and photo books—what iPhoto '09 now calls "keepsakes." Numerous programs can help you edit and organize photos. But iPhoto is the undisputed champion of creating high-quality printed products in an easy fashion.

The beauty of iPhoto's prints, cards, calendars, and books, apart from their quality printing on heavy, glossy paper, is that they help bridge the gap between the analog and digital worlds. Many people still prefer prints displayed in a traditional photo album, and there's no denying the attraction of a glossy color calendar on the wall that's displaying your photos or the slickness of a professionally printed postcard showing your latest photographic favorite on the front.

In addition, with a modern inkjet printer, anyone can create prints that rival those ordered from a commercial service.

Whatever your preference, by the time you're done with this chapter, you'll be able to turn your digital photography collection into stunning prints, cards, books, and calendars.

Printing Photos Overview

Many people prefer to print their photos on inexpensive color inkjet printers rather than waiting for online orders.

To print photos:

1. Select one or more photos to print and choose Print from the File menu ($\boxed{\text{Cmd}}\boxed{\text{P}}$) to bring up the print settings dialog (**Figure 10.1**).

2. Select the desired theme from the list.

3. From the four pop-up menus, choose the appropriate printer, printer-specific presets, paper size, and print size.

4. Either click Print to print right away with the default settings (jump to step 9), or click Customize to switch to the print project interface, which makes a Printing album in the Recent list (**Figure 10.2**).

5. From the Themes, Background, Borders, and Layout pop-up menus in the toolbar, choose settings to lay out your photos.

6. Enter text if the layout provides it; you can tweak text settings by clicking the Settings button in the toolbar.

7. To make temporary adjustments to an image, select it, click the Adjust button, and use the buttons and sliders in the Adjust window as you would in the normal Adjust and Effects windows in edit mode (**Figure 10.3**).

8. When you're ready, click the Print button. iPhoto displays the standard Mac OS X Print dialog (**Figure 10.7**, on page 160).

9. Verify your printer and preset settings, enter the number of copies to print, and access other settings from the pop-up menu under the page range controls. Click Print when done.

   iPhoto sends your photos to the printer.

Figure 10.1 Choose basic printing options in the print settings dialog, and then click Print. Or click Customize to set advanced options before printing.

Figure 10.2 In the print project interface, you can choose alternate themes, backgrounds, borders, text settings, and layouts, including those that put multiple photos on a single page.

Figure 10.3 Make non-permanent adjustments to photos using the modified Adjust window.

PRINTING PHOTOS OVERVIEW

Click to view   *Click to view*
page layouts.   *available photos.*

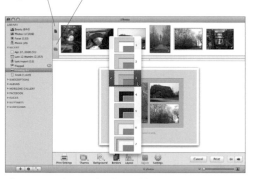

Figure 10.4 Choose the desired border design from the Borders pop-up menu.

Figure 10.5 Choose the desired page layout from the Layout pop-up menu.

Figure 10.6 Change settings for the entire print project in the settings dialog.

Designing Print Projects

iPhoto enables you to print not just a single photo at standard sizes, but also multiple photos with themed frame styles, colored backgrounds, and text. While you're designing your prints, they appear in a special Printing album in the Recent list in the source pane; you can perform other tasks and return to the Printing album at any time.

To design a print project:

1. In the print project, click a page.

2. From the Themes pop-up menu on the toolbar, choose the desired theme (if you want to switch from the currently selected theme).

3. From the Background pop-up menu, choose the color for your background.

4. From the Borders pop-up menu, choose the desired border style (**Figure 10.4**).

5. From the Layout pop-up menu, choose the desired page layout (**Figure 10.5**).

6. Click the photo icon to switch from viewing pages to viewing the available photos, and then drag photos to the desired spots in your layout.

7. Tweak each photo so it is zoomed and centered appropriately; for details, see "Editing Photos on Pages," on page 176.

8. Enter text in any provided text boxes, and change text settings as you would in any other program.

9. Click an arrow button or press ⬅ or ➡ to move to another page, and repeat steps 3–8.

✔ Tip

■ Click Settings to change font settings for all the pages of your print project, among other options (**Figure 10.6**).

Previewing Prints

Ink and paper for color inkjet printers are expensive, particularly glossy photo paper. If you're unsure about what's going to print, it's best to preview the output before committing it to expensive paper.

To preview prints:

1. In the second Print dialog, choose Open PDF in Preview from the PDF pop-up menu (**Figure 10.7**).

   iPhoto "prints" the selected photos to a temporary PDF document called "Untitled" and opens it in Apple's Preview application (**Figure 10.8**).

2. Click the thumbnails on the right side to see other pages, and when you're done, close the window or, if you like what you see, click the Print button.

✔ Tips

- If you click the blue triangle button in the upper right of the Print dialog, it toggles the Print dialog between contracted and expanded states. In the contracted state, there's a Preview button that has the same effect as choosing Open PDF in Preview from the PDF pop-up menu.

- You can save the temporary document in the Preview application if you want a PDF version, or just choose Save as PDF from the Print dialog's PDF pop-up menu.

- Previewing in this fashion won't help you determine if your photos will fit within the margins of your printer. Also, any printer-specific changes you make in the settings (such as forcing black ink on a color printer) won't be reflected in the preview. See if your printer has an economy or draft mode you can use to test printer-specific features on a single page of photos.

Figure 10.7 Choose Open PDF in Preview from the PDF pop-up menu to view your prints.

Figure 10.8 Your print preview opens in Preview.

Test, Test, Test!

A few things can affect how a photo looks when it comes out of your printer:

- ◆ Printer capabilities, both what they can do physically and what their drivers allow, vary by brand and model.

- ◆ Inkjet printers print very differently on different types of paper, and it's important to match the print settings to the type of paper you're using.

It may take several tries to determine the best combination of options. You may be able to try some in economy mode on cheap paper, but in the end, you may have to expend some ink on a few sheets of expensive photo paper. To reduce the waste and cost, keep good notes for subsequent printing sessions.

PREVIEWING PRINTS

Inkjet Printing Tips

How can you achieve the best quality prints? Along with repeated testing, try these tips for working with your photos and your printer:

◆ Use a good quality inkjet printer. Printers designed to print photos do a better job than general-purpose printers (but may not print text as well). Also consider dye-sub printers, which are more expensive but print wonderful colors. For printer reviews, see `www.printerville.net`.

◆ Make sure your print head is clean and aligned. If your printouts don't look quite right, try cleaning the print head.

◆ Use good paper. Modern inkjets lay down incredibly small drops of ink, and standard paper absorbs those drops more than photo paper, blurring printouts.

◆ Make sure to print on the correct side of the paper (it's usually whiter or shinier).

◆ Don't handle the surface of the paper that will be printed on. Oils from your skin can mess up the printout.

◆ Remove each sheet from the output tray after printing, particularly with glossy films, and be careful not to touch the surface until it has dried.

◆ In the Print dialog, make sure you're using the highest resolution and other appropriate settings. In particular, aim for settings that favor quality over speed.

◆ When printing black-and-white photos, make sure to print with only black ink.

Paper Types

Computer superstores sell a vast number of different types of inkjet papers. What should you buy? You're almost certain to get good results with paper made by the manufacturer of your printer. Papers from other manufacturers will likely work well too, but aren't as guaranteed. The basic paper types include:

◆ Plain paper. Use it only for drafts or text; photos won't look great.

◆ Matte paper. These papers are heavier than plain paper and have a smooth, but not glossy, finish. Matte paper can be very good for photos.

◆ Glossy photo paper and film. These papers, which come in a bewildering variety of types and weights, are heavier yet and have a glossy surface that looks like standard photo paper. Glossy film is actually polyethylene, not paper. Use glossy paper for your best prints.

◆ Specialty papers. You can buy papers that look like watercolor paper, have a metallic sheen, are of archival quality, or are translucent. Other specialty papers can be ironed onto T-shirts, are pre-scored for folding, have magnetic backing, and more.

If you like printing photos on your own printer, I strongly encourage you to buy a variety of papers and see what you like. Also fun to try is a sample pack from Red River Paper, an online paper vendor at `www.redrivercatalog.com`.

Printing Standard Prints

Printing standard print sizes on special paper can be tricky, even in iPhoto.

To print standard print sizes:

1. In the print settings dialog, select the Standard theme.

2. From the Paper Size pop-up menu, choose the size that matches the paper on which you're printing (**Figure 10.9**).

3. From the Print Size pop-up menu, choose the size that matches how large you want your photo to print (**Figure 10.10**).

4. If you wish to print multiple photos on a page, click Customize, click Settings, and choose from the Photos Per Page pop-up menu (**Figure 10.11**). (Your print size setting must be enough smaller than your paper size setting.)

5. Click Print, and continue as normal.

An explanation of a tricky topic:

By choosing the paper size, you tell iPhoto about the paper that the printer has loaded, which may or may not be different from the size of the photo you want to end up with.

If you want to print on 4" x 6" paper, you would choose 4 x 6 from the Paper Size pop-up menu (the choices there are printer-specific). But don't choose a 4 x 6 print size. Instead, choose Standard from the Print Size pop-up menu to print the largest possible area on the available paper.

In contrast, if you want two 5" x 7" photos on the same 8.5" x 11" piece of photo paper so you can cut them out, use US Letter for the paper size, and set the print size to 5 x 7.

✔ Tip

■ Check Show Crop Marks in the settings dialog to make it easier to cut out photos.

Figure 10.9 When printing standard-sized prints, first choose the paper size on which you're printing from the Paper Size pop-up menu.

Figure 10.10 Then choose the desired print size from the Print Size pop-up menu.

Figure 10.11 To put more than one photo (either the same one or different ones) on a page, choose the desired option from the Photos Per Page pop-up menu in the Settings dialog.

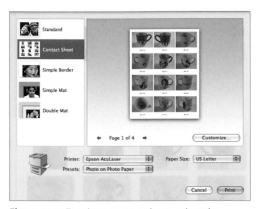

Figure 10.12 To print a contact sheet, select the Contact Sheet theme, and click Customize.

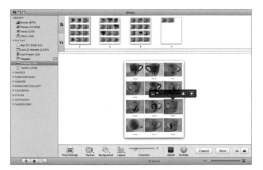

Figure 10.13 Set the number of columns with the Columns slider.

Figure 10.14 In the settings dialog, select which pieces of metadata should print with the photos.

Printing Contact Sheets

Contact sheets are traditionally used to look at a number of photos at once, which is handy for comparing different versions of the same picture, or for letting relatives who don't have a computer pick which photos they'd like you to order for them as prints. Printing contact sheets is a bit different from other types of prints.

To print contact sheets:

1. Select a number of photos, and choose Print from the File menu ([Cmd][P]) to display the print settings dialog.

2. In the print settings dialog, select the Contact Sheet theme (**Figure 10.12**), and click Customize.

3. In the toolbar, select the desired number of columns from the Columns slider, and, if necessary, zoom photos in their frames (**Figure 10.13**).

4. Click the Settings button in the toolbar, and in the settings dialog choose the items you want to print under each photo, along with the font options (**Figure 10.14**).

✔ Tips

■ To print multiple copies of the same photo, don't use the Contact Sheet theme. Instead, select Standard, choose the desired size from the Print Size pop-up menu, click Customize, click Settings, choose Multiple of the Same Photo Per Page, and click OK. (You may need to enter a custom size; remember that your photos are likely a 4 x 3 aspect ratio.)

■ The maximum number of photos that can print across the page is 10; that gives you 13 rows for a total of 130 pictures.

PRINTING CONTACT SHEETS

Setting up an Apple ID

Before you can order anything from Apple, you must have an Apple ID with 1-Click ordering enabled. If you haven't previously set up an Apple ID, you can create one within iPhoto.

To set up an Apple ID:

1. Click the Order Prints button to display the Order Prints window.

2. Click the Set Up Account button.

   iPhoto displays the Apple Account Sign-in dialog (**Figure 10.15**).

3. Click the Create Account button.

   iPhoto displays the first of three dialogs that collect the data necessary to create an account (**Figure 10.16**). The first asks for your email address and password, the second collects billing information, and the third garners shipping information.

4. Enter the necessary information, clicking the Step button to move through the process until you're done.

✔ Tips

- If the Order Prints button isn't showing, choose Order Prints from the View menu's Show in Toolbar submenu.

- Remember that your Apple ID is always your email address.

- Choose a password that can't be easily guessed. Otherwise miscreants could go in, change your shipping settings, order prints or books with your credit card, and switch back without you realizing.

- If you have trouble with your Apple ID, visit `http://myinfo.apple.com/` and confirm or re-enter your settings. You can also set up an Apple ID at this site if necessary.

Figure 10.15 To create a new Apple ID, click the Set Up Account button in the Order Prints window to bring up the Apple Account Sign-in dialog. Then click the Create Account button.

Figure 10.16 Enter your sign-in information, billing details, and shipping address in the dialogs that appear.

Strong Passwords

Apple requires that your password be at least six characters long, but you can make it stronger by ensuring that it contains numbers and punctuation along with uppercase and lowercase letters. One good strategy is to take a phrase you'll remember, like "Take me out to the ball game!" and use the first letter of each word, adding numbers where possible. The above phrase could be turned into this strong password: `Tmo2tbg!`

Whatever you choose, do not use a proper name or a word that will appear in the dictionary—they're too easy to guess.

Figure 10.17 Verify and change your Apple ID settings in the Edit Account dialog.

Figure 10.18 To enter a new shipping address, choose Add New Address from the Address pop-up menu, and then enter the new address in the Edit Shipping Addresses dialog.

Forgotten Passwords

If you forget your password, enter your email address in the Apple ID field in the Apple Account Sign-in dialog, click the Forgot Password? button, and go through the necessary Web pages. Apple sends you an email message containing your password.

Using Your Apple ID

Once you have your Apple ID set up, you can use it with Apple's ordering services. It's also useful for some of Apple's online tech support services and ordering from the iTunes Store or Apple Store. iPhoto usually remembers your Apple ID, but if not, you can always sign in manually.

To sign in using your Apple ID:

1. In one of iPhoto's Order windows (for prints, books, cards, or calendars), click either the Account Info button or the Set Up Account button to display the Apple Account Sign-in dialog (**Figure 10.15** on the previous page).

2. Enter your Apple ID and password, and then click the Sign In button.

   iPhoto displays the Edit Account dialog (**Figure 10.17**).

3. If 1-Click purchasing is turned off, select the Enable 1-Click Purchasing checkbox.

4. Verify that everything else looks correct (if not, click the Edit button next to the incorrect data and make the necessary corrections), and then click Done.

✔ Tips

■ You can switch between Apple IDs using the method above with two sets of email addresses and passwords. This is handy if multiple people want to order items on separate accounts.

■ You can add additional shipping addresses by clicking Edit Shipping in the Edit Account dialog, choosing Add New Address from the pop-up menu, and filling in the details (**Figure 10.18**). Switch between the addresses by choosing the desired one from the Ship To pop-up menu in an Order window.

Preparing to Order Prints

Since iPhoto's snazzy zoom and crop interface isn't available when ordering prints, you will want to spend some time preparing your photos for printing by cropping them to the appropriate aspect ratios for prints. But what if you don't want to crop the originals permanently? Follow these steps.

To prepare photos for printing:

1. Make a new album, and add the photos that you want to order prints of.

2. Switch to the album, and edit each photo as desired, other than cropping.

3. In organize mode, select all the photos ([Cmd][A]) and choose Duplicate from the Photos menu ([Cmd][D]) to make copies (for details, see "Duplicating Photos," on page 85).

4. Select just the copies in your album ("Duplicating Photos" explains this too).

5. Drag them to the source pane to create a new album of just the copies (append the word "Prints" to its name to be clear), and then return to the previous album and delete it (or keep it, if you have some other use for it).

6. Go through the photos in the "Prints" album, this time cropping each to the desired aspect ratio.

7. If you're printing photos in different sizes, manually group them by size in the album. That makes keeping track of them in the Order Prints window easier.

   Now you're ready to order the prints (see the next page).

Pixels and Prints

You may have noticed that iPhoto reports how large your photo is in pixels in the Information pane. But how does that match up with print sizes that you order from Apple? You mostly don't have to care, since iPhoto displays a low-resolution warning icon when a photo doesn't have enough pixels to print well at the desired size. For reference, here are the pixel sizes at which iPhoto starts adding the warning icon, given both in terms of the 4 x 3 aspect ratio of uncropped photos and with the appropriate cropping for the size at which you want to print.

Note that these are the *minimum* recommended resolutions. The larger your photos and the more they exceed these minimums, the better the final quality.

◆ For wallet-sized prints (which are about 2.4" x 3.4"), you need at least 337 x 450 pixels (when cropped to the above aspect ratio, keep the long side above 450 pixels).

◆ For a 4" x 6" print, you need at least 675 x 900 pixels (when cropped to 4 x 6, keep the long side above 900 pixels).

◆ For a 5" x 7" print, you need at least 788 x 1050 (when cropped to 5 x 7, keep the long side above 1050 pixels).

◆ For an 8" x 10" print, you need at least 1200 x 1600 (when cropped to 8 x 10, keep the short side above 1200 pixels).

◆ For 16" x 20" prints, you need at least 1600 x 2132 (when cropped to 16 x 20, keep the short side above 1600 pixels).

◆ For 20" x 30" prints, you need at least 1800 x 2400 (when cropped to 20 x 30, keep the long side above 2400 pixels).

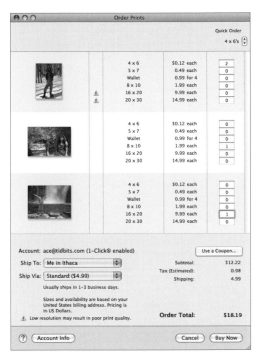

Figure 10.19 To order prints, select one or more photos, click the Order Prints button, and in the Order Prints dialog, enter the number of prints of each photo that you want. When you're ready, click the Buy Now button.

International Shipping Details

Apple currently supports print, book, card, and calendar orders in the United States, Canada, Japan, Europe, Australia, New Zealand, Singapore, and Hong Kong.

However, you can send orders only to addresses within your shipping region. So if you live in the United States and wish to send a calendar to a friend in Scotland, you must first ship it to yourself and later mail it to your friend.

Ordering Prints

Once you've prepared your photos, it's time to order prints.

To order prints:

1. Make sure you're connected to the Internet, select one or more photos, and click the Order Prints button.

   iPhoto opens the Order Prints dialog (**Figure 10.19**).

2. For each picture, enter the number of each size print you'd like to order.

   iPhoto automatically updates the total cost as you add and subtract prints.

3. Choose the appropriate shipping address and method from the Ship To and Ship Via pop-up menus.

4. Check your order carefully to make sure you're getting the right number of each print, and confirm that each photo can print at the size you've selected.

5. Click the Buy Now button.

   iPhoto uploads your pictures and alerts you when it's done.

✔ Tips

- If the Order Prints button isn't showing, choose Order Prints from the View menu's Show in Toolbar submenu.

- Uploading takes a long time on a slow Internet connection because iPhoto uploads full-size images for best quality.

- If you want mostly 4" x 6" prints, click the Quick Order 4 x 6's arrows at the top right to increase or decrease the number of 4" x 6" prints of each photo.

- If you see a yellow warning icon next to a size you want, see "Dealing with Warning Icons," on page 198.

Creating Cards Overview

Of cards, books, and calendars, cards are the easiest to create, since they have room for only a few photos and minimal text.

To create a card:

1. Select the photo or photos that you want to appear on your card.

2. Click the Card button in the toolbar.

3. In the card design dialog, choose Greeting Card or Postcard from the pop-up menu at the upper left, select a theme, and click Choose (**Figure 10.20**).

   iPhoto creates your card (**Figure 10.21**).

4. For the front of the card, choose the desired background, orientation, and design from the Background, Orientation, and Design pop-up menus, and add and format text as desired (see pages 178–183 for instructions on different ways to work with text).

5. When you're done, click the Buy Card button, and run through the process of ordering your card. See "Ordering Cards, Calendars, and Books," on page 185.

✔ Tips

- If you're not sure which of several photos you might want to use, or if you're working with a theme with multiple photo frames, select several photos before creating the card, and drag different photos into the photo frame(s) to see how they look.

- Greeting cards are 5" x 7" with a picture on the outside and text on the inside; postcards are 4" x 6" with a picture on the front and room for text or text and an address on the back.

- For tips on editing photos in a card, see "Editing Photos on Pages," on page 176.

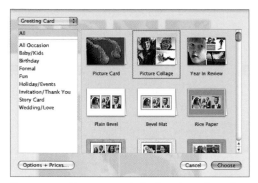

Figure 10.20 Choose your desired card type from the pop-up menu and pick a theme from the scrolling list of themes.

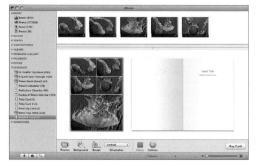

Figure 10.21 iPhoto creates the card in the Keepsakes list of the source pane, showing the front and inside of the card in the display pane.

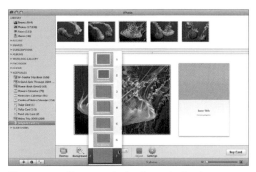

Figure 10.22 Choose a design from the Design pop-up menu to change the look of your card.

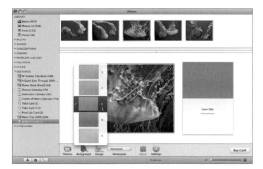

Figure 10.23 Choose a color from the Background pop-up menu to change the color of your card.

Designing Your Card

iPhoto provides only a few ways you can change the design of your card.

To design a card:

1. Select the front of your card by clicking it.

2. From the Orientation pop-up menu, choose either Horizontal or Vertical.

3. From the Design pop-up menu, choose a design (**Figure 10.22**). Repeat until you've found the design you like.

4. Select the back/inside of your card by clicking it in the display pane.

5. From the Design pop-up menu, choose a design. Repeat as necessary until you've found the design you like.

6. If you don't like any of the designs, click the Themes button and choose a new theme from the card design dialog.

7. From the Background pop-up menu, choose a complementary background color (**Figure 10.23**).

8. Enter text in the provided text boxes and, if you don't like the default text format, reformat it as desired.

✔ Tips

- I recommend sticking with the fonts that Apple's designers chose. Otherwise, you risk picking a font that may not look as you expect on the finished card.

- You can enter text only in the provided text boxes. Different themes may offer additional places to enter text, but in general, text options are limited with cards.

- With postcards, the back of the card can accept either a design that provides room for general text or a design that provides space for an address and a stamp.

Creating Calendars Overview

Calendars are a bit more involved to create than cards, though less so than books. Here's the basic process:

To create a calendar:

1. Select the photos that you want to appear in your calendar.

2. Click the Calendar button in the toolbar.

3. In the calendar design dialog, select a theme from the list of themes, and click Choose (**Figure 10.24**).

4. iPhoto then displays the calendar options dialog; set the options for when to start the calendar, how many months it should contain, and what holidays and calendar events should be included on it automatically (**Figure 10.25**).

   iPhoto creates your calendar in the Keepsakes list in the source pane (**Figure 10.26**).

5. For each calendar page, set the number of photos and the design using the Layout pop-up menu. Drag photos from the vertical photo list to frames in the calendar page or to particular dates in a month. You can drag photos from frame to frame or date to date to move them around, or off the page entirely to put them back in the available photo list.

6. When you're done, click the Buy Calendar button and run through ordering your calendar. See "Ordering Cards, Calendars, and Books," on page 185.

✔ Tip

- To save time placing photos, arrange the photos in an album before selecting the album and creating the calendar.

Figure 10.24 Select a theme from the scrolling list of themes and click the Choose button.

Figure 10.25 Set the options for your calendar.

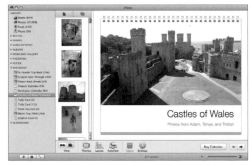

Figure 10.26 iPhoto creates the calendar in the Keepsakes list, showing the cover in the display pane, with the available photos to the left.

Changing Start Dates

Unfortunately, when you change the start date of a calendar (as you might, if you want to give the same calendar as a mid-year anniversary present and an end-of-year holiday gift), iPhoto removes all photos you've added to individual dates, forcing you to replace them manually.

Click to view
page layouts.

Click to view
available photos.

Click to view one
page at a time.

Click to view two
pages at once.

Figure 10.27 Use the buttons above the vertical list to switch between showing calendar pages and available photos (showing above). Use the buttons below the list to switch between showing both calendar pages (top and bottom, showing above) and just the top or the bottom page in the display pane.

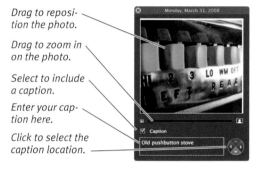

Drag to reposition the photo.

Drag to zoom in on the photo.

Select to include a caption.

Enter your caption here.

Click to select the caption location.

Figure 10.28 Double-click a photo on a date to zoom in, reposition it within the square, add a caption, and position the caption location.

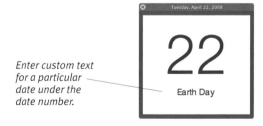

Enter custom text for a particular date under the date number.

Figure 10.29 Click a date to open a window in which you can enter custom text. You can apply font styles and colors to the custom text, but not to the date number.

Designing Calendar Pages

Depending on the theme you select, there may be quite a few design options for individual calendar pages. Follow these steps:

To design a calendar page:

1. Select a page by clicking it in the display pane or in the vertical list (**Figure 10.27**).

2. From the Layout pop-up menu, choose a page type, which generally involves the number of photos on the top page.

3. If you don't like any of the page types, click the Themes button and choose a new theme.

4. Drag photos from the available photo list to photo frames on the top page or to individual dates on the bottom page. Move or delete photos as desired. Photos can appear more than once.

5. Double-click photos to zoom and position them, and, for those on dates, to add captions (**Figure 10.28**).

6. Enter text in any provided text boxes, and add text to individual dates by clicking a date and typing the text in the date window (**Figure 10.29**).

✔ Tips

- When viewing calendar pages in the vertical list, you can click the top or bottom page of the thumbnail to select it (use the controls explained in **Figure 10.27**), which helps when choosing page designs.

- Some themes offer independent designs for the top and bottom pages; others apply the design to both pages at once.

- Captions can appear only in cells adjacent to their pictures.

- For tips on editing photos, see "Editing Photos on Pages," on page 176.

Creating Books Overview

Because books offer the most flexibility, they require the most effort to create. But fear not; iPhoto still makes the process far simpler than laying it out by hand would be. Here's my recommended process:

To create a book:

1. Make a normal album with the photos you want in your book (see "Creating Albums," on page 39 and "Adding Photos to Sources," on page 46). You can drag more photos to the book later if you forget any.

2. Arrange the photos in the album in the rough order you want them to appear in the book (see "Sorting Photos," on page 48). Make sure no photos are selected when you're done.

3. Click the Book button in the toolbar (if the window is narrow, choose Book from the Keepsakes pop-up menu instead).

4. In the book design dialog, choose a book size from the Book Type pop-up menu and select a theme. The dialog shows a preview of each book size and theme (**Figure 10.30**).

   iPhoto creates your book in the Keepsakes list in the source pane (**Figure 10.31**).

5. For each book page, set the number of photos and the design using the Layout pop-up menu, and add text as desired. You can drag photos from frame to frame to move them around or off the page entirely to put them back in the available photo list.

6. When you're done, click the Buy Book button, and run through the process of ordering your book. See "Ordering Cards, Calendars, and Books," on page 185.

Figure 10.30 Choose your desired book type from the Book Type pop-up menu, and pick a theme from the scrolling list of themes.

Figure 10.31 iPhoto creates the book in the Keepsakes list, showing the cover in the display pane, with available photos and pages above.

Avoid Autoflow!

Should you let iPhoto lay out your book automatically by clicking the Autoflow button? Only if you're short on time and want a quick result. It's much harder to rearrange photos on pre-built pages (so use automatic layout only if your photos are already in the correct order). Also, iPhoto can't guess how many related photos you've given it or which photos are likely to look good together in a two-page spread, so expect to spend time fixing every page.

There's no harm in trying an automatic layout, but if you don't like it, delete the book and start over, rather than trying to fix each page. I never use Autoflow.

CREATING BOOKS OVERVIEW

Figure 10.32 Choose the number of photos you want to appear on the page from the Layout pop-up menu.

Figure 10.33 Choose a background color from the Background pop-up menu.

✔ More Tips

- After the cover page (and inside flap, for hardcover books), which is required, the other page designs are optional.

- If an entire page is gray in the Layout pop-up menu, the page contains a background photo, with text and other photos optionally on top. You can set opacity by clicking the photo and using the opacity slider under the zoom slider.

- Many of the page designs assume an aspect ratio of 4 x 3, so if you use a non-standard cropping ratio, photos may not line up as you expect. A different page design or photo arrangement might help, or you may have to zoom in on the photo and reposition it within the frame.

Designing Book Pages

If you choose to lay out your photos on pages manually (and you should), you need to make a number of choices about how each page will look.

To design a page:

1. Select a page by clicking it.

2. From the Layout pop-up menu, choose a design, which usually involves the number of photos you want to appear on the page (**Figure 10.32**).

   iPhoto changes the design of the selected page, pushing already placed photos up to the available photo list if you reduced the number of available photo frames.

3. Add, remove, or rearrange photos within the available frames.

4. From the Background pop-up menu, choose a color (**Figure 10.33**).

5. Repeat steps 2–4 until you have the page looking exactly as you want.

✔ Tips

- Each theme offers a new map page design, and the Travel theme has numerous map designs. For more detail, see "Putting Maps in Books," on page 78.

- Each theme offers different page design possibilities. Spend some time looking at each one to get a feel for which you like the most. For an extremely detailed look at each theme's page designs, check out Liz Castro's iPhoto Book Themes site at www.lizcastro.com/iphotobookthemes/.

- Images can appear multiple times; a white checkmark indicates if an image has been used already.

- The more photos in a page design, the smaller they appear on the page.

DESIGNING BOOK PAGES

Adding, Deleting, and Moving Book Pages

No matter how many photos you use to create a book, iPhoto creates the book with 20 blank pages. You should fill up those pages, since you'll pay for blanks, but what if you need more, or what if you find yourself with extras at the end?

To add a page or page spread:

◆ Click the Add Page(s) button or choose Add Page from the Edit menu.

iPhoto adds either one page, if you're viewing a single page at a time, or a two-page spread, if you're viewing page spreads, to the right of the currently selected page or spread (**Figure 10.34**).

To delete a page:

◆ While viewing pages (not available photos) in the scrolling list, select a page, choose Remove Page from the Edit menu or press Delete. Click Delete if iPhoto asks if you want to delete the page.

To move a page or page spread:

◆ While viewing pages (not available photos) in the scrolling list, drag a page or page spread (it depends on your current view) from one position in the scrolling list to another position (**Figure 10.35**).

iPhoto rearranges the pages in the book to match.

✔ Tip

■ Remember that you can choose Undo (Cmd Z) from the Edit menu if you add or delete pages by mistake.

Click to view book pages.

Click to view available photos.

Press Delete to remove the page.

Click to add a page or page spread.

Click to view individual pages.

Click to view page spreads.

Figure 10.34 Use the controls in book mode to set whether you're seeing pages or available photos in the scrolling list, to set whether pages appear alone or as two-page spreads, and to add new pages.

Figure 10.35 To rearrange pages, drag them from position to position in the scrolling list.

Arrangement Tips

Think carefully about the best arrangement of photos and pages in your book. A chronological layout may work well for vacation photos, whereas mixing shots of people might make more sense for party photos.

For the best layouts, pay attention to the photos that will appear on the same page to make sure they overlap appropriately and have compatible colors. Also consider not just one page at a time but the entire two-page spread, and think about the direction people are facing when placing multiple photos on a page. (Control-click a photo and choose Mirror Image to make people face the opposite direction.)

Note that page designs can change when you swap landscape and portrait photos.

Figure 10.36 To add a photo to a page, creating a new frame in the process, drag a photo to a blank portion of the page, as I'm doing on the right-hand page.

Figure 10.37 To add a photo to an existing frame, drag it to the destination frame, as I'm doing to the lower left corner frame in this calendar page.

Arranging Photos on Book and Calendar Pages

As you design pages in books and calendars, you must arrange photos so they appear in the right order.

To arrange photos on pages:

◆ To change the number of photo frames on a page, choose a different page type from the Layout pop-up menu.

If the new page type has fewer frames, iPhoto pushes already placed photos back into the available photo list.

◆ To add a photo to a page manually, increasing the number of photo frames on the page, drag it from the available photo list or from another page to a blank portion of the page (**Figure 10.36**).

◆ To remove a photo from a photo frame, drag the photo from the frame to the area outside the page, or to the available photo list.

iPhoto removes the photo from the frame, putting it either at the beginning of the available photo list or where you dropped it. The frame may or may not disappear, depending on the number of remaining frames.

◆ To add a photo to a frame, drag it either from the available photo list or from another visible frame, to the desired frame (**Figure 10.37**).

If the destination frame is empty, iPhoto assigns the photo to that frame. If the destination frame is already occupied, iPhoto swaps the two photos.

◆ To change how a photo overlaps with an adjacent photo, (Control)-click it and choose Move to Front or Send to Back from the contextual menu that appears.

Editing Photos on Pages

While you're laying out and arranging photos in cards, books, and calendars, you may discover that a particular photo would look better if it were cropped more heavily or otherwise edited. You can easily make non-permanent crops (zooming into a photo) or switch to edit mode for other changes.

To zoom and center photos:

1. Select a photo to reveal the zoom slider above the image (**Figure 10.38**).

2. Drag the slider to the right to zoom into the image, essentially cropping it further without actually changing the original.

3. Drag the image itself within the frame to center the photo. If you haven't already zoomed in, click the hand button first (to make it gray) to move a portrait photo in a landscape frame.

4. Click anywhere outside the photo when you're done.

To edit photos:

1. Double-click a photo, or (Control)-click it and choose Edit Photo from the contextual menu that appears (**Figure 10.39**).

2. Make your changes, and when you're done, either click the Done button or double-click the photo to return.

✔ Tips

- In certain cases, you may need to re-center photos within their frames even if you haven't zoomed; certain page designs cut off the edges of photos.

- To fit a photo within its frame (after you've zoomed, or if it's wrong to start with), (Control)-click it and choose Fit Photo to Frame Size from the contextual menu that appears.

Figure 10.38 To zoom into a photo, click it (double-click in calendar dates), drag the zoom slider to the right, and then drag the photo around to re-center it, as I've done in the large picture on the right-hand page above. Since it's a background photo, I've also decreased its opacity; only background images get the opacity slider.

Figure 10.39 To make other editing changes, either double-click the photo or Control-click it and choose Edit Photo. When you're finished, click the Done button to return to the book, card, or calendar that you're creating.

Zooming Is Cool!

I adore iPhoto's zooming and centering capabilities, since many photos look better in print, card, book, and calendar layouts when they're zoomed further than they were cropped initially. Although zooming acts like cropping, and may cause a yellow warning icon to appear if there isn't enough data in the zoomed portion to print well, it's entirely non-destructive and doesn't affect the original photo.

Figure 10.40 When a page design calls for a photo to be printed larger than its resolution allows, iPhoto places a warning icon on the offending image.

Figure 10.41 To make the warning icon disappear, change the page design so the printed size better matches the resolution of the image. In this example, adding more photos decreased the size of each photo to the point where at least some of them would print at a decent quality (these are 640 x 480 photos from an Apple QuickTake 150 from 1996).

Text Warning Icons

If you see a small, yellow, triangular warning icon next to a text box while designing pages (**Figure 10.41**), it's because the text doesn't fit in the box. The font size is predetermined by the theme, but you can switch to a different font or shorten the text.

Dealing with Warning Icons

One problem that can appear any time you print a digital photo is poor quality, or rather, your inability to predict the quality of a print. Numerous variables can play a part in reducing the quality of a printed image, but iPhoto tries to help prevent one of the most common—printing an image at a size larger than is appropriate for the image's resolution. When you have an image that's too low resolution for the proposed size, iPhoto displays a triangular warning icon to alert you to the problem (**Figure 10.40**).

Ways to deal with a low-resolution warning icon:

◆ Choose a different page design so the photo with the warning icon shrinks small enough that the icon disappears (**Figure 10.41**).

◆ Move the image to a different location on the current page or another page where it will appear at the necessary smaller size.

◆ Cropping a photo or zooming it makes it more likely that the image won't be large enough to print properly. To remove cropping, select the image, and from the Photos menu choose Revert to Original. Remember that this will remove all your changes, not just the cropping. Try again after cropping the image less heavily.

◆ If you run into this problem regularly, make sure your camera is set to take pictures at its highest resolution.

◆ If you decide to live with a low-resolution warning icon, note that the icon won't appear on the printed page.

Entering and Editing Text

Once you have laid out all your pages to your satisfaction, you can enter or edit the text that appears with the photos.

Ways to enter or edit text:

◆ Click a text box and either enter new text or edit the existing text. While you're editing, iPhoto displays a selection rectangle around the text box (**Figure 10.42**).

◆ You can use all the standard editing techniques and commands that you've become accustomed to as a Mac user—commands like Cut, Copy, and Paste, not to mention double- and triple-clicking.

◆ You can check the spelling of your text. See "Checking Spelling as You Type," on page 183.

✔ Tips

■ If you leave iPhoto's placeholder text alone, those text boxes won't appear in the final book. Photos don't take over the empty space; it just prints blank.

■ iPhoto can pick up existing album names, titles, and descriptions for books if Automatically Enter Photo Information is selected in the settings dialog.

■ iPhoto no longer tries to simplify editing by zooming in on the page in the display pane so the text displays larger. Now you must zoom in manually, using the size slider in the display pane (**Figure 10.43**).

■ If you copy and paste text, the font-related information of the copied text accompanies the pasted text, which may not be desirable.

Figure 10.42 To edit or enter text, click a text box and enter new text or edit the existing text. If there is too much text in the text box, a warning icon appears to alert you when you click out of the box. No scroll bars will appear; you must edit the extra text blindly.

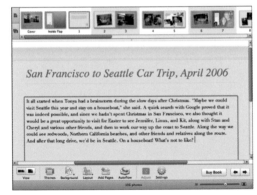

Figure 10.43 It's helpful to zoom in using the size slider so you can see what you're typing.

Smart Quotes, Easily

In Mac OS X 10.5 Leopard, Apple has added a Smart Quotes feature that automatically turns single and double hash marks into true apostrophes and quotation marks. To turn it on, Control-click any text block and from the Substitutions submenu, choose Smart Quotes so it gets a checkmark next to it.

The Wrong Way

Here it's a cold afternoon in March. Mary is gazing out over the GRAND CANYON at sunset--check out the sweater Grandma Bunny actually <u>knitted</u> for her. The other folks in this picture are:

* My friend Samuel from work.

* Mary's cousin JoAnn.

* JoAnn's husband, who goes by "Chuck".

Copyright (c) 2009 Joe Schmoe

The Right Way

Here it's a cold afternoon in March. Mary is gazing out over the Grand Canyon at sunset—check out the sweater Grandma Bunny actually *knitted* for her. The other folks in this picture are:

• My friend Samuel from work.

• Mary's cousin JoAnn.

• JoAnn's husband, who goes by "Chuck."

Copyright © 2009 Joe Schmoe

Typing Text "Correctly"

You're going to zoom into your photos perfectly and arrange them just so—are you then going to write text that looks downright trashy? Follow a few simple rules to make sure your text looks as good as your pictures and iPhoto layouts (if you don't believe me, compare the example captions to the left). For details, snag a copy of Robin Williams's classic book *The Mac is not a typewriter.*

Rules for classy looking text:

◆ Put only one space after periods, commas, question marks, parentheses, or any other punctuation.

◆ Use true quotation marks (" ") instead of double hash marks (" "). To get them, type Option [and Option Shift [.

◆ Use true apostrophes (' ') instead of hash marks (' '). To get them, type Option] and Option Shift].

◆ Punctuation goes inside quotes.

◆ Instead of double hyphens (--), use an em dash (—). Press Option Shift -.

◆ If you want to put a copyright symbol (©) in your book instead of (c), get it by typing Option G.

◆ To make a list, use bullets (•) rather than asterisks (*). To type a bullet, press Option 8.

◆ In text boxes that have relatively long lines of text, edit to prevent the last line from containing only a single word.

◆ Avoid underlining text. Instead, use italics, which may require that you select an italic version of the font you're using.

◆ Use uppercase sparingly, and only in titles. Uppercase text is hard to read.

Changing Fonts, Styles, and Sizes Globally

Although Apple hired professional designers to create the card, calendar, and book templates, iPhoto makes it possible to change the font, style, and size of text for different categories of text. Be careful when modifying these defaults, though, because Apple's font choices are highly intentional, and if you change them too much, the results may not look as elegant as you'd like.

To change fonts, styles, and sizes:

1. When creating a card, calendar, or book, click the Settings button to show the settings dialog (**Figure 10.44**, **Figure 10.45**, and **Figure 10.46**). For calendars, click the Styles button, if necessary.

2. To change the look of different classes of text, choose from the various pop-up menus to change the font and style, and enter new sizes in the size fields.

3. Click OK to apply your changes.

✔ Tips

- The classes of text often change for different themes.

- If you muck up the text settings badly, click Restore Defaults to reset them.

- Using certain Type 1 PostScript fonts can cause your book order to be cancelled. For more information, see http://support.apple.com/kb/TA22924.

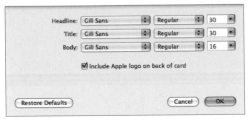

Figure 10.44 Cards have relatively little text, and thus provide only a few categories you can modify. Deselect the Include Apple Logo on Back of Card checkbox if you don't want to advertise Apple's role in making your gorgeous card.

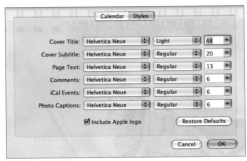

Figure 10.45 Calendars offer quite a few more categories of text to modify. Be careful, because some caption and event text is very small, and not all fonts work well at small sizes.

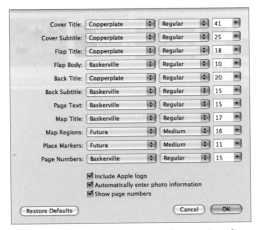

Figure 10.46 Along with a number of categories of text, books offer the option to include photo titles and descriptions automatically, and to turn page numbers on and off.

Figure 10.47 Select the font, style, and size from the Family, Typeface, and Size columns in the Fonts window.

Changing Fonts, Styles, and Sizes per Text Box

iPhoto also provides several ways to modify the font, style, and size of selected text.

To change fonts, styles, and sizes:

1. Select the text you want to change.

2. Open the Fonts window by choosing Show Fonts ([Cmd][T]) from the Edit menu's Font submenu.

3. In the Fonts window, you can choose a font from the Family column, a style from the Typeface column, and a size from the Size column (**Figure 10.47**).

    iPhoto changes the currently selected text to match your choices.

To change just styles:

◆ Select some text, and from the Edit menu's Font submenu, choose Bold ([Cmd][B]) or Italic.

◆ [Control]-click the selected text, and choose Bold, Italic, Underline, or Outline from the contextual Font submenu.

✔ Tips

■ Bold and Italic are dimmed in the menus if the current font has no Bold or Italic typeface. Verify in the Fonts window.

■ iPhoto does not provide keyboard shortcuts for Italic, Underline, or Outline.

■ The Restore Defaults button in the settings dialog also overrides any individual font changes you've made.

■ Be judicious in your changes; excessive use of fonts and styles generally looks lousy, and I strongly encourage you to print a page or two on your own printer before buying a card, calendar, or book whose fonts you've changed.

Copying Font and Style Information

If you've set the font, style, and size for one piece of text, you can copy that to any other bit of selected text easily.

1. Select the text whose settings you want to use elsewhere.

2. Choose Copy Style ([Cmd][Option][C]) from the Edit menu's Font submenu.

3. Select the text whose settings you want change.

4. Choose Paste Style ([Cmd][Option][V]) from the Edit menu's Font submenu.

    iPhoto changes the currently selected text to match the font, style, and size of your original selection.

Changing Text Color

Although it's not obvious, iPhoto provides controls to change the color of text as well.

To change colors:

1. To open the Colors window, (Control)-click a text box and choose Show Colors from the Font submenu (**Figure 10.48**).

   or

   In the Fonts window, click the text color button.

   iPhoto opens the Colors window (**Figure 10.49**).

2. Select the text to which you want to apply a color, and click a color in the color wheel.

   iPhoto changes the color of the text.

✔ Tips

- You can apply color only to selected text, not to classes of text in the settings dialog.

- To copy a color from elsewhere on the screen to the color box, click the magnifying glass icon, and then click a color anywhere on the screen.

- Drag the color box to one of the cells of the color swatch collection to save it for repeated use. Clicking one of the color swatches applies it to the selected text.

- Copying fonts also copies colors.

- Use color carefully and sparingly—it's too easy to make a book garish by applying too much color. You don't want your text to compete with your photos.

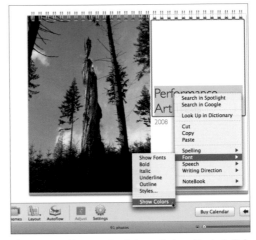

Figure 10.48 To open the Colors window, Control-click a text box, and from the Font submenu, choose Show Colors.

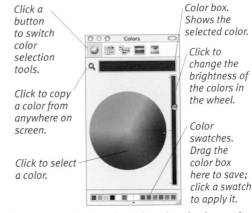

Click a button to switch color selection tools.

Click to copy a color from anywhere on screen.

Click to select a color.

Color box. Shows the selected color.

Click to change the brightness of the colors in the wheel.

Color swatches. Drag the color box here to save; click a swatch to apply it.

Figure 10.49 Click a color in the color wheel to put it in the color box and apply it to the selected text.

Figure 10.50 Note how iPhoto has underlined the misspelled words in red.

Figure 10.51 To replace a misspelled word with one of Mac OS X's guesses, Control-click the word and choose a guess from the contextual menu.

Checking Spelling as You Type

You won't be typing much in iPhoto, but since its editing environment is crude, typos are likely. The last thing you want in a beautifully designed card, calendar, or book is a glaring typo, so I recommend you use Mac OS X's built-in spell checker to verify the spelling of your titles and captions as you type them.

To check spelling as you type:

1. Click a text box, and from the Edit menu's Spelling submenu, verify that Check Spelling While Typing has a checkmark next to it.

2. Type your text in any text box.

   iPhoto displays a red line underneath any words that aren't in the system-wide Mac OS X spelling dictionary (**Figure 10.50**).

3. Control-click a word with a red underline to display a contextual menu that enables you to replace the word with one of Mac OS X's guesses, ignore the misspelling for this launch of iPhoto, or learn the spelling by adding it to your system-wide Mac OS X dictionary (**Figure 10.51**).

✔ Tips

- Check Spelling While Typing is on by default and stays on all the time.

- If you quit iPhoto and come back to a book later, you must check spelling manually to find errors in existing bits of text. To do this, click in each text box and choose Check Spelling from the Edit menu's Spelling submenu (Cmd;). I recommend using the keyboard shortcut.

- Ignore Spelling isn't particularly worthwhile—iPhoto forgets ignored text between launches.

Talking Captions

For longer spans of text, select all the text (Cmd A), Control-click it, and from the Speech submenu, choose Start Speaking. iPhoto will read your text to you, which can help identify mistakes.

Printing on Your Own Printer

iPhoto makes it easy to print a card, calendar, or book on your own printer, which is faster than waiting for Apple to deliver the finished product, though books and calendars lack bindings, of course.

To print on your own printer:

1. While in a card, calendar, or book, choose Print from the File menu (Cmd P).

   iPhoto displays the standard Print dialog (**Figure 10.52**).

2. Select the options you want (switch among sets of options using the pop-up menu under the page range fields).

3. Click the Print button.

✔ Tips

■ You can print individual pages from a book layout to mix photos and text on a single page in ways beyond print projects.

■ I also particularly like printing the date pages from calendars for posting in schools or other organizations.

■ It's difficult to print cards, since you need to print one page, wait for the ink to dry, and then flip the paper and print the second page on the other side, and the two sides may not match up. Test before assuming it will work!

■ Choose Open PDF in Preview from the PDF pop-up menu to see what your output will look like before printing. I recommend that you do this, especially since it simplifies printing only selected pages.

■ Choose Save As PDF from the PDF pop-up menu to generate a PDF instead of printing. It's a nice way to share a photo layout with friends via email.

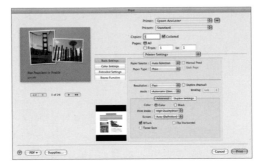

Figure 10.52 To print a book on your own printer, choose Print from the File menu.

Printing Selected Pages

If you want to print just a few pages in your book, you may find it difficult to figure out exactly which page numbers to enter into the Print dialog. That's because iPhoto doesn't assign a page number to the cover, and the inside cover is never printed. Follow these steps for a more obvious approach:

1. Choose Print from the File menu (Cmd P) to bring up the Print dialog.

2. Choose Open PDF in Preview from the PDF pop-up menu to make iPhoto create a PDF and automatically open it in Apple's Preview application.

3. In Preview, review exactly which pages you want to print, paying attention to the page numbers in the page drawer.

4. In Preview, choose Print from the File menu and enter the appropriate page numbers in the Pages fields. Set any other printing options you want, such as number of copies or print quality.

5. Click Print to send your pages to the printer.

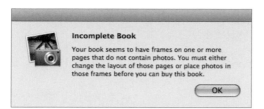

Figure 10.53 If you haven't finished placing photos on your pages, iPhoto warns you with a dialog like this.

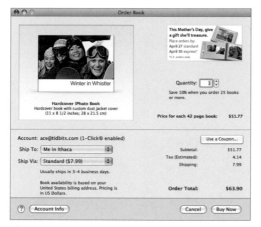

Figure 10.54 Convey the details of your order to Apple in the Order window.

Pricing and Shipping Details

Prices vary by style, size, and number of pages; read Apple's pricing page at www.apple.com/ilife/iphoto/prints.html for details.

Shipping costs vary by the number of items you order and the type of item, but note that per-item shipping costs are less for subsequent items (in other words, if you buy two copies of a book, you'll pay only a little more to receive the second one, instead of double the normal shipping charge).

Ordering Cards, Calendars, and Books

Once you've designed a card, calendar, or book, ordering it from Apple is easy.

To order a card, calendar, or book:

1. Select the item you want to order, and verify that each page looks right.

2. Make sure you're connected to the Internet, and click the Buy button.

    iPhoto assembles the print job, warning you if some photos won't print well, if some default text hasn't been edited, if other text doesn't fit, or if a book or calendar isn't complete (**Figure 10.53**).

    iPhoto then opens the Order window (**Figure 10.54**).

3. Enter the number of items you want to order in the Quantity field.

    iPhoto automatically updates the total cost as you add and subtract items.

4. Choose the appropriate shipping address and method from the Ship To and Ship Via pop-up menus.

5. Click the Buy Now button.

    iPhoto uploads your pictures and alerts you when it's done.

✔ Tips

- Hardcover books now have photo-wrapped covers and matching dust jackets, so you can't choose cover color.

- Uploading can takes a long time because iPhoto uploads full-size images.

- If you're warned about low-resolution images, see "Dealing with Warning Icons," on page 177.

- If this is your first order, review the Apple ID setup details on pages 164–165.

TROUBLESHOOTING

The Trouble with Bugs

Many iPhoto problems that I've seen people report seem to be specific to their photos, a particular iPhoto Library, their Mac, or the phase of the moon, and I have been unable to reproduce them. I still include here the potential problem and any solutions I've heard of or can think of, but this uncertainty makes it impossible for me to say when or if Apple has fixed the incorrect behavior. As such, some of the problems and solutions listed in this chapter may no longer apply to iPhoto '09; there's simply no way to tell.

I continue to include these suggestions even when I can't verify them because bugs are slippery, and just because I can't reproduce a particular problem in this or any other version of iPhoto doesn't mean that you won't experience it. And then one of the suggestions in this chapter may save your bacon (or at least your photos).

Also keep in mind that updates to iPhoto very well may eliminate even those problems I've confirmed in iPhoto '09, so be sure to use Software Update to check for new versions on a regular basis.

The world of iPhoto is no more a perfect place than the real world. No one, iPhoto's developers least of all, wants problems, but bugs are a fact of life, and you may have a problem with iPhoto at some point.

One advantage iPhoto has in this respect is that it saves your changes frequently and automatically, so you're unlikely to lose much work even if it does crash. Put simply, if iPhoto crashes (and it has crashed on me a number of times while I was writing this book), just relaunch the program and pick up where you left off. Also be sure to click the Report button in the crash dialog and report the crash to Apple so it can be fixed. If the crashes happen regularly, you may need to do some troubleshooting. One way or another, keep good backups! (See "Backing up Your Photos," on page 26.)

Of course, most of the problems you might encounter won't result in a crash. It's more likely you'll have trouble importing photos from an unusual camera, printing a photo at the exact size you want, or dealing with thumbnails that don't display properly. Those are the sorts of problems—and solutions—I'll focus on in this chapter.

General Problems and Solutions

Some problems you may experience in iPhoto aren't related to particular activities. Others are, and subsequent pages in this chapter will address issues with importing, editing, slideshows, printing, and more.

Performance Problems

If you find iPhoto slow to perform certain operations, try these tricks. Some are obvious (if expensive), others less so:

◆ Turn off title, rating, and keyword display using the View menu.

◆ Shrink thumbnails to a smaller size.

◆ Use the triangles next to events in Photos view to hide photos you don't need to see.

◆ Quit other programs that are running. In my experience, there is usually one culprit, which you can identify by launching Activity Monitor from your Utilities folder and clicking the CPU column title to see which applications are using the most processor time.

◆ Restart your Mac by choosing Restart from the Apple menu. Restarting is especially helpful if you don't have much free disk space, which cramps Mac OS X's virtual memory techniques.

◆ Check your disk with DiskWarrior (www.alsoft.com/DiskWarrior/); sufficient disk corruption can cause huge performance problems on startup.

◆ Add more RAM to your Mac. iPhoto works with 512 MB of RAM, but it likes a lot more, and RAM is cheap. I always recommend at least 1 GB these days.

◆ Buy a faster Mac. That's always fun.

Some Photos Disappear

Some people have reported troubles with photos disappearing, even when the files are still present in the iPhoto Library. Try the following:

◆ Make sure the photos aren't just in the Trash; it's easy to delete inadvertently.

◆ Hold down Cmd Option while clicking the iPhoto icon in the Dock to launch it. This causes iPhoto to display the Rebuild Photo Library dialog.

  Try each of the options, and see if one of them fixes the problem. For more info, see http://support.apple.com/kb/HT2638.

◆ With iPhoto as the frontmost application, choose Enter Time Machine from the Time Machine menu in the menu bar. Navigate back in time through Time Machine's backups to the point where you see the missing photos, then click the Restore button.

◆ If you have the photo elsewhere on your Mac or on another computer, just import it again.

All Photos Disappear

What if none of your photos appear at all? First, try the options listed just above, and if they don't help or aren't possible, try these:

◆ Make sure you're using the correct iPhoto library. Locate the one you want in the Finder and double-click it to open it.

◆ Create a new iPhoto library and import the contents of the Originals folder (and, if desired, the Modified folder) inside the corrupted iPhoto library package. Control-click it and choose Show Package Contents to get at those folders (see "iPhoto Directory Structure," on page 19). This won't preserve anything but the photos, unfortunately.

Flaky Behavior or Crashes

Sometimes iPhoto just acts strangely, and I've come up with a few ways of dealing with weird behavior (make sure you have a backup before deleting any files!):

◆ Quit iPhoto and relaunch it.

◆ Restart your Mac by choosing Restart from the Apple menu.

◆ Quit iPhoto. From the Preferences folder inside your user's Library folder, drag the file com.apple.iPhoto.plist to the Desktop and launch iPhoto again. Deleting this file can even resolve missing or truncated text problems with books, cards, and calendars; for details, see http://support. apple.com/kb/TS1616.

◆ Hold down Cmd Option while clicking the iPhoto icon in the Dock to launch it. In the Rebuild Photo Library dialog, try each of the options, quitting and relaunching in between attempts, and see if one of them fixes the problem. For more info, see http://support.apple.com/kb/HT2638.

◆ Use iPhoto Library Manager's Rebuild Library command, which uses the AlbumData.xml file written by iPhoto to re-create the library. This is a completely different method from what iPhoto uses. (It's at www.fatcatsoftware.com/iplm/. iPhoto Library Manager's help has other useful troubleshooting information too.)

◆ Run Disk Utility and use the buttons in the First Aid pane to verify and repair both permissions and the disk.

◆ Delete and re-install iPhoto.

◆ Try creating a new iPhoto library and re-importing your photos from the Originals and Modified folders.

Other Problems

Here are a few other general problems and their solutions:

◆ Don't attempt to read a newer iPhoto library with an older version of iPhoto, or corruption could ensue.

◆ If other iLife apps can't see your photos, or if some photos or albums are missing, read this support article for things to try: http://support.apple.com/kb/TS1192.

◆ If you have trouble with iPhoto's photo sharing or the sharing tools that upload data, shut off or bypass your firewall to see if it's blocking necessary ports.

◆ If iPhoto complains about being unable to establish a connection when uploading to MobileMe, make sure the date is set correctly in the Date & Time preference pane in System Preferences.

◆ If mailing a photo in Apple's Mail doesn't result in an enclosure, and another user on the Mac has successfully attached a photo in the same session, restart the Mac and try again.

◆ If you've ended up with duplicate photos, you can delete them with the $7.95 Duplicate Annihilator from Brattoo Propaganda Software (www.brattoo.com/propaganda/index.php?s=1169727148&action=software). Make a backup before running this program!

Report Your Problems!

Report any problems you may have by choosing Provide iPhoto Feedback from the iPhoto menu and then filling in Apple's Web-based feedback form.

Importing Problems and Solutions

I've had little trouble importing photos into iPhoto. However, because importing involves interacting with an unpredictable outside world of cameras, card readers, and files of varying formats, problems can occur.

Camera or Card Reader Isn't Recognized

Mac OS X and iPhoto support most common digital cameras and card readers, but not all of them. And sometimes iPhoto may not recognize specific memory cards, even if it recognizes the card reader in general. Try the following tips:

- Make sure the camera is turned on, in review mode, and plugged in via USB properly. I know it seems obvious, but we've all made this mistake before.

- Use Software Update, accessible in System Preferences, to make sure you have the latest version of Mac OS X, since Apple continually adds support for more digital cameras and card readers.

- If your camera is incompatible with Mac OS X and iPhoto, buy a card reader that supports the memory card used by your camera.

- If your user account can run only certain applications, that may prevent you from importing in iPhoto. The only fix is for an administrator-level user to increase the capabilities of your account in the Accounts and Parental Controls preference panes.

- Some cameras must be placed in Picture Transfer Protocol mode to communicate with iPhoto. And if that doesn't work, try other modes. Check the manual for help.

- Older versions of iPhoto have had trouble with some large memory cards. People have resolved the issue by reformatting the card in the camera, using a memory card reader, or using smaller cards.

- Try reformatting the memory card in the camera and taking a picture before connecting it to the Mac again. Keep in mind this will destroy any photos already on the card!

- If you have two cameras connected at once, or a camera and a scanner, iPhoto may become confused about which device to use. Connect only one device at a time if this causes trouble for you.

Nothing Appears after Import

If nothing appears in iPhoto after you import files from your hard drive, try these solutions:

- Instead of using the Import to Library command in the File menu, drag the images (or a folder containing them) onto iPhoto's display pane.

- Like all Mac OS X applications, iPhoto is sensitive to proper permissions. So, if you've moved your iPhoto Library and are trying to import from another user, verify in the Finder's Get Info window for the iPhoto Library package and all enclosed folders that the appropriate user has Read & Write permissions.

- The photos might be duplicates, which iPhoto imports only if you tell it to do so. See Chapter 2, "Importing and Managing Photos," starting on page 11.

- If the files you imported were located in the iPhoto Library package, iPhoto may assume they've already been imported and won't do so again. To solve the problem, move the files out of the iPhoto Library package and try again.

Damaged Photos Warning Appears during Import

Sometimes when you import photos, you may see an error dialog complaining about unreadable photos. It can occur for a variety of reasons:

- You're accidentally importing non-graphic files, such as aliases to photos, HTML documents, or other data files.

- The image files may actually be damaged. See if you can open them in Preview or GraphicConverter. If so, you may be able to convert them to another format and eliminate the corruption.

- If your files are in an unsupported format, try using GraphicConverter to convert the images to JPEG. Similarly, if RAW images from your camera aren't supported by iPhoto, see if your camera manufacturer makes a utility that will convert them to a supported format.

- Sometimes the problem may relate to a communications failure between your camera or card reader and your Mac. Try plugging the camera or card reader directly into one of the Mac's USB ports rather than into the keyboard's USB port or a port on a USB hub.

- iPhoto can display the damaged photo error message if your hard disk is full. Since iPhoto duplicates every photo when importing from files, if you're importing hundreds of megabytes of photos from files, it's by no means unthinkable that you could run out of disk space. Clear some space and try importing again.

- Photos taken with Apple's QuickTake 100 and QuickTake 150 digital cameras must be converted from the special format Apple used into the JPEG format.

Other Importing Problems

Here are a miscellany of importing problems and solutions that don't fit larger categories:

- iPhoto may crash if you disconnect your camera while photos are transferring.

- If iPhoto fails to warn you about duplicates, it may be because the date and time on your camera are wrong.

- Make sure there are no aliases among files you are importing; they can cause crashes.

- iPhoto 2 won't recognize discs burned in later versions of iPhoto, although the later versions can recognize older discs.

- If iPhoto complains about not being able to upgrade your library on the first launch, the problem may be related either to incorrect permissions or to locked files. For instructions on how to solve this problem, see `http://support.apple.com/kb/TS1318`.

- If you import a misnamed file—a TIFF file with a `.jpg` filename extension, for example—iPhoto may display the picture strangely when editing, refuse to let you order prints, or even crash. Delete the misnamed picture from your Photo Library; then rename it appropriately in the Finder before importing it again.

- If you have erased your camera and need to recover the original photos, check out the $29 PhotoRescue (a free version will tell you if it's going to work). Learn more at `www.datarescue.com/photorescue/`. Also try the $39.95 ImageRecall from `www.flashfixers.com/software/` or the $29.95 MediaRECOVER from `www.mediarecover.com`.

Editing Problems and Solutions

Most photo editing problems stem from using another program to edit the photos.

Photos Don't Open in an External Program

Although it is unlikely that you'll run into this problem, it could be frustrating. Here are a few reasons it could happen:

◆ If you have changed the name of the photo's file in the Finder, it may not open when double-clicked in iPhoto. The solution? Change the filename back to what iPhoto expects, and don't mess with any filenames within the iPhoto Library. It's a bad idea!

◆ Double-check to make sure iPhoto's preferences are set to open photos in an external program (see "Using an External Editor," on page 110), that the program is present on your hard drive, and that you can launch it and open photos normally.

Photos Don't Appear When Edited or Magnified

There are a few reasons why iPhoto might show only a black screen or fuzzy exclamation point when you edit or magnify a photo:

◆ Changing the photo's filename in the Finder can cause this problem. Don't do it!

◆ A corrupted photo can cause iPhoto to freak out. Editing and saving the original file in another application might eliminate the corruption, or you could delete the corrupt photo and import it again, assuming you have another copy.

iPhoto Doesn't Allow Editing

Some people have reported importing images from a CD that they later couldn't edit in iPhoto. As a workaround, convert the images in GraphicConverter from JPEG to TIFF, for instance, and see if you can import and then edit those versions.

Also verify that the permissions on the files allow your user to write to the files. To check, select them in the Finder, choose Get Info from the File menu (Cmd I), and look in the Permissions area.

Revert to Original Dimmed

You may see the Revert to Original command in the File menu dimmed after you've made a change. This can happen if you drag a photo from iPhoto to another program to edit the photo. If you do that, iPhoto will be unable to track changes you've made and Revert to Original will be dimmed. There's no workaround, other than making sure to open photos for editing in external applications properly from within iPhoto. See "Using an External Editor" on page 110.

Thumbnails Are Corrupted or Cause Crashes

If a thumbnail doesn't reflect edits, is entirely black, or causes iPhoto to crash, hold down Cmd Option while clicking the iPhoto icon in the Dock to launch it. In the Rebuild Photo Library dialog, select the first two checkboxes to rebuild all thumbnails.

RAW File Facts

Apple's support for RAW files in iPhoto has caused some confusion. The following facts may shed some light on it for you:

◆ RAW files are considered to be "digital negatives" that aren't to be modified, so changes you make are always saved to a secondary file. As a result, on import, iPhoto converts the RAW file to JPEG and stores the RAW file itself in the Originals folder. Alternatively, you can set iPhoto to save edited RAW files as 16-bit TIFFs.

You *never* work on the RAW file directly, only on its JPEG or TIFF stand-in. If you wish to throw out your edits and start a new copy from the RAW file again, choose Reprocess RAW from the Photos menu.

◆ Because of the large size of uncompressed RAW files and the JPEG conversion that occurs during import, the import process can take a longer time with RAW files.

◆ When you edit a RAW file, iPhoto displays a RAW badge at the bottom of the display pane or in the toolbar in full screen view.

◆ Scrolling may seem slower when browsing through large thumbnails of RAW files. The problem is that when you're using a thumbnail size larger than the actual thumbnails, iPhoto must load the original photo to create the thumbnail. That's a slower process. To speed up scrolling, press 1 while in organize mode to zoom to thumbnail size (press 0 to zoom to the smallest size).

◆ To export a RAW file in RAW format, choose Original from the Format pop-up menu in the Export Photos dialog.

◆ For more info, see http://support.apple.com/kb/TA22895.

Slideshow Problems and Solutions

Slideshows can run into a variety of problems; try these solutions:

◆ PowerPC G4- and some PowerPC G5-based Macs don't support all of iPhoto '09's slideshow themes. See http://support.apple.com/kb/TS2576.

◆ Some transitions, like Cube and Flip, may not work on older Macs with less capable video cards.

◆ Music purchased from the iTunes Store and used in a slideshow can be heard only on authorized computers. Either pick different music or convert tracks (burn to CD and re-import into iTunes) for use on other computers.

◆ If slideshows look wrong, try switching to "Thousands" of colors in the Displays pane in System Preferences.

◆ If a slideshow takes a long time to start, it may be because of a very large music file you've set to play. Pick a smaller file to speed start time.

◆ If slideshow transitions are slower than you've set, it may be because your photos are too large or your screen resolution is too high. Setting a lower resolution in the Displays preference pane or using smaller photos should speed transitions.

◆ If you can't see your iTunes Library when selecting music for a slideshow, launch each of these applications in this order: iTunes, iPhoto, iMovie, and then iDVD.

◆ If Windows users see error -8992 when trying to play your QuickTime movie, have them turn off DirectDraw Acceleration in the Video Settings screen of the QuickTime Settings control panel.

RAW FILES AND SLIDESHOWS

Printing Problems and Solutions

Many printing problems you'll experience will be specific to your particular printer and setup, so read your printer manual carefully and be sure to test before printing at the highest quality on expensive paper.

Prints Don't Appear Correctly on the Paper

You may have trouble getting prints to show in exactly the right location on the paper. Try these solutions to the problem:

◆ Set the paper size and print size appropriately in the pop-up menus in the print settings dialog. This is key for unusual paper sizes.

◆ Make sure the margins are set correctly for your printer and paper combination.

◆ Verify that you load paper into your printer properly. This solution helps particularly with unusual paper sizes.

Printing calendars on your own printer may result in similar problems. Solve the problem by saving a PDF of the calendar and then printing from Preview. For more details, see `http://support.apple.com/kb/TS1073`.

Photos Print at Incorrect Sizes

Even if you ask iPhoto to print a standard size print, the image that comes out of the printer might not be the size you want. This can happen if you change the layout to print multiple pages per sheet of paper in the Print dialog's settings.

Poor Print Quality

The main complaint with printing occurs when print quality doesn't meet your expectations. Here are a few suggestions for addressing print quality problems:

◆ Make sure your inkjet cartridges aren't clogged. Once my black ink cartridge clogged and it took me an hour to figure out that the clog caused color photos to print oddly. Your printer manual should tell you how to clear clogs.

◆ Change your ink cartridges. It's possible that one is low on a specific color and not yet reporting the problem.

◆ Use different paper. You'd be amazed how much better print quality is on paper designed for photo printing.

◆ Make sure your paper is loaded correctly to print on the printable side. It's usually whiter or glossier than the other side.

◆ Make sure you select the appropriate settings in the Print dialog for your printer to use high-quality mode.

◆ CMYK files, which you can create in some programs (but won't come from a standard digital camera), may not print correctly. Try converting them to RGB.

◆ Verify that the problems aren't inherent to the original image. If so, you may have to edit the image to correct the issue.

Print and Book Problems and Solutions

A few common problems have cropped up when working with prints and books.

Can't Enable 1-Click Ordering

Early on, some people had trouble enabling 1-Click ordering within iPhoto, even though they had a 1-Click account with Apple that worked on Apple's Web sites. To fix the problem, try one of these solutions:

◆ Connect to `http://store.apple.com/`, click the Account link, and log in to your Apple Store account. Click the "Change Account Information" link, log in again if necessary, and then change your password (changing other data wouldn't hurt either). The goal here is to force the Apple database to update so you can connect to it via iPhoto. (If changing your account on the Apple Store doesn't have the desired effect, try running through the same procedure at `http://myinfo.apple.com/.`)

◆ Follow the above procedure, but instead of clicking "Change Account Information," click "Change 1-Click Settings." Again, make some changes and toggle 1-Click ordering off and on again to see if that enables iPhoto to connect.

◆ If you can set up a new email address easily, create it and then add a new Apple ID that uses the new email address. This should work, but isn't an ideal solution, since then you have to keep track of an extra email address.

Errors During Ordering

You may encounter a few problems during the process of ordering items from Apple:

◆ If you see an error dialog complaining that a network connection could not be established, verify that your Internet connection is working by loading a page in a Web browser or by checking your email.

◆ You may see a confusing error message that says, "The changes to your account information could not be saved." Ignore the message, and enter your credit card information again, making sure the card hasn't expired. If that doesn't work, try a different credit card.

◆ If you see an alert that your password is invalid, but it works fine in the Apple Store, change your password to be less than 30 characters. The Apple Store allows 32-character 1-Click passwords, whereas iPhoto allows only 30-character 1-Click passwords.

◆ Different aspects of iPhoto may request access to your password keychain during ordering. That's totally fine.

◆ If you have a firewall that blocks port 80, try turning your firewall off, or allowing data to pass through on port 80, to solve upload errors.

◆ For the latest tips from Apple, see `www.apple.com/support/photoservices/account_troubleshooting/.` (You must log in to see this page.)

Photos Don't Upload

Some people have had trouble uploading photos to Apple's servers to have them printed or turned into a book or other item. Here are a few things to try:

◆ Try again later. Many Internet problems come and go, so a second try an hour or a day later may succeed.

◆ If possible, see if the problem occurs when uploading to MobileMe as well. If not, the problem may be limited to the specific servers used for prints or other printed items.

◆ If possible, verify that you can upload a large file using a different program. If that fails, the problem is likely with your Internet connection. If it works, the problem is probably in iPhoto.

◆ If iPhoto complains about an error while accessing your account information, make sure the date and time on your computer are set properly in the Date & Time pane of System Preferences. It's a good idea to select Set Date & Time Automatically in that preference pane to eliminate the problem in the short term. If your Mac is several years old and loses track of the date and time regularly, you need to buy it a new clock battery. Macs with dead clock batteries can suffer all sorts of weird problems.

◆ Contact Apple via the Web forms available from www.apple.com/support/photoservices/.

Apple Has Trouble Processing Your Book or Photos

There are several problems that can prevent Apple from printing photos you've uploaded, the two most common of which are damaged files and files that contain a question mark in the filename. You should receive email telling you about the problem, but a few common issues include:

◆ If a photo has a ? in the filename, it won't print. Export the photo, change the filename, re-import, and delete the original.

◆ Damaged photos may not print. To identify damaged photos, connect to Apple's Web site at www.apple.com/internetservices/yourorderstatus/, where you can look for missing or partial thumbnails for the order in question. Once you've identified the damaged files, try exporting them, opening them in another application, saving a copy of each, and re-importing the copies to eliminate the corruption.

◆ If you order a print of an image that indicates it may be subject to another person's copyright, Apple may put your order on hold pending verification that you have the right to make a copy of the photo. You must complete and submit an iPhoto Print Consent form; Apple will tell you how to do this when you're contacted.

◆ Using certain Type 1 PostScript fonts can cause your book order to be cancelled. For more information, see http://support.apple.com/kb/TA22924.

- If over half of the page numbers in a book are hidden by photos, Apple may cancel your order. It's easiest to deselect the Show Page Numbers checkbox in the Settings dialog before placing the order, although you could also change the theme or page design to one in which photos don't cover the page numbers.

- If you receive email from Apple saying your order can't be processed, you can wait for Apple to contact you with details, or you can try to figure out what went wrong, cancel the order, and then resubmit it. Apple gives you up to 90 minutes to cancel the order yourself; do this by logging in with your Apple ID to www.apple.com/internetservices/yourorderstatus/ and clicking the Cancel Order link.

Order Doesn't Arrive or Is Damaged

There are several ways to learn more about your order and to contact Apple if you experience problems with an order:

- Check the status of your order at www.apple.com/internetservices/yourorderstatus. You need your Apple ID and password to sign in.

- Contact Apple via the Web forms available from www.apple.com/support/photoservices/. Be sure to include the text of your confirmation message from Apple so they have your order details.

Prints or Books Aren't What You Expect

It's highly frustrating to order prints or books that aren't of the quality you expect. Follow these tips to avoid common problems:

- Prints ordered via iPhoto may come back darker than is ideal. This may be because Mac and PC monitors have different color contrast settings, something called *gamma*. Macs usually use a gamma of 1.8, whereas PCs use a darker gamma of 2.2. The belief is that Kodak serves more PC customers and has thus tweaked its equipment so PC users don't think their prints look washed out.

  You can adjust your monitor to use PC gamma settings when working with photos. In the Color view of the Displays pane in System Preferences, click the Calibrate button to run the Display Calibrator Assistant. Then work through the Display Calibrator Assistant, picking 2.2 Television Gamma in the third screen. When you're done, save the profile you created, and select it in the Color view of the Displays preference pane.

- Prints use a three-color process whereas books use a four-color process. Because black is added to photos in books, they can appear slightly darker in books than when ordered as prints.

- If prints in your order from Apple are garbled, the problem may be that the photos were modified in another application (like Photoshop) to use CMYK or grayscale format. To fix the photos, use another application to change the color space to RGB, which Apple requires for ordered prints and books.

- For the latest tips from Apple, see www.apple.com/support/photoservices/product_troubleshooting/.

PRINT AND BOOK PROBLEMS AND SOLUTIONS

Dealing with Warning Icons

Let's say you want to print a photo in a card, calendar, or book, or via Apple's online print service, but iPhoto is displaying a warning icon on the page thumbnail or next to a specific size you want in the Order Prints window. What can you do to resolve this situation?

Ways to handle warning icons:

◆ You can simply print at a smaller size. When ordering prints, try a smaller size (**Figure 11.1**); with a card, calendar, or book, choose a different page design or rearrange the photos so the offending one prints at a smaller size (**Figure 11.2**). Or, don't zoom into the photo as far.

◆ If the photo is too small because you cropped it, you can select it, choose Revert to Original from the Photos menu, and crop it again to a larger size. I recommend this procedure primarily if you think you're right on the edge of receiving the warning icon.

◆ You can also increase the size of your image using GraphicConverter or Adobe Photoshop. The way these programs scale the photo up might look better than iPhoto's method, though it's harder.

✔ Tips

■ For exact details about how many pixels photos must have to print at different sizes, see "Preparing to Order Prints," on page 166.

■ To learn how image resolution relates to what comes out of a printer, take a look at "Understanding Resolution," starting on page 204.

Figure 11.1 Note how the three images showing here have warning icons applied to different print sizes. The first (heavily cropped) image can print well only at wallet size. The second (slightly cropped) won't print well at 8" x 10" or larger. The third image (uncropped) drops out at 16" x 20".

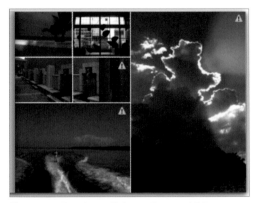

Figure 11.2 Note how all these photos, which were taken with my old QuickTake 100 at 640 x 480 pixels, show low-resolution warning icons in this book layout, except the three smaller photos in the upper left. A 640 x 480 image must be quite small to print acceptably.

Figure 11.3 Start with Apple's iPhoto support pages for general help and pointers to other resources.

Figure 11.4 If all else fails, ask for help on Apple's iPhoto discussion boards.

Help Resources

I'm sure other problems and solutions will become known after I finish writing. Along with iPhoto's online help (choose iPhoto Help from the Help menu), a variety of Internet resources provide assistance.

Places to look for more help:

◆ Check Apple's iPhoto support pages at `www.apple.com/support/iphoto/` (**Figure 11.3**) and `www.apple.com/support/iphoto/customerservice/`.

◆ Search in Apple's Knowledge Base using the Search field on the pages listed above. Narrow your search by adding terms, so if you're having trouble importing RAW files, search for "import RAW" or something similar.

◆ Try asking a question on Apple's iPhoto Web-based discussion forums linked at `http://discussions.info.apple.com/` (**Figure 11.4**). In my experience, these discussions are good for straightforward questions; harder questions may go unanswered. When posting, state your problem clearly and include relevant information while at the same time keeping the question concise.

◆ For order-related problems, contact Apple via the Web forms available from `www.apple.com/support/photoservices/`. Make sure you have your order details at hand.

◆ Check out *TidBITS*, the free weekly Web site and newsletter I publish. It contains tons of useful information on all sorts of topics, including digital photography. Visit `www.tidbits.com` and search on "iPhoto" or "photography" to see relevant articles. You can also subscribe to receive issues in email.

HELP RESOURCES

Deep Background

Right off the bat, let me say that you don't need to read this appendix. It's deep background, the kind of detail that you might wish to delve into when you're attempting to understand how iPhoto works, perhaps because you've just printed a photo and you're unhappy with the results.

The following pages contain "Understanding Aspect Ratios," "Understanding Resolution," and "Understanding Color Management." Each of these discussions examines an aspect of digital photography from which iPhoto, for the most part, tries to shield you. That's great most of the time, but if you're trying to understand how cropping removes information from a photo, thus making it print at a lower quality, you'll want to come here for the explanation.

Lastly, although I've called this appendix "Deep Background," these topics are so complex that entire books have been written about each one. If these discussions leave you with more questions, I'd encourage you to visit a library or bookstore and browse its collection of books on photography, digital imaging, and prepress. I especially recommend *Real World Scanning and Halftones, Third Edition,* by David Blatner, Conrad Chavez, Glenn Fleishman, and Steve Roth.

Understanding Aspect Ratios

iPhoto makes it easy to select and crop a portion of a photo using a specific aspect ratio, but why is this important? It matters because aspect ratios differ between traditional and digital photos.

An aspect ratio is the ratio between the width of the image and its height, generally expressed with both numbers, as in the line from Arlo Guthrie's song "Alice's Restaurant Massacree" about "Twenty-seven, *eight-by-ten*, color glossy photographs with circles and arrows and a paragraph on the back of each one."

The aspect ratio of 35mm film is 4 x 6 (using the standard print size rather than the least common denominator of 2 x 3) because the negative measures 24mm by 36mm. Thus, traditional photographs are usually printed at sizes like 4" x 6", 5" x 7", or 8" x 10", all of which are close enough to that 4 x 6 aspect ratio so photos scale well. When there's a mismatch between the aspect ratio of the original negative and the final print, either the image must be shrunk proportionally to fit (producing unsightly borders) or some portion of the image must be cropped. (The alternative would be to resize the image disproportionally, which makes people look like they're reflected in a funhouse mirror.)

The equivalent of film in digital photography is the *CCD* (charge-coupled device), which is essentially a grid of many light-sensitive elements that gain a charge when exposed to light. Through much digital wizardry, the camera translates those charges into the individual dots (called *pixels*) that, put together, make up the image. Zoom in on a picture all the way, and you can actually see these pixels. So if your digital camera uses a CCD that can capture a picture composed

Figure A.1 This is a 4 x 3 image with a 4 x 6 landscape selection. A bit of the bottom of the image would be lost, which is fine.

Figure A.2 This is a 4 x 3 image with a 5 x 7 landscape selection. Very little of the bottom of the image would be lost to cropping.

Figure A.3 This is a 4 x 3 image with an 8 x 10 landscape selection. Losing the right side of the image would be somewhat problematic.

Figure A.4 This is a 4 x 3 portrait image with a 4 x 6 portrait selection. A bit on the left would be lost, which is fine (a better crop would take some from the left, the right, and the top).

Figure A.5 This is a 4 x 3 portrait image with a 5 x 7 portrait selection. A very small amount on the left would be lost, which is fine.

Figure A.6 This is a 4 x 3 portrait image with an 8 x 10 portrait selection. A better crop would have cut off Tristan's feet, rather than coming so close to the top of his head.

Figure A.7 This is a 4 x 3 portrait image with a square selection. As you can tell, the square selection is a lousy choice for this image.

of 1600 pixels wide by 1200 pixels high, basic math shows that your photos will have a 4 x 3 aspect ratio.

Why did digital camera manufacturers choose a 4 x 3 aspect ratio when 4 x 6 is the 35mm film standard? It matches the aspect ratios of early computer monitors. Early common monitor resolutions were 640 x 480, 800 x 600, and 1024 x 768, all having a 4 x 3 aspect ratio. Displaying a photo at full screen size without cropping thus requires a 4 x 3 aspect ratio. (And why did computer monitors use a 4 x 3 aspect ratio? Because that's the aspect ratio used by televisions. However, since HDTV uses a 16 x 9 aspect ratio, many monitors now use that or 16 x 10.)

Hopefully the choices in iPhoto's Constrain pop-up menu make more sense now. If you're starting from a photo with a 4 x 3 aspect ratio, and you want a 20" x 30" print (a 4 x 6 aspect ratio), there's no way to print that photo without adding borders or cropping because of the mismatch in aspect ratios. The same applies to other standard print sizes—they don't match the 4 x 3 aspect ratio of most digital photos. Rather than suffering borders or automatic cropping, it's better to crop the image yourself so you can be sure the important parts are retained. **Figure A.1** through **Figure A.7** show how cropping a 4 x 3 image at the other common aspect ratios works for two sample images (results will vary by image).

The 4 x 3 aspect ratio plays an important role in output too, since iPhoto's book designs generally assume 4 x 3 images. The books vary the final image size depending on the page design, and you can zoom in and re-center the image to crop temporarily, but as long as the aspect ratio of your images remains 4 x 3, the layout will work as Apple intended. You can use different aspect ratios in a book, but the layout may not work well.

UNDERSTANDING ASPECT RATIOS

Understanding Resolution

Understanding how the dimensions of a digital photo relate to what comes out of a printer is hard. That's why iPhoto merely alerts you with a warning icon when a photo won't print well at a specific size. Read these two pages to learn why iPhoto displays warning icons; "Dealing with Warning Icons," on page 177 offers help.

Pixels and Dots

Every digital photo is made up of a rectangular grid of points, called *pixels,* each of which can display one of sixteen million colors or several hundred shades of gray. For instance, photos from one of my cameras are 3264 pixels wide by 2448 pixels high. Monitors also display rectangular grids of pixels, say 1900 pixels wide by 1200 pixels high.

Not all of a 3264 x 2448 photo can fit on a 1900 x 1200 monitor when every pixel in the image is mapped to a pixel on the monitor. To display a photo so it fills a monitor, iPhoto removes pixels on the fly, a process called *downsampling.*

You can't perform the same one-to-one mapping when it comes to print, though, because most printers (which have only four or six colors) can't display a pixel's exact color in a single dot. Instead, they use collections of single-colored dots to fool the eye into seeing that color. For this reason and other more complex ones, the main fact to grok is that, in general, the more pixels in the image, the better it will look printed.

This fact is particularly relevant when you're printing images at large sizes. For instance, why does an image that looks fine when printed at 4" x 6" appear fuzzy at 8" x 10"?

Imagine a knitted blanket. If you stretch it to make it larger, you can see through the holes between the strands of yarn. Expanding a

Figure A.8 The original image at 100 percent.

Figure A.9 Shrink the image to 17 percent of original size and the loss of detail caused by downsampling makes it hard to see the stripes on the penguin's tie.

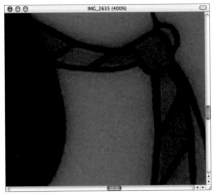

Figure A.10 Expand the image to 400 percent of the original and the fuzziness added by interpolation becomes evident.

Figure A.11 The original 1600 x 1200 pixel image, with a small area to crop selected.

Figure A.12 Crop the image to 206 x 183 pixels and you can see how the horse looks much fuzzier due to all the interpolation necessary to expand it to the desired size.

photo to print at a larger size works similarly, except the printer fills in each hole with dots of roughly the same color as the dots surrounding the hole, a process called *interpolation*. The more pixels in the image, the smaller the holes that need to be filled, and the less interpolation is necessary.

Downsampling vs. Interpolation

Downsampling onscreen works well, since it's easy to remove similarly colored pixels without changing the image much. Even though the photo loses pixels and thus some detail, quality doesn't suffer too much (**Figure A.8** and **Figure A.9** on the previous page). Along with the fact that onscreen images are extremely bright because monitors *emit* light, whereas paper *reflects* light, minimal downsampling helps explain why photos look good on monitors at full size.

Interpolation, particularly on a printer, is different. There's no way to avoid adding dots that didn't exist before when expanding a photo, and because those dots exist only by virtue of the dots around them, they make the image look fuzzier (**Figure A.8** and **Figure A.10** on the previous page). Interpolation simply cannot add details to the image that weren't originally present. Scale an image too large, and iPhoto warns you that so much interpolation will be needed that you won't like the result.

Cropping Implies Interpolation

Cropping exacerbates the problem because it removes pixels, making the photo smaller and requiring more interpolation to expand the image back up to the desired size.

To see this, compare the original image in **Figure A.11** with **Figure A.12**, which shows a heavily cropped version of the same image, displayed at the same size as the original. Notice how the cropped horse is fuzzier.

UNDERSTANDING RESOLUTION

Understanding Color Management

iPhoto 5 first introduced tools for manually adjusting color saturation, temperature, and tint. Why did it take Apple so many versions to add these tools? Color correction of any sort is devilishly difficult to do right (and as you may have noticed, even the automatic Enhance tool gets it wrong at times). Color correction suffers from two basic problems: color is highly perceptual and different devices render color in different ways.

Color Perception

Everyone sees color in different ways. My wife and I, for instance, frequently disagree on whether a given color is green or blue, and the fact that my opinion generally seems to match what others think as well doesn't change her perception of a different color. Plus, at least 10 percent of the population suffers from some level of color blindness that makes it impossible to perceive differences between colors that others can distinguish.

The conditions in which color is perceived also make a huge difference, as you have probably realized if you've ever purchased a shirt in a store lit with fluorescent lights and were surprised by how the shirt looked when you tried it on at home under incandescent lights. Similarly, when painting a room, you have to consider how the color will look in sunlight during the day and with artificial lighting at night. The differences can be striking.

The lesson here is that you cannot define color objectively—there is no right answer. Always keep that in mind, and it will remove some of the stress about achieving the "perfect" color in your photos.

Rendering Color

Digital cameras, computer monitors, inkjet printers, and commercial photo processing equipment all use different methods of rendering color. Even with monitors, there's little common ground between CRT-based monitors and LCD flat-panel monitors, and sometimes even between LCD monitors from different manufacturers.

When you take a picture with your camera, look at it on your Mac, print a copy on your printer, and order a large print of the image from Kodak, you would like the colors in the image to match closely at each step. The engineers designing these devices have managed to make the color produced by each one match fairly well, but not perfectly. Here's how it works.

Imagine a three-dimensional graph, with the X-, Y-, and Z-axes representing the amount of red, green, and blue in every possible color. (Don't worry about this turning technical; that's as bad as it gets.) Now imagine an amorphous blob in the graph that represents the specific set of colors any given device can capture (for digital cameras) or display (for monitors or printers). That blob is called the *gamut,* and every device has a gamut that's at least slightly different.

The problem with matching color across completely different devices is that each device can render only colors in its gamut. When a color, say a specific dark blue, falls into an area where there's overlap between gamuts, each device does the right thing and renders the exact same dark blue. However, when a color falls outside the set of colors a device can render, it's a problem. The device cannot render a color outside its gamut, so it makes an educated guess about what color to render instead.

Color-Matching Systems

Many efforts have been made to address this problem, but the one you're most likely to have heard about, being a Mac user, is Apple's ColorSync technology. The particular approach it uses to make educated guesses about which colors to render on different devices is immaterial; suffice to say that its goal is consistency. In theory, if you have chosen or set up a ColorSync profile for your monitor and your printer, for instance, it should help ensure that the colors you see on your monitor match those printed by your printer.

Without getting into too many details, you can calibrate your monitor by choosing System Preferences from the Apple menu, clicking the Displays preference pane, clicking the Color button, and clicking the Calibrate button to run and work through the Display Calibrator Assistant. Then, when you're printing, look for a ColorSync setting in the Color Management pane of the Print dialog. Whether it's present or not depends on your printer driver, but if the setting is present at all, it's usually the default. That's all there is to basic use of ColorSync, and on the whole, it works pretty well.

You may not be limited to ColorSync's educated guesses about how to render color (my Epson inkjet's Photo-Realistic mode sometimes produces better results), and in fact, none of the commercial photo processing companies, including Kodak, uses it. Why not? Two reasons.

First, photos are displayed on monitors and on paper totally differently. Monitors *emit* light, causing photos to be extremely bright. Paper *reflects* light, so unless you shine a floodlight on a photo, you can't come close to the amount of light emanating from a monitor.

Second, as I noted, color is highly perceptual, and Kodak and other photography companies have done incredible amounts of research to determine not so much how to match colors exactly, but how to print photographs that meet people's expectations.

In the end, the problem of matching color perfectly among devices is just too hard. Even with technologies like ColorSync, the differences between a photo on a light-emitting monitor and light-reflecting paper mean that the photo-processing companies have a better chance of satisfying customers if they concentrate more on producing a photograph that looks desirable than on matching colors perfectly in an imperfect world where everyone sees color differently.

Should You Correct Colors?

Color correction is complex, and the necessary tools are also usually complex. Apple did a good job with giving iPhoto basic color-correction tools in the Adjust window, and many photos can be improved with judicious color correction. Of course, iPhoto's tools are still limited in comparison to those in programs like Adobe Photoshop; in particular, iPhoto's tools always affect the entire image, rather than letting you select a portion of the image to correct.

Now that you know how hard it is to achieve reliable, predictable results, should you color correct your photos using iPhoto or another program? It depends on how much you want to play. For those who don't like to fuss, don't bother. If you like fiddling with your photos so you can make them just right, go ahead. And for the majority of us who fall between those two poles, I recommend doing manual color correction on those images you like the most and that will benefit from it the most. Remember, the "right" color is the one that looks right to you.

Taking
Better Photos

iPhoto and your digital camera will make you a better photographer, for the simple reason that the best way to improve a skill is constant practice. Thanks to iPhoto, it's easier to take and review photographs than ever before.

But you need not discover all the ways you can take better photos on your own. Having the best equipment for the kind of photos you want to take will help, as will learning some of the basics of different types of photography. This appendix offers that advice, ranging from choosing the best camera for your needs to tips on how to take great pictures of kids. (Hint: The posed portrait is unlikely to work.)

So skim these few pages to find tips that you can use to create better photos with minimal extra effort.

What Kind of Photographer Are You?

When choosing the camera that will help you take the best photos, it's important to choose one that matches the kind of photos you actually take. But what sort of photographer are you? In one way of thinking, there are two types of photographers: artistic and documentary (and as is usually the case, most people overlap somewhat).

You're an artistic photographer if:

◆ You care more about the overall look of a photo than the subject of the picture (**Figure B.1**).

◆ Objects and landscapes fill many of your photos and stand alone as aesthetic representations of your reality.

◆ Display and print quality is of the utmost importance. You regularly print and display your best photos.

◆ You're willing to take time to set up the perfect shot, and you do things because they give you photo opportunities.

You're a documentary photographer if:

◆ Who or what appears in the photo is more important than the overall look (**Figure B.2**).

◆ The most common subjects of your photos are people and places, and they usually fit into and support a larger story.

◆ You're willing to trade quality for convenience, ease of use, or speed of shooting.

◆ You don't have the free time or patience to set up shots, and you prefer to snap a few pictures quickly, hoping that at least one will turn out well. You carry your camera to record events or in the hope of getting a good shot.

Figure B.1 There's not much of a story in this photo—I was just intrigued by the color of the leaf underneath the new-fallen snow. We're definitely looking at an artistic photograph here.

Figure B.2 In contrast, here we have a picture of me and my grandmother at my 35th birthday party. Whether or not it's a good photo is almost immaterial—what's important is that it reminds me of a special meal with my family. It's a pure documentary photograph.

Choosing a Camera

Once you've determined what sort of photographer you really are (and that may be different from the type of photographer you'd like to be in an ideal world), working through the variables that differentiate digital cameras becomes significantly easier.

Form Factor

Digital cameras come in a wide variety of sizes, and for documentary photographers, small size can be important so the camera fits in a pocket and so the fact that you're taking pictures doesn't overwhelm the event. In contrast, artistic photographers are often willing to carry larger cameras because of their increased quality and flexibility. Most cameras fall in a middle ground, so it's best to hold the camera to see how it feels in your hand before buying it.

Megapixels/Quality

Within the form factor that matches your shooting style, you should usually try to get the most megapixels (larger cameras have larger CCDs and can thus capture more pixels). But lens quality and other variables make a difference too, and the best way to learn about those issues is to read detailed camera reviews. Artistic photographers need to pay the most attention to quality issues.

Lens Capabilities

For documentary photographers, this mostly comes down to whether or not the camera has a decent optical (ignore digital) zoom for capturing far away events. For artistic photographers, zoom capabilities are important for those times when you simply can't (or shouldn't) get close enough to the subject (such as a grizzly bear). Also important are macro capabilities for stunning close-ups of flowers, insects, and other small objects.

Extra Features

Extra features may be important: documentary photographers may appreciate a movie capability, whereas artistic photographers might look for the capability to use an external flash or different lenses. Also pay attention to factors like the camera's battery type. AA batteries are cheap and easily found, and you can buy good rechargeable batteries, but the smallest cameras generally have their own battery packs and chargers.

Price

Everyone has a budget, and here's where you must decide how much to pay. Documentary photographers will pay more for truly tiny cameras with decent quality, whereas artistic photographers pay more for quality, manual controls, and support for additional lenses. Although more money will buy a better camera, you can take good pictures with almost any camera.

Interface

Some cameras are easier to use than others, which is important for documentary photographers who need to be able to set options quickly before missing a particular shot. Artistic photographers care more about control, so the camera interface should help them twiddle manual settings easily.

Speed

Digital cameras can be quite slow, with a few seconds to start up, a lag between when you press the shutter release and when the picture is taken, and a noticeable lag between shots. Documentary photographers in particular should look for faster cameras, so as to avoid missing that perfect shot due to camera lag. Artistic photographers interested in action shots should also pay attention to speed or risk losing great photos.

Where to Read Camera Reviews

After you've determined roughly what kind of camera you want, you have a few choices. You can go to a store and buy whatever the salesperson recommends after hearing your story. You can depend on a friend who has already researched a similar type of camera. Or you can do the research yourself. Be forewarned—if you're not a camera buff, you may find reading numerous camera reviews overwhelming, thanks to the incredible detail provided. I've found the sites below useful for reviews, buyer's guides, news, discussions, and other digital photography information.

Camera review sites:

◆ *Digital Photography Review* has an especially detailed feature search tool and a useful way of comparing the specs on different cameras, side-by-side.

  Find it at: `www.dpreview.com`

◆ *Digital Camera Resource Page* offers an extensive camera database through which you can search to find cameras with your desired specifications. Reviews are all on one page, making them easy to read, unlike the other three sites.

  Find it at: `www.dcresource.com`

◆ *Imaging Resource* stands out from the pack with its Comparometer, which lets you compare sample photos taken with different cameras. The site also offers an easy-to-use model comparison tool.

  Find it at: `www.imaging-resource.com`

◆ *Steve's DigiCams* offers detailed reviews and a nice summary page listing the cameras the writers believe are the best in each of a number of categories.

  Find it at: `www.steves-digicams.com`

A Better Starting Point

Honestly, camera reviews make me crazy, since I don't have a background in traditional photography to help me understand all the jargon. I've tried to lay out the basics here, but if you want more information about how to think about the right camera for your needs and how to understand the camera reviews, I recommend Larry Chen's *Take Control of Buying a Digital Camera,* one of the Take Control ebooks. Larry also provides advice on evaluating image quality and gives you a comparison worksheet to help you track the different cameras you're considering. Read more at `www.takecontrolbooks.com/buying-digicam`.

Camera Accessories

Although all you need to take good photos is a camera, there are some accessories that can help at times.

Bigger Memory Card

Most cameras ship with small memory cards, and you may feel as though you should shoot at a lower resolution to save space. Don't do it—just buy a larger memory card. Visit www.dealram.com to compare prices at multiple vendors for the type of memory card your camera uses.

USB Card/PC Card Reader

If you have friends with digital cameras, a USB or FireWire card reader that accepts all the types of memory cards can make it easy to share photos of an event on the spot, without having to mail them around later. Folks with laptop Macs might also look for a PC Card or ExpressCard adapter that lets you plug your memory card right into the laptop.

Alas, attachments to download photos into an iPod have all faded away, but if you're looking for a photo backup solution while travelling, check out the Photo Safe II or Picture Porter Elite from Digital Foci. For more info, visit www.digitalfoci.com.

Monopod/Tripod

In low-light situations, if you don't use the flash, you risk your photos coming out blurry. The solution? Attach the camera (most have the appropriate threaded mount) to a monopod or a tripod. Documentary photographers are less likely to want to use even a monopod (which is smaller and faster to use than a tripod) because of it getting in the way, whereas artistic photographers are more likely to accept a little extra annoyance in exchange for the highest quality photos. Either way, make sure it's easy to use.

Extra Batteries

It's unfortunately common to run out of power at a bad moment, particularly if you're using your camera's flash or LCD display a lot. Avoid missing great photos because your camera is dead by carrying an extra battery pack or set of batteries. Proprietary battery packs tend to be expensive, but my experience is that it's worth buying the camera vendor's battery rather than one from an independent manufacturer. Other cameras take standard AA batteries; you can use any normal battery, but it's cheaper and more environmentally friendly to use rechargeable batteries, such as those available from Quest Batteries; visit www.questbatteries.com.

Lens Cleaning Kit

Those of us who have used only digital cameras may not realize that it's well worth getting a special lens cleaning kit that can remove dust and dirt from your lens and LCD (and for cameras with removable lenses, the CCD inside). Normal cloth might cause scratches. Any camera store should be able to recommend a lens cleaning kit.

Printer

With iPhoto, you can always order prints from Apple. But you may want to print them yourself, perhaps for instant gratification, greater control, or privacy reasons. For that you'll need a color printer. There are a number of different technologies, such as inkjet, laser, and dye-sublimation. Inkjet printers are the most common, offer excellent quality, and come in a wide variety of sizes, but have high per-print materials costs. Dye-sublimation printers have the best quality for photos, but can be expensive. And color laser printers are the cheapest to run for many prints, but may not have as good print quality. You can learn more at camera review sites, which also often review photo printers.

General Photo Tips

No matter what type of photos you take, a few general tips will take you a long way:

◆ Consider the Rule of Thirds. Divide the image into a 3 x 3 grid and try to position the main subject of the photo where the lines intersect (**Figure B.3**). If your photo will have strong horizontal (as in a horizon) or vertical lines (as in a building), try to keep them on the horizontal or vertical lines. Centering can work, but tends to be a bit dull for anything but portraits.

◆ Pay attention to where the light comes from and try to avoid shooting into strong light. It's better to shoot with light at your back (make sure your subjects aren't squinting) or to one side whenever possible. If you have to take a picture of people who have the sun behind them, turn on your flash to light up their faces, which will otherwise be too dark.

◆ Don't be afraid to shoot from odd angles or unusual heights. Digital cameras encourage experimentation, and playing around can produce some great shots.

◆ Avoid a busy background that will distract the eye from the subject of the photo (**Figure B.4**).

◆ Keep the camera steady, particularly when you're shooting in low light without the flash. The beauty of the LCD screen on the camera is that you can set the camera on a solid object to shoot, even when it's not at a comfortable height.

◆ Remember that the flash on most small digital cameras works well only to about 10 feet. Relying on room light is tricky, but the more light you can throw on the subject in a normal room, the better.

Figure B.3 Note how the heads of Tristan and his cousin Madeline are at the intersections of the grid, increasing visual interest and emphasizing their interaction.

Figure B.4 This photo shows the value of an uncluttered background—the blank wall helps the eye focus on the man in the scene. Note too that the fact that he's only half in the frame increases the power of the photo. Sometimes in photography, as in graphic design, some "white space" can improve the image.

Figure B.5 Portrait orientation makes all the difference for this picture of the long, deep gorge that runs through Cornell University.

Figure B.6 This close-up of my wife's face works in large part because it's so close and out of focus.

More General Photo Tips

Here are a few more tips that can help:

◆ Try to match the orientation of the subject to the orientation of the photo (**Figure B.5**). Landscape orientation, where the photo is wider than it is tall, usually works best for landscapes (with specific exceptions, such as the gorge in **Figure B.5**), whereas portrait orientation, where the photo is taller than it is wide, works best for people. Computers and TVs generally use landscape orientation, so keep that in mind if you plan to do a lot of slideshows.

◆ Try to avoid posing your subjects. Most people aren't very good at describing exactly what they want the person in the photo to do, and most people aren't good at adopting a specific pose without it looking forced. Give it a try and you'll appreciate how hard professional photographers and models work.

◆ Figure out exactly what interests you about a scene before shooting. That helps you set up the shot and find different ways of emphasizing the subject.

◆ Take lots of photos—they don't cost anything. This is especially important when the scene is changing, but even with shots you set up, it's worth taking a few, just in case one shot works better than another.

◆ As a corollary, try alternative ways of taking a given picture, such as with and without the flash. Do this enough and you'll start to figure out when to use certain settings for your desired effect.

◆ Don't be afraid to get close and fill the frame with the subject, even when it means cutting off parts of people's bodies or faces (**Figure B.6**).

Portrait Photo Tips

For many of us, pictures of people make up the bulk of our photo collections. Use these tips to improve your portraits of family and friends in the future:

◆ Get closer. A lot of portraits are taken from too far away, lessening the impact of having that particular person in the photo. Of course, since getting closer isn't always feasible, a good zoom lens can help.

◆ When you're taking pictures of traveling companions, break the previous rule a bit so you can add context to the shot. Signs work well for reminding you of where and when a picture was taken, particularly if they're in other languages.

◆ For candid snapshots, which are often the best kind, make sure you have enough light and just point the camera in the right direction and shoot from the hip (**Figure B.7**). Lots of these shots will be terrible, but the effort of tossing them is well worth the occasional amazing shot you'll get.

◆ Don't warn people in advance that you're going to take a photo unless you want forced smiles. If you need people to look at you, prefocus your camera by pressing the shutter release button halfway, then say something to get their attention. As soon as they look at you, and before they realize you're taking a picture, press the button the rest of the way down.

◆ In group photos, make everyone crunch together and overlap. The presentation is much more interesting than if everyone just lines up by height (**Figure B.8**).

Figure B.7 I took this photo while holding the camera at my waist and walking normally down the street.

Figure B.8 This group photo from my family reunion works well because the different levels provided by the stairs help everyone overlap neatly.

Figure B.9 Getting a cat and a child both looking photogenic at the same moment can be tricky unless you're willing to take lots of shots.

Figure B.10 The fact that the camera is on Tristan's level, about a foot off the ground, provides a good perspective.

Figure B.11 Since Tristan loved trains, these abandoned mine trains at the Last Chance Basin Mining Museum in Juneau, Alaska, were a big hit. He asked me to take this photo and even agreed to pose in it.

Child and Pet Photo Tips

People may be the most common subjects of photos, but I'll bet most of those photos are pictures of children. And those folks who don't have children around often seem to replace kid photos with pet photos. Children and pets require similar shooting styles:

◆ Adults are usually capable of at least that oh-so-familiar forced smile, but kids often don't want to participate, and it's almost impossible to convince pets to pose. Give it up and shoot surreptitiously.

◆ When kids or pets are playing, they may not notice you, so work fast and take lots of pictures, perhaps with your camera's burst mode (**Figure B.9**). Try to avoid calling out names, since that will almost certainly break the spell.

◆ If the kids or pets realize what you're doing, just be patient and stay prepared in case you get another chance.

◆ If you plan to take pictures of children, encourage them to wear brightly colored clothing. Lots of color can make your photos more eye-catching.

◆ With both kids and pets, get down on their level (**Figure B.10**). Otherwise you end up shooting the tops of their heads.

◆ At zoos or similar attractions, try to photograph the child reacting to, or interacting with, the animals.

◆ It can be great fun to involve kids in the decisions about what pictures to take, particularly if you're on a trip. Ask them what they'd like you to take pictures of, and let them set the scene (**Figure B.11**).

◆ Outdoor photos often work the best, perhaps because it's easier to get good, uncluttered backgrounds.

Landscape Photo Tips

There are places where it seems almost impossible to take a bad photo (glaciers and mountain vistas, for instance), but a few tips can help improve other landscape pictures:

◆ Take advantage of the long light early in the morning (less haze) or just before dusk (sunset colors), since you get more interesting shadows and interplay between light and dark. Try to keep the sun at your back or your side.

◆ Try to keep the horizon level, although iPhoto can straighten a photo if an otherwise good photo is marred by a bit of skew (**Figure B.12**).

◆ Keeping the Rule of Thirds in mind, if the land is the subject of your photo, make two-thirds of the photo be land, with one-third sky. If the sky is the focus of the photo (sunset photos can produce the most amazing colors), then reverse those proportions so the sky fills most of the frame.

◆ Try to include an object in the foreground to catch the eye, rather than leaving the entire landscape in the far distance (**Figure B.13**). A foreground object has the added advantage of indicating the magnitude of the scenery.

◆ When possible, eliminate distracting elements, such as telephone poles or electric lines. Otherwise, try to use them in the composition of the photo.

◆ Try using reflections in water or windows for interesting effects and perspectives (**Figure B.14**).

Figure B.12 It's hard to take a bad picture of a glacier... unless you can't hold the camera straight. iPhoto's Straighten tool can fix this shot.

Figure B.13 The misty woods in the background evoke a mood, but Tristan running away from the camera down the mown strip in the field lends focus.

Figure B.14 This picture, although seemingly a normal landscape of trees and the sky, is actually a reflection in a pond, giving the scene added depth.

Figure B.15 Having Tristan pose in front of our cruise ship, with its name visible in the background (though hard to read at this size), made for a perfect travel picture.

Figure B.16 Make sure to have other people take pictures of you. You'll especially appreciate having done this if you decide to make a book of your trip in iPhoto.

Travel Photo Tips

Although the tips for landscapes and portraits apply equally well when you're traveling, a few special tips can help improve your vacation photos:

◆ Include your traveling companions in the shots when possible, because without them, you could just buy a postcard.

◆ Take photos that remind you of an area or event. Shoot details such as buildings, signs, or natural landmarks, but take them from your perspective and, when possible, with your traveling companions (**Figure B.15**).

◆ Don't get sucked into the trap of posed shots of your companions in front of whatever the local attraction may be. Have some fun and keep it light, partly so you get better shots, and partly so your traveling companions don't get sick of your camera.

◆ Ask one of your companions, or a passer-by, to take pictures that include you. Otherwise it may seem as though you weren't along on the trip (**Figure B.16**).

◆ Take pictures of the people you meet (it's best to ask for permission first), and make notes so you remember each person later.

◆ Plan ahead so you can take lots of photos. That may entail carrying an extra memory card or two, bringing a rechargeable digital wallet drive to store photos, or lugging a laptop along (at which point you can upload photos of your travel photos for friends and family back home). It's also worth doing a bit of culling every night to free space used by bad shots.

INDEX

INDEX